SEE BRITAIN BY TRAIN

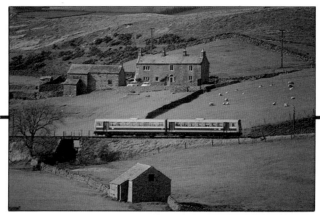

Scenic railway journeys described by
PAUL ATTERBURY

Published by The Automobile Association,
Fanum House, Basingstoke, Hampshire RG21 2EA

The Automobile Association acknowledges the
assistance given in the preparation of this
book by British Rail

---CONTENTS---

THE WEST COUNTRY
8-27

SOUTH & SOUTH EAST ENGLAND 28-43

WALES
44-59

© The Automobile Association 1989
Mapping © The Automobile Association 1989
All cartography based on the AA's Automaps database.

Filmset by Avonset, Midsomer Norton, Bath
Printed and bound by Purnell Book Production Ltd. Member of BPCC plc

The contents of this publication are believed correct at the time of printing. Nevertheless, the publishers cannot accept responsibility for errors or omissions, or for changes in details given.

ISBN 0 86145 760 9

Researched and written by
Paul Atterbury
Preserved Railways text by
Peter Semmens
Additional research by
Virginia Langer
Original concept by
Martin Boddy

SEE BRITAIN BY TRAIN

Cover: (main picture) *Inverness-Kyle of Lochalsh – Loch Carron*   Photo: Andrew Vines
(inset) *Dovey Junction-Pwllheli – Barmouth Bridge*   Photo: Richard Owen
Title page: *Clapham, North Yorkshire, on the Leeds – Morecambe route*   Photo: D J Fowler
This page: *Crianlarich-Oban – Loch Awe*   Photo: Dennis Hardley

MAP OF ROUTES

The British Rail routes featured in this book are shown on the map in the six regions into which the book is divided (see below). Stations at the beginning and end of each route are marked in red type. Other routes in the British Rail network are shown in black. The map also indicates the page(s) on which each route is described. See also Contents page.

- The West Country
- South & South East England
- Wales
- Central England & East Anglia
- The North Country
- Scotland
- Other British Rail routes

USING THE TRAINS

RAIL INFORMATION

British Rail operates Britain's national rail network covering England, Scotland and Wales. On the fast, regular InterCity mainline services you can easily cover long distances. And off the main routes, modern Express trains are being introduced, with new rolling stock to take you in comfort through spectacular scenery.

TICKETS

Tickets can be purchased in advance or at the time of travel. Full details of prices of rail tickets including any special offers, together with information about train services can be obtained from British Rail stations and Travel Centres and BR Appointed Travel Agents.

There is a range of rail tickets available, whether you want to spend a day out or take a longer trip. The ideal way to tour Britain by rail is with a Rail Rover ticket. Choose from the comprehensive All Line Rover ticket, available for 7 or 14 days, or from a range of Regional or Local Rail Rovers available for 3, 7, or 14 days, depending on the area you choose. These tickets let you plan anything from a short excursion to a two-week holiday. Rail Rovers can offer substantial savings and with only a few peak time travel restrictions, offer a simple and economic way of seeing Britain by train.

Alternatively there is a wide range of Saver tickets available between most British Rail stations. These tickets can offer attractive reductions off the Standard Return fares.

For many people there is an added bonus. Holders of Young Persons, Senior Citizen and Disabled Persons Railcards can get discounts off the price of a wide range of British Rail tickets. A Network Card offers discounted travel in the Network SouthEast area. Families can make substantial savings with the Family Railcard. Overseas visitors should enquire about the BritRail Pass, which must be bought before leaving home.

Children under five travel free provided that not more than four accompany each fare paying passenger. Children aged between five and 15 travel at half fare.

At many stations – and in restaurants on the train – Barclaycard/Visa, Access and American Express can be used.

Dogs and most other domestic pets can accompany passengers in most circumstances, but a fare is charged if larger animals travel in passenger carriages.

Seats on most InterCity trains can be reserved at major stations or at travel agents.

ON THE TRAIN

DISABLED FACILITIES

Principal stations are fully accessible to wheelchairs. On older trains there is limited access for wheelchairs, with entry via the guard's compartment, but most modern carriages have wide or sliding doors for direct wheelchair access. Some have a removable seat space for a wheelchair.

SMOKING

On most trains there are smoking and non smoking sections, or carriages.

LUGGAGE

Most carriages are equipped with adequate storage space for luggage and other personal possessions, but bulky items can travel in the guard's compartment, sometimes upon payment of a fee.

BICYCLES

On many trains a bicycle can be taken free of charge. On certain routes there are restrictions and charges because of limited luggage space and the needs of other passengers. Reservations are required on most InterCity trains and some cross-country services. These restrictions vary from route to route and details should be obtained from stations before travelling.

EATING

Most long-distance trains have a buffet (or even a restaurant) on board, where you can get meals, hot and cold snacks and drinks 'on the move'. A trolley service of light refreshments and drinks is provided on most cross-country routes. Refreshment facilities are found at stations in most large towns and cities, see Trains Information, page 6, and Index.

SLEEPING

Sleeper services operate on a number of routes between England and Scotland and to the West Country. Many sleeper services also have Motorail facilities, with passengers' cars travelling on the same train.

On main line InterCity routes, some carriages have telephones, operated by credit cards.

CARS AND TAXIS

PARKING

Parking facilities are available at most stations. Stations with no car park are marked accordingly in the Index.

CAR HIRE

In association with British Rail, Hertz offer immediate and comprehensive car rental facilities at 100 principal stations during normal office hours (marked accordingly in the Index). Cars can also be arranged to be available at virtually any BR station provided they are booked at least 24 hours in advance. Further details are available from Hertz or British Rail stations.

TAXIS

Stations with a taxi rank are marked accordingly in the Index.

PRESERVED RAILWAYS

British-Rail tickets are not valid on preserved railways and separate ones need to be purchased, although special tickets are sometimes available covering the BR journey and the preserved railway. Brief operating details are given with the preserved railways featured in this book but many preserved railways run some services out of season which may vary from year to year and cannot be detailed in this guide.

USING THE BOOK

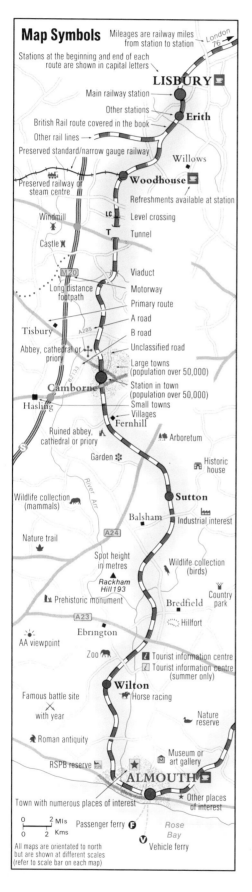

Map Symbols

Mileages are railway miles from station to station

Stations at the beginning and end of each route are shown in capital letters

LISBURY

Main railway station

Other stations

Erith

British Rail route covered in the book

Other rail lines

Preserved standard/narrow gauge railway

Willows

Preserved railway or steam centre

Woodhouse

Refreshments available at station

Windmill

LC — Level crossing

T — Tunnel

Castle

M20 — Viaduct

Long distance footpath — Motorway

Primary route

A road

Tisbury — B road

Abbey, cathedral or priory — Unclassified road

Large towns (population over 50,000)

Camborne — Station in town (population over 50,000)

Hasling — Small towns

Villages

Fernhill

Ruined abbey, cathedral or priory — Arboretum

Garden — Historic house

Wildlife collection (mammals)

Sutton

Balsham — Industrial interest

A24

Nature trail

Spot height in metres — Wildlife collection (birds)

Rackham Hill 193

Prehistoric monument — Bredfield — Country park

A23 — Hillfort

Ebrington

AA viewpoint

Zoo — Tourist information centre

Tourist information centre (summer only)

Wilton — Horse racing

Famous battle site with year — Nature reserve

Roman antiquity

Museum or art gallery

RSPB reserve

ALMOUTH

Other places of interest

Town with numerous places of interest

0   2 Mls
0   2 Kms

Passenger ferry

Rose Bay

Vehicle ferry

All maps are orientated to north but are shown at different scales (refer to scale bar on each map)

SEE BRITAIN BY TRAIN is presented as a series of railway journeys through some of Britain's loveliest countryside. The book is divided into six regions. Each journey takes the form of a detailed map of the route and a text describing what can be seen from the train window with, where relevant, historical or background information.

THE MAPS

The maps show the railway line and its immediate surroundings, with railway features, roads, geographical features, towns, villages and places of interest clearly marked. All maps are orientated to the north, but are shown at different scales (refer to the scale bars).

THE ROUTES

The text is written in the form of a particular journey with a declared direction of travel, eg, from Inverness to Aberdeen, but with reference to points of interest that can be seen from both sides of the train.

ABBREVIATIONS USED IN TEXT

BH	Bank Holiday
BR	British Rail
EH	English Heritage
Etr	Easter
m	miles
NT	National Trust
NTS	National Trust for Scotland
RSPB	Royal Society for the Protection of Birds
SDD	Scottish Development Department
TIC	Tourist Information Centre
w/end	weekend

TRAINS INFORMATION

Attached to the text for each journey are details of train frequency and length of journey in time and railway miles. The information applies to all trains running between approximately 7.30am and 7.30pm. However, there may be seasonal variations; and since British Rail timetables are revised twice a year, it is always advisable to check journey details at the station. The availability of on-train refreshments is indicated in the text; the maps indicate stations where platform refreshments are usually available. The Index shows parking, buffet, taxi and car hire facilities at stations.

FEATURES

Each regional section has introductory pages with information about the railway history of the region, local railway architecture and walking in the area. On most routes there is a special feature on things to Look Out For from the train.

THE PRESERVED RAILWAY

A number of preserved or private railway companies (shown on the Contents page in italics) are featured in the book, many of which use steam for haulage. These have direct, or bus, connections with the British

Rail network. For details of others see the lists published in railway magazines or the annual guides to preserved railways.

WHEN TO GO & WHAT TO TAKE

The amount that can be seen on any one journey is naturally affected by the weather, the time of day and the season. In general, far more can be seen in winter, when the leaves are off the trees, but spring and autumn are when the colours are at their best. It is hard to look from both sides of the train at once so some things are bound to be missed. The best thing is to make the journey more than once. The spotting and identification of particular places and things of interest can be helped by binoculars and by the use of the relevant Ordnance Survey 1:50000 maps. Taking photographs from moving trains is very hard, and generally not recommended, and at all times passengers should obey basic safety rules, such as not leaning out of windows.

PLACES TO VISIT

A selection is given of places to visit near the stations along each route. These are open all year unless otherwise stated, but readers should contact the Tourist Information Centres listed for fuller details of opening times.

CARS AND BICYCLES

The aims of the book are to make the railway journey more enjoyable and to encourage the use of the train as the preferred means of exploring the most scenic parts of Britain. However, information is also given to encourage further exploration on foot, by bicycle, by bus or by car. Addresses are given below of relevant organisations such as the Regional Tourist Boards, the National Trust, English Heritage, the Forestry Commission, and other bodies concerned with wildlife, nature conservancy, etc. Details of car-hire facilities are given on page 5. Information on cycling routes and places to hire bicycles can be obtained from the Cyclists' Touring Club. See page 5 for information on taking bicycles on trains.

WALKING

For each railway route in this book Walks are suggested which can be reached easily from nearby stations. For details, contact the local Tourist Information Centre. They carry information and route descriptions of many walks in the vicinity, and can give advice about any difficulties which may be encountered. They may also have information on guided walks. Occasionally, information on walks may be available at railway stations.

Many of the official long distance paths (Pennine Way, South West Peninsula Coast Path, etc) are accessible from the stations featured in the book, and appear on the maps. Further information is available from the Countryside Commission (address below). Ordnance Survey maps or a good footpath guide are necessary for those intending to follow them for any substantial distance. Some are for experienced walkers only.

WALKING AND CYCLING ON DISUSED RAILWAYS

Over 8,000 miles of railways have been closed in Britain since 1947. Of this total there are still thousands of miles untouched since the track was lifted, quietly left as linear nature reserves. Increasingly, the potential of these lines to form a national network of footpaths, cycleways and bridle paths is being developed, and currently over 1,000 miles of disused railway lines have been reopened to the public. The routes open at present range from under a mile to over 20 miles in length, and can be found in virtually every part of Britain, in both urban and rural surroundings. Some stand on their own, some connect with other footpath networks.

By their nature the routes are predominantly level and fairly easygoing and there is always plenty to see in terms of landscape, urban settings, railway history, and natural history. A selection of disused railways officially designated as footpaths is given in the introduction to each region. Sustrans, the railway and cycle route company (address below), can supply detailed information on railway paths.

ADDRESSES

		Regional Tourist Boards	London	Thames & Chilterns
Cadw	National Trust for Places of Historic Interest or Natural Beauty		26 Grosvenor Gardens London SW1W 0DU	The Mount House Church Green Witney Oxon OX8 6AZ
Brunel House Fitzalan Road Cardiff CF2 1UY		Cumbria		
The Countryside Commission	36 Queen Anne's Gate London SW1H 9AS	Ashleigh Holly Road Windermere Cumbria LA23 2AS	Northumbria Aykley Heads Durham DH1 5UX	
John Dower House Crescent Place Cheltenham Gloucestershire GL50 3RA	National Trust for Scotland 5 Charlotte Square Edinburgh EH2 4DU	East Anglia Toppesfield Hall Hadleigh Suffolk 1P7 7DN	North West The Last Drop Village Bromley Cross Bolton Lancashire BL7 9PZ	Wales Brunel House 2 Fitzalan Road Cardiff CF2 1UY West Country 37 Southernhay East Exeter Devon EX1 1QS
Cyclists' Touring Club 69 Meadrow Godalming Surrey GU7 23HS	Nature Conservancy Council Northminster House Peterborough PE1 1UA	East Midlands Exchequergate Lincoln LN2 1PZ	Scotland 23 Ravelston Terrace Edinburgh EH4 3EU	Yorkshire & Humberside 312 Tadcaster Road York YO2 2HF
English Heritage PO Box 43 Ruislip Middlesex HA4 0XW	Royal Society for the Protection of Birds The Lodge Sandy Bedfordshire SG19 2DL	Heart of England 2/4 Trinity Street Worcester WR1 2PW Isle of Man Department of Tourism & Transport 13 Victoria Street Douglas	South East Warwick Park Tunbridge Wells Kent TN2 5TA South The Old Town Hall Leigh Road Eastleigh Hampshire SO5 4DE	
Forestry Commission 231 Corstorphine Road Edinburgh EH12 7AT	Sustrans Ltd 35 King Street Bristol BS1 4DZ			

THE
WEST
COUNTRY

Spectacular coastal views are a feature of many West Country routes:
the St Ives branch line, Cornwall, is a classic seaside journey

THE GENIUS OF BRUNEL

RAILWAY HISTORY AND ARCHITECTURE

CORNWALL PLAYED A significant part in the development of Britain's railways. By the 18th century tin and copper mines were the backbone of the county's industry. Many used tramways to transport the ore to the north and south coasts, and the steam pump had ensured that Cornish engineers led the world in steam technology. However, railways in Cornwall were isolated and independent, and it was not possible to travel by train from London to Penzance until 1859.

The building of the railway west from London was largely the work of Isambard Kingdom Brunel, the most inspired and adventurous of the Victorian railway engineers. In 1833 Brunel, who had never designed a railway before, was employed by the Great Western Railway to build a line from London to Bristol, and he resolved that it would be 'the finest work in England'. The first trains ran from London to Bristol in June 1841; a year later Queen Victoria took her first rail journey, to London from Slough. The Great Western's fast and comfortable service was greatly helped by the 7-foot gauge that Brunel had chosen instead of the conventional 4 foot 8½ inches. Brunel took personal charge of every aspect of the construction, and no other railway in Britain carried so clearly the stamp of one engineer.

Isambard Kingdom Brunel (opposite above) left his stamp on the Great Western Railway network with designs such as Saltash Viaduct (opposite below: the 1859 opening); Box Tunnel (right) and Bristol Temple Meads (below right)

Shipping and the South Wales coal trade were major GWR interests but the West Country was the company's financial heart. The railway developed a large-scale tourist business and was largely responsible for the creation of the Cornish Riviera. The Great Western retained its autonomy and style through the 1923 Groupings and the 1948 formation of British Railways. Even now the westward lines from Paddington have a character of their own.

A surprising variety of his engineering features are still in regular use. His masterpiece, the revolutionary Royal Albert Bridge over the Tamar at Saltash, is still the best way to enter Cornwall. The lesser buildings that he designed, stations at Mortimer, Stroud and Chepstow, for example, all clearly bear the Brunel stamp. And the railway's entry into Bath with its excellent bridges and tunnels, and the stone-lined cutting, is entirely sympathetic to the city's architecture.

WALKING IN THE REGION

The Dartmoor and Exmoor National Parks and the South West Peninsula Coast Path offer the best walking in the West Country and they can all be reached by train. Both Dartmoor and Exmoor National Parks offer a programme of guided walks. The Two Moors Way connects the two Parks. For details of all Walks suggested on the routes in the following pages, contact the local Tourist Information Centres. See also page 7.

Railway walks in the West Country are a good way to explore the lesser known landscape, river valleys and coastline of the region. A selection of the closed railways now designated as official footpaths is given below:

Barnstaple to Braunton (3 miles), part of the former Barnstaple to Ilfracombe branch line incorporated in the North Devon Coast Path

Blandford Forum to Sturminster Newton (5 miles) and Midsomer Norton to Radstock (2 miles) and other sections of the former Somerset and Dorset line from Bath to Broadstone

Plym Bridge to Bickleigh (2 miles) and other parts of the former Plymouth to Tavistock line

Wadebridge to Padstow (6 miles) and other parts of the former Launceston to Padstow line

Yatton to Cheddar (10 miles), the Cheddar Valley Walk along part of the former Yatton to Shepton Mallet line

To the Cornish Riviera

EXETER – PENZANCE *Exeter – Plymouth* *52 miles*

The journey from Exeter to Plymouth is a memorable exploration of the many faces of Devon. It starts in a cathedral city, tours the traditional English seaside at Dawlish and Teignmouth and then, turning inland, it crosses rolling hills and river valleys, and flanks the southern frontier of Dartmoor before entering the great maritime city of Plymouth. Sit on the left for this journey.

Exeter

At Exeter St David's the two rail routes to the west come together. The high speed trains from Paddington continue their journey to Cornwall, but Exeter is now the terminus for trains from Waterloo. St David's is a splendid station, full of period detail behind its imposing façade and notable for the traditional panelled waiting room, but Exeter Central is more convenient for the city. The medieval cathedral, with its 300ft-long vaulted nave is near by. Beyond the remains of the city walls is a rich range of 18th- and 19th-century buildings, marking the period of Exeter's prosperity as a seaport. The ship canal made all this possible and its basin is lined with fine old warehouses, one now the home of the famous maritime museum.

The train follows the Exe to its estuary, passing Powderham Castle and park, and Starcross, where one of the few remaining pumping houses for Brunel's inauspicious atmospheric railway is now a museum. There are good views across the estuary to Exmouth as the train approaches the sandy dunes of **Dawlish Warren**.

Dawlish

At Dawlish the train becomes a scenic part of the seaside, with the line sandwiched between the beach and the red sandstone cliffs and running in and out of the rocky tunnels and cuttings. This is a classic stretch, made particularly evocative by the beach huts and boats, the birds and the old-fashioned holiday atmosphere. Dawlish is a pretty, early Victorian resort. The train continues to Teignmouth, with good views of the pierced rock formation known as the Parson and Clerk. The South Devon Coastal Footpath also follows the line.

Teignmouth

Little of this Regency resort can be seen from the train as it passes the old port with its quays built in 1821 for shipping Dartmoor granite. Leaving Teignmouth, the train turns west along the Teign estuary, with views to the steep hills of the southern shore.

Newton Abbot

The line leaves the estuary and enters Newton Abbot with the racecourse to the north. Little remains of the medieval town, for Newton Abbot was greatly expanded following the arrival of the railway in 1846, and its terrace housing still has an early industrial air. Bradley Manor, a 15th-century house, is just west of the town. Leaving Newton Abbot, the line swings west after the junction with the Paignton branch (see right),

TRAINS
(1 hr 10 mins approx)
Mon–Fri 17; Sat 14;
Sun 9
Refreshments: usually

**Tourist Information
Centres** (*summer only)
Dartmouth Royal
Avenue (08043) 4224
Dawlish The Lawn
(0626) 863589
Exeter Civic Centre, Paris
St (0392) 265297
Newton Abbot 8
Sherborne Rd
(0626) 67494
Paignton The Esplanade
(0803) 558383
Plymouth Royal Parade
(0752) 264849
Teignmouth The Den, Sea
Front (06267) 79769
Torquay Vaughan Parade
(0803) 27428
Totnes The Plains
(0803) 863168

**For all information on
Plymouth see page 14**

Walks
*South West Peninsula Coast
Path* join between
Dawlish and Dartmouth.
Dartmoor National Park
(see pages 10–11), from
Buckfastleigh or by car
from any station.
River Dart Country Park
(Dartmoor) by car from
Buckfastleigh, Newton
Abbot, Totnes.

Places to Visit
Dartmouth Castle, EH;
steamer trips to Totnes
Dawlish Museum
(May–Sep)
Exeter Cathedral;
Maritime Museum;
Royal Albert Memorial
Museum. *By train/car*
Brunel Atmospheric
Railway Museum (Apr–
Oct). *By car* Powderham
Castle (May–Sep)
Newton Abbot Bradley
Manor, NT (Apr–Sep).
Paignton Kirkham House,
EH (Etr–Oct); Oldway
Mansion; Zoo
Teignmouth Teign Valley
Glass Studios
Torquay Torre Abbey
(Apr–Oct)
Totnes Castle, EH;
Elizabethan Museum
(Etr–Oct); Motor
Museum (Apr–Oct). *By
car* Bowden House
(Apr–Sep); Buckfastleigh
for Buckfast Abbey,
Butterfly Farm
(Etr–Oct), Steam &
Leisure Park; Dartington
Cider Press Centre;
Dartington Hall

London-Penzance train on the spectacular stretch near Dawlish

and winds its way through a typical Devon landscape of wooded hills, little streams and thatched cottages.

Totnes

The train crosses the River Dart and enters Totnes. This is a good place to break the journey, an attractive small town easily explored on foot, with a castle and a good range of buildings from the 15th century onwards. This is also the station for the Dart Valley Railway's steam trains to Buckfastleigh (see below), and for visits to Dartmoor, six miles to the west. West of Totnes, the train continues through the typical Devon countryside. The Victorian church at Tigley can be seen to the north and then the line curves round South Brent, where the church with its Norman tower stands right by the River Avon. Dartmoor can now be seen to the north and then the train passes the little town of Ivybridge, high up on a curving viaduct. Another excellent viaduct carries the line over the Yealm valley, near Cornwood. The train then enters **Plymouth**, passing the ruins of Plympton Castle and Saltram House, with its Adam interior, in the woods to the south.

The Norman motte and bailey castle at Totnes

DART VALLEY RAILWAYS

Buckfastleigh & Totnes 7 miles
Totnes BR Station – Buckfastleigh.
Tel (0364) 42338. Operates: Etr, end May–Aug, Mon–Fri. Sat, Sun from Buckfastleigh (phone for details).
Single journey: 30 mins

Paignton & Dartmouth 7 miles
Paignton (beside BR station) – Kingswear (ferry Kingswear – Dartmouth).
Operates: Etr, end May–Aug (phone (0803) 555872 for details).
Single journey: 30 mins

See panel page 12 for **Tourist Information Centres, Walks** and **Places to Visit**

Brunel's Atmospheric Railway

This amazing invention was designed to haul trains on the very steep inclines between Newton Abbot and Plymouth. It consisted of a pipe between the rails in which ran a piston, fitted to the engine. Pumping houses sucked the air out, forming a vacuum. But problems plagued the project and it was abandoned in 1848.

DART VALLEY RAILWAYS

The Dart Valley is noted for its scenery, and is served by the private railway's two separate lines. The Paignton & Dartmouth Railway, running along the coast for nearly seven miles from Paignton, once carried such prestigious trains as the 'Torbay Express', while the Buckfastleigh & Totnes line was just a rural branch that served the middle valley for 98 years before being closed by BR.

Trains leave **Totnes** for **Buckfastleigh**, and run up the valley to **Staverton Bridge**, the station for the Old Mill which is now part of the Dartington Hall Trust. Just over six miles from the junction, the train reaches Buckfastleigh terminus, at one end of the old town. Buckfast Abbey is less than a mile away.

No other preserved railway can boast such spectacular views as the Paignton & Dartmouth. Three-quarters of a mile from **Paignton** the coast is reached, with the beach served by **Goodrington** station. From here the line climbs steeply, and the view opens up. As the train crosses the spectacular Hookhills and Broadsands viaducts, the coast beyond Exmouth is visible with occasional glimpses of the contrasting red cliffs of Devon and white cliffs of Dorset.

Beyond **Churston** lies the quarter-mile Greenway Tunnel, the exit from it being high above the Dart estuary, with the Royal Naval College on the far side.

From the terminus at **Kingswear** a ferry crosses to Dartmouth from where, at the right state of the tides, pleasure vessels leave for Totnes.

THE PAIGNTON BRANCH 8¼ miles

Leaving the main line south of Newton Abbot, the Paignton branch climbs steeply, passing Kingskerswell Church, to **Torre** station, a pretty building in typical Brunel style. Torquay now spreads to the south as the line drops to the coast, and the grounds of 12th-century Torre Abbey just before **Torquay** station. The line then runs by the shore to **Paignton**, with good views across Torbay, to Torquay and to Brixham.

TRAINS

(17 mins approx)
Mon–Sat 21; Sun 19

Buckfastleigh-Totnes train by the Dart with 45-XX locomotive

The beautiful old Smeaton's Lighthouse adorns Plymouth Hoe

TRAINS
(1 hr 15 mins approx)
Mon–Sat 14; Sun 9
Refreshments: usually

Tourist Information Centres (★summer only)
Bodmin Mount Folly Sq
(0208) 6616
Looe★ Fore St, East Looe
(05036) 2072
Lostwithiel Liddicoat Rd
(0208) 872207
Plymouth★ Civic Centre,
Royal Parade
(0752) 264849

Truro Boscawen St
(0872) 74555

For all information on Truro see page 16

Walks
The South West Peninsula Coast Path join at Looe, Par and Plymouth.
Country Park Mount Edgcumbe, by ferry from Plymouth

Cycling (see pages 5–7)
Plym Valley Cycle Path

Places to Visit
Bodmin Parkway
Lanhydrock House
(Apr–Oct) & Gdns, NT
Liskeard Merlin Glass of Liskeard (Feb–Dec).
By bus from station
Dobwalls Theme Park
(Etr–Oct). *By car*
Carnglaze Slate Caverns,
St Neot (Apr–Sep);
Hurlers stone circle;
Trethevy Quoit
(prehistoric burial);
Lostwithiel Restormel
Castle, EH
Plymouth City Museum & Art Gallery; Drake's Island (May–Sep) (ferry); Merchant's House Museum; Plym Valley Railway Steam Centre; Smeaton's Tower (May–Sep). *By ferry/bus* Mount Edgcumbe House (Etr/Apr–Oct) & Park. *By car/bus* Dartmoor Wildlife Park & Falconry Centre, Sparkwell. *By car* Antony House (Apr–Oct) & Gdns, NT, Torpoint; Saltram House, NT (Apr–Oct) & Gdns, Plympton
St Austell Automobilia (Etr–Oct). *By car/bus* Wheal Martyn Museum (Apr–Oct)
St Keyne Paul Corin's Mechanical Music Centre (May–Sep)

Par-Newquay See page 19

Truro Penzance See pages 16–17

EXETER – PENZANCE   *Plymouth – Truro*   53¾ *miles*

The journey from Plymouth to Truro is a voyage through Cornish history, from Anglo-Saxon Christianity to 19th-century industrialisation, via medieval castles and great mansions. The train travels across the heart of the county, winding through the hills and striding across the river valleys on great viaducts, the whole route a living memorial to Victorian engineering.

Two bridges across the Tamar – Brunel's masterpiece, opened in 1859, carries the railway, and behind it the modern Suspension Bridge carries road traffic

Plymouth

This excellent city makes the most of its natural harbour formed by four rivers, the Plym, the Tavy, the Tamar and the Lynher. A maritime city for centuries, Plymouth is full of history, from Drake to modern frigates. Treats include Smeaton's original Eddystone lighthouse, a fine 17th-century citadel, some Tudor houses round the Barbican, a wealth of 18th- and early 19th-century buildings, civic and naval, great Edwardian hotels and over 200 churches. The older parts, the Hoe, Stonehouse and the Barbican, are a mile south of Plymouth station, but the naval dockyards are best approached from **Devonport** station. A good outing is to take the ferry from Stonehouse to Devil's Point for Mount Edgcumbe house and park with its views across the Sound.

Saltash

The train leaves Plymouth, passes through Devonport suburbs high above the Hamoaze and the naval dockyards, with views across to Torpoint, and then slows for the approach to Brunel's great bridge across the Tamar. This marvellous structure, the only railway suspension bridge in the world, was completed in 1859, and the two huge curving spans, carrying the single track 100ft above the river, still dominate their surroundings and the little streets and quays of Saltash, far below. The parallel road bridge was opened 102 years later. Brunel's bridge is best seen from the west, as the train descends the steep approach curve through Saltash station. From Saltash the train runs above the Lynher estuary, crossing Antony Passage on the first of the many viaducts between here and Truro.

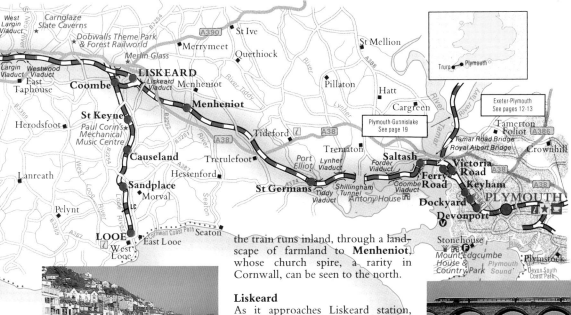

the train runs inland, through a landscape of farmland to **Menheniot**, whose church spire, a rarity in Cornwall, can be seen to the north.

Liskeard

As it approaches Liskeard station, with the town spread over the hills to the north, the train crosses the Looe branch (see left) on a high viaduct. From Liskeard the line winds through hills until it reaches the wooded valley of the Fowey river, which it then follows to **Bodmin Parkway** station. The town of Bodmin is three miles to the north west. Stop here for Lanhydrock House and Gardens. The train continues to Lostwithiel, with Restormel castle, one of the best examples of military architecture in Cornwall, to the north.

Lostwithiel

Dominated by its large church, the town is spread beside the Fowey, which is crossed by a 14th-century bridge. The best view of the town is from the train as it crosses the river to the south of the station. The line now runs towards the sea.

Par

Par station, old-fashioned and full of interest, is the stop for the Newquay branch (page 19) and for visits to Fowey, Gribbin Head and Polruan, four miles to the east via the A3082. Par church, the first building designed by the Victorian architect G E Street, is to the east of the station. From Par the train runs beside the sea. Mining and china clay prompted the development of Par, Charlestown and St Austell in the 19th century, but Carlyon still has its sandy beaches.

St Austell

St Austell is the capital of the china clay trade, and the white spoil tips can be seen on the horizon to the west of the station. Also visible as the train goes west are the ivy-clad ruins of the old mine chimneys.

Truro

A remote landscape surrounds the track as the train passes Probus, whose magnificent church tower can be seen high on a hill to the south. After the Tresillian river, cuttings and tunnels hide the landscape, allowing the train to make a rather secret approach to Truro. Suddenly the city appears, spread below the elevated track around its great Victorian cathedral.

The 13-arch viaduct at St Germans

LOOK OUT FOR

The most striking feature of the line westwards from Plymouth are the great **viaducts** that carry the train high above the river valleys and across the rolling hills. There are no less than 34 major viaducts between Saltash and Truro. When the Cornwall Railway was first opened in 1859, many of the viaducts along its route and along the routes of the other linking railways in Cornwall and Devon were built from timber. These complex structures in yellow pine, often supported on slate or granite piers, were all designed by Brunel. The decision to use wood was prompted by economy but they were so well engineered that many survived into this century. The last timber viaduct, at College Wood on the Falmouth branch, was finally rebuilt in stone in 1934. Today, the ivy-clad piers of the original viaducts can sometimes be seen standing beside their stone or brick replacements. Good viaducts to look out for are west of St Germans, over the A38, over the Gover valley, west of St Austell, two over the River Fal, seven miles west of St Austell, and over the Tresillian river west of Probus.

Looe, with its old buildings and pretty lanes, popular with holidaymakers

THE LOOE BRANCH 8¾ miles

TRAINS
(30 mins)
Mon–Fri 7; Sat 9; Sun (summer only) 4

The branch line to Looe is both eccentric and attractive, a Victorian survival that is an enjoyable anachronism in the late 20th century. The start sets the tone for the whole journey, the train departing from a pretty white-painted terminus across the road from the main **Liskeard** station. It sets off down a steep hill and under the viaduct that carries the main line, and on down to **Coombe Junction Station** on the china clay line. The train then reverses, the guard having changed the points, and follows the wooded valley of the Looe river, full of wild flowers, to **St Keyne**, with its Holy Well up on the hillside to the west. When the line was built, it followed the route of the old Liskeard–Looe Canal, and traces of this can still be seen, notably the canal bed, the narrow stone bridges, and the old locks, clearly visible south of St Keyne and south of Sandplace, where the canal used to join the estuary. Remote halts at **Causeland** and **Sandplace** seem to serve nowhere, but to the east of Sandplace is Tudor Morval House with its pretty church near by. From Sandplace the line runs beside the estuary to its terminus at **Looe** station, to the north of the picturesque fishing village.

St Germans

After crossing the River Lynher by a fine viaduct the train reaches St Germans, with its charming and original Brunel station of 1859. This little town is well worth a visit, for its setting, for the old quays, for its picturesque almshouses and above all for its marvellous Norman church. The cathedral of Cornwall was here in Anglo-Saxon times until 1050. To the north is Port Elliot, a former priory converted into a house by Sir John Soane from 1802. From St Germans

TRAINS
(42 mins approx)
Mon–Sat 14; Sun 7
Refreshments: usually

Tourist Information
Centres (*summer only)
Falmouth The Moor
(0326) 312300
Hayle★ A30 Southern
Cross Self-Serve, Loggans
Moor (0736) 755485
Penzance Station Rd
(0736) 62207
St Ives Street-an-Pol
(0736) 796297
Truro Boscawen St
(0872) 74555

Walks
The Cornwall Coast Path
join at Falmouth, Hayle,
Penzance or St Ives.
The Tinners' Way, from St
Ives to St Just

Cycling (see pages 5–7)
Penzance–Land's End–
Penzance

Places to Visit
Camborne By bus
Camborne Geological
Museum; Cornish
Engines, East Pool, NT
(Apr–Oct). *By car*
Carwynnen Quoit
Falmouth Art Gallery;
Maritime Museum
(Etr–Oct); Pendennis
Castle, EH
Hayle Paradise Park (rare
birds); Towans Railway
(May–Sep)
Penzance Egyptian
House; Penlee House
Museum & Gallery.
By bus Newlyn Art
Gallery. *By car* ancient
sites Chysauster, EH,
Lanyon Quoit & Men-
an-Tol, Madron;
Trengwainton Gdn, NT
(Mar–Oct)
Redruth Carn Brea. *By bus*
Cornish Engines, see
Camborne
St Ives Barbara Hepworth
Museum & other art
galleries; Museum
(May–Sep)
Truro Cathedral; County
Museum. *By car* Probus
Demonstration Gdn;
Trelissick Gdn, NT
(Mar–Oct)

EXETER – PENZANCE   *Truro – Penzance   25¾ miles*

From Truro to Penzance the train travels through a dramatic landscape, a powerful mixture of natural elements combined with the man-made scars of the mining industry. Now a part of history, these have acquired a romantic appeal and seem as remote as the many prehistoric monuments of the region. The line links together picturesque old harbours, sandy beaches and remote river valleys, to capture the particular flavour of West Cornwall.

Truro
An enjoyable lively city, full of late Georgian architecture, Truro has a particular appeal that has much to do with its position at the head of the estuary. It still has the atmosphere of a port, its older centre contained by the harbour to the south, and the railway to the north. The focal point, and the natural starting point for any exploration, is the Cathedral, the only Victorian cathedral of note in England and the first in Cornwall since 1050. The train leaves the large brick station and soon the Falmouth branch swings away to the south (see right).

Redruth
East of Redruth the landscape becomes more industrial, a strange blend of rocky outcrops and old mines. All around are the ruined engine houses and chimneys, built for the great steam pumps that kept the tin mines clear of water. Ivy-clad and sombre, these have a picturesque quality that is part of the character of Cornwall. Redruth has a powerful industrial atmosphere, its Victorian terraces well seen from the viaduct west of the station. In these surroundings it is easy to forget that the Atlantic coast is only four miles to the north. West of the town the landscape is dominated by the great mound of Carn Brea, crowned by a monument to Lord de Dunstanville, its engine houses looking down on Church Town, actually Redruth's parish church with its 15th-century tower.

Camborne
Redruth and Camborne are virtually one town, linked by the railway and the A30. In Camborne's centre, beside the old A30, is a preserved steam pumping engine, its great iron beam piercing the side of the stone engine house. A convenient reminder of Cornwall's pre-industrial history is the Stone Age burial chamber, or quoit, at Carwynnen, two miles to the south, one of the many prehistoric monuments in the area. After Camborne, the train leaves the industrial landscape behind, and passes the former Gwinear Road station, where the track of the long-closed branch to Helston swings away to the south. Also to the south is Gwinear Church, set among trees.

Hayle
The train drops down towards Hayle, with views across Phillack church to St Ives bay. Hayle, built round its large enclosed harbour, is an important town in the industrial history of Cornwall. The first steam-powered railway in Cornwall was opened here in 1834 and Harvey's of Hayle were the leading builders of steam pumps and mine engines, and from Hayle harbour these great iron monsters were shipped all over the world. Today it is quiet, the harbour silted and disused, and full of gentle decay.

St Erth
The line runs beside the Hayle estuary to St Erth, an isolated station well to

---

THE ST IVES BRANCH 4¼ miles

TRAINS
(12 mins)
Mon–Fri 19; Sat 17
Sun (summer only) 14

This short journey starts at **St Erth** and the train runs along beside the estuary, with views across to Hayle. A Park-and-Ride system to St Ives operates from **Lelant Saltings. Lelant**, its church up above the line, was once a seaport. The train then comes out into St Ives Bay, its route high on the cliffs with wonderful views towards Godrevy Point. It is a classic seaside journey. The great sands of Port Kidney are followed by **Carbis Bay**, where there is a halt, and then the train rounds Porthminster Point and comes to a halt at **St Ives** station, well to the south of the town, but with the harbour straight ahead.

The St Ives train passing is a familiar sight to holidaymakers on the beach

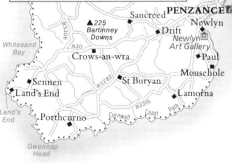

the north of its village. It is worth the short walk, for the village has a pretty setting and 18th-century cottages beside the old bridge over the Hayle. The branch for St Ives (see opposite page) leaves the main line here. Leaving St Erth, the train cuts across Cornwall at its narrowest point, a few miles linking the Atlantic with Mount's Bay on the south coast.

Penzance

The approach to Penzance is a fitting end to a remarkable journey. The train circles round Mount's Bay, with Marazion to the east, and runs along the edge of the sandy beach. St Michael's Mount is a dramatic centre-piece for the splendid view. This is a journey to take at different times and seasons, for the light on the Mount is constantly changing. Penzance is ahead, the town spread along the shore to the south, and the journey ends at the handsome stone station, with its glazed trainshed recently restored. The town centre is to the south, beyond the harbour, and easily reached on foot. It is an attractive, independent sort of town, with good early 19th-century buildings spread over the hillside. Notable are the market hall of 1844, St Mary's Church, and the Regency terraces west of the main street, but Penzance's most famous landmark is inevitably the façade of the extraordinary Egyptian House.

East Pool whim beam engine, near Camborne

LOOK OUT FOR
Reminders of **Cornwall's industrial past** are a feature of the landscape, particularly around Redruth–Camborne. Copper and tin mining made the area prosperous, but with the collapse of the industry, many miners emigrated and the mines, with their characteristic chimneys, were left to decay.

The famous rocky pile of St Michael's Mount, with its picturesque grouping of monastic buildings

Falmouth harbour, important as a yachting centre and as a working port. The Killigrew family were major movers behind the growth of the port in Tudor times and there is a monument to them in the town dating from 1737

THE FALMOUTH BRANCH
12¼ miles

TRAINS
(24 mins)
Mon–Fri 12; Sat 11; Sun 7

The Falmouth branch leaves the main line west of **Truro**, and it is a delightfully rural journey. Much of the route is elevated, giving good views across the wooded valleys and fields of fruit trees as the train descends steadily towards the sea. A high viaduct just before **Perranwell station** looks down towards the former port of Devoran, long closed by the silting of Restronguet Creek. A hundred years ago this was a hive of activity, with its own railway network, ships loading at the quays and the iron foundry at nearby Perran Wharf producing great steam pumping engines. The line continues high up, passing through tunnels and over another viaduct, and then drops steeply to **Penryn**, where the elevated station offers an excellent view over the little town. The train enters **Falmouth** in a rather private way until suddenly the great harbour comes into view, still busy with shipping. It is a fine harbour, its entrance guarded by Henry VIII's great castles at Pendennis and St Mawes, its development from a fishing village dating from the 16th century. The town is attractively ranged round the harbour and easily reached.

Barnstaple ●—● Exmouth

West Country Branches

Four highly varied West Country branch lines capture the atmosphere of the English rural railway at its best, a marvellous way to see the countryside. At the same time, they all have considerable historical interest, for each was once part of a far greater network of West Country railways.

EXETER–BARNSTAPLE 38¾ miles

Leave from **Exeter St David's.** The train follows the River Yeo to Crediton and Colebrooke, and then, after Lapford, the fast-flowing Taw with its mills, old bridges and wooded banks thick with wild flowers. This is the best section, the landscape of Tarka the Otter. Most of the stations and halts are by request only, so tell the guard where you want to get off. The A377 follows the line closely, with easy access to villages *en route*. **Crediton** is the only place of any size, a pleasant market town whose red sandstone church has a memorial to Sir Redvers Buller, the reliever of Ladysmith. After **Yeoford**, a branch leads to Okehampton. Now used only by stone trains from Meldon Quarry, this was the Southern Railway's main line to Plymouth. **Lapford** has a pretty church and mill, but the best church is at **King's Nympton**, with its excellent Renaissance and later woodwork. Just north is Junction Pool, the attractive meeting of the Mole and Taw. At Bishop's Tawton the train passes between the church

with its octagonal spire and the Tudor gatehouse of Tawstock Court, and then the valley opens out as **Barnstaple** comes into view. A blend of seaport and market town, it stands on the Taw estuary. It is a good station for visits to Exmoor by car.

EXETER – EXMOUTH
11¼ miles

Leave from **Exeter** (either station) and sit on the right. The train joins the Exe at **Topsham**, a pretty village, and then travels along the shore with views to Powderham and Starcross. Look out for the assault course at the Marine Training Centre at **Lympstone Commando**, then a clock tower after **Lympstone** station, and finally **Exmouth**, a pleasant old port with a sandy beach. Just to the north, off the B3180, is A la Ronde, a delightful 18th-century folly.

Built in 1798, A la Ronde contains a good Regency gallery

TRAINS
Exeter–Barnstaple
(1 hr 50 mins approx)
Mon–Fri 7; Sat 8; Sun 4

Exeter–Exmouth
(30 mins approx)
Mon–Sat 23; Sun 10

Tourist Information Centres (★summer only)
Barnstaple Library, Tuly St (0271) 47177
Exeter Civic Centre, Paris St (0392) 265297
Exmouth★ Alexandra Terr (0395) 263744

For all information on Exeter see page 12

Walks
Exmoor National Park, varied walking, including guided (see pages 10–11), by car from Barnstaple
Braunton Barrows dune and estuary nature reserve, reach by car from Barnstaple
South West Peninsula Coast Path join at Barnstaple, Exmouth
Taw Valley from stations/halts north of Eggesford
Two Moors Way, access Morchard Rd, Copplestone

Places to Visit
Barnstaple St Anne's chapel (Jun–Sep). *By car* Arlington Court, NT (Apr–Oct); Marwood Hill Gdns
Exmouth By car/bus A la Ronde (Apr–Oct); Country Life Museum (Etr–Sep). *By car* Bicton Park Gdn (Apr–Oct); Wonderful World of Miniature (model trains) (Apr–Oct)

BARNSTAPLE
Bishops Tawton
Cobbaton
Chapelton
Atherington Umberleigh
High Bickington
Chittlehamholt
Portsmouth Arms
Burrington Kings Nympton
Chulmleigh
Chawleigh
Eggesford
Wembworthy
Lapford
Morchard Bishop
Down St Mary
Morchard Road
Copplestone
Coleford
Colebrooke Crediton
Yeoford
Newton St Cyres

Junction Pool
Kings Nympton
Two Moors Way

River Taw
River Mole
River Bray
River Dart
River Yeo
River Dalch

0   2 Mls
0   2 Kms

The Church of All Saints at Eggesford – one of several delightful churches along this line – contains two outstanding memorials

Salisbury – Exeter
See pages 24-25

Exeter – Penzance
See pages 12-17

EXETER
St James Park
Exeter Cen
Exeter St David's
Exeter St Thomas
Polsloe Bridge
Pinhoe
Clyst St Mary
Topsham
Exton
Lympstone Commando
Lympstone
Powderham Castle
Clock Tower
A la Ronde Country Life Museum
Starcross
Exmouth
Brunel Atmospheric Railway Pumping House Museum

A step back in time: Morwellham's assayer

PLYMOUTH–GUNNISLAKE
14¾ miles

This is one of the least known delights of the West Country. The train leaves **Plymouth** with good views over the harbour and the warships in the naval dockyard, and then branches off the main line to pass under Brunel's Saltash Bridge. The line then runs beside the Tamar and crosses the Tavy, with views west to Landulph Church, before starting the climb towards **Bere Ferrers.** It is a remote little town, surrounded by rivers, and with a pretty station decorated with old railway signs. From here the train starts to climb seriously, winding its way through rocky cuttings spanned by old stone bridges to **Bere Alston**, a terminus where the train reverses. This was once the Southern Railway's main route to Exeter, via Tavistock and Okehampton. The train is now high above the twisting Tamar, and Cotehele House and Quay can be seen below, accessible from **Calstock** station. The great Calstock viaduct carries the train into Cornwall, 117ft above the Tamar, and then the line climbs on up, with occasional glimpses of Morwellham Quay and its museum far below. It reaches **Gunnislake** in a typical Cornish landscape over overgrown mine chimneys. These were the line's *raison d'être* and it once went to Callington, to serve the huge mines on Kit Hill.

TRAINS
(50 mins approx)
Mon–Sat 6; no Sunday service

Places to Visit
Calstock Cotehele House, NT (Apr–Oct); Morwellham Quay Museum

For all information on Plymouth see page 14

LOOK OUT FOR
It was the **copper, tin** and **china clay** deposits that justified the building of many Cornish railways in the 19th century. The tin and copper mines have closed, but the landscape around Gunnislake is dotted with the chimneys of the old mine engines, now broken and overgrown. Cotehele and Morwellham have both been preserved, with a large industrial museum, Morwellham Quay Museum, at the latter, and further south are Par and Charlestown, seaports built for the export of both ores and china clay.

PAR – NEWQUAY *20¾ miles*

The train leaves the main line at **Par** and passes the semi-circular engine shed at St Blazey. It climbs through woods, with a fast-flowing river falling noisily below, and then passes under the great Treffry Viaduct, built in 1825 for a mine tramway, now a footpath which can be seen across the river south of Treffry. After **Luxulyan**, the train enters a wilder moorland landscape, with china clay mines dominant as the line passes **Bugle** and **Roche**, with its 14th-century chapel on top of a rocky crag, and crosses the wilderness of Goss Moor. The china clay pits which fill the horizon west of Luxulyan and Bugle, have a certain romantic grandeur, with the white conical spoil tips looking like strange mountain ranges. To the north is the Iron Age fort, Castle-an-Dinas associated with King Arthur. Rolling hills with occasional views of the sea take over the approach to **Newquay**, renowned for the surfing on its Atlantic beaches.

Both quays in Newquay Harbour offer good fishing for bass and flounder, and boats are available for offshore fishing

TRAINS
(48 mins approx)
Mon–Sat 6; Sundays (summer only) 4

Tourist Information Centre
Newquay Cliff Rd
(0637) 871345

Walks
South West Peninsula Coast Path from Par.

Places to Visit
Newquay Aquarium (May–Sep); Zoo. *By car* Trerice House, NT (Apr–Oct)
Roche/St Columb Road By car Castle-an-Dinas hillfort

Across Wessex

BRISTOL – WEYMOUTH *Bristol – Yeovil 59½ miles*

TRAINS
(1 hr 40 mins approx)
Mon–Fri 6; Sat 7; Sun 6
Refreshments: some

**Tourist Information
Centres** (*summer only)
Bath Abbey Church Yard
(0225) 462831
Bradford-On-Avon Silver
St (02216) 5797
Bristol Colston St
(0272) 293891/260767
Bristol Airport
(027587) 4441
Frome Cattle Market Car
Park (0373) 67271
Trowbridge★ St Stephens
Place (0225) 777054
Westbury★ Edward St
(0373) 827158
Yeovil Johnson Hall,
Hendford (0935) 22884

**For all information on
Yeovil see page 22**

Walks
Avon Walkway 27 miles
along Avon, can be
joined at Bristol and
Bath.
Cotswold Way Join at Bath
Kennet & Avon Canal
Towpath starts in Bath.

Places to Visit
Bath Abbey; Costume
Museum; Pump Room;
Roman Bath Museum.
By car American
Museum, Claverton
Bradford-on-Avon St
Lawrence Saxon Church;
Tithe Barn (Apr–Oct)
(*bus*).
Bruton By car Stourhead
Bristol Arnolfini Gallery;
Bristol and Clifton
Cathedrals; City Docks;
City Museum & Art
Gallery. *By car* Clifton
Suspension Bridge; Zoo
Frome By car/bus Longleat
House and Safari Park;
By car East Somerset
Railway, Cranmore
Westbury By car Bratton
Camp and White Horse

*SS Great Britain in
Bristol Docks, like the
GWR a product of
Brunel's genius*

A journey that links such interesting towns and cities as this one has to be special. It explores England's history from before the Romans to the legacy of Brunel and the Great Western Railway, via the splendid stone elegance of the 18th century. The landscape ranges from the dramatic to the domestic, with the steep Avon valley, the rolling farmland of Wiltshire and Somerset, the ancient hills of Hardy's Dorset and finally the seaside at Weymouth. For the best views, sit on the left from Bristol.

Bristol
With its churches, Georgian and Victorian architecture, rich commercial buildings and revived dock area, Bristol's temptations include the zoo, theatres and galleries, shopping precincts and many museums. Above all it is the city of Brunel, with his suspension bridge at Clifton, his *SS Great Britain*, and his magnificent GWR terminus at Temple Meads.

The line follows the twisting Avon, through rock cuttings and tunnels. Hanham Court dominates the river to the north near **Keynsham** and at Saltford the manor is glimpsed, one of England's oldest inhabited houses. To the south is Newton Park (1762), now a training college, seen shortly before the train enters the castellated portal of Twerton Tunnel.

Bath
The train makes a fine entrance to Bath, high above the Avon which is crossed twice on curved viaducts, and circling to the south with the 18th-century terraces in golden stone spread over the hills to the north. The Abbey, the Roman Baths and Pump Room, and the Assembly Rooms can be identified from the train. Leaving Bath the train passes through Sydney Gardens in an elegant cutting spanned by decorative stone bridges. After Bathampton, and with Bathford church up on a hill to the north, the train branches from the main line, to follow the winding Avon. This is a magnificent stretch, with Claverton and the American Museum, and charming **Freshford**, with its medieval bridge, set on the wooded hills. The

*The Great Bath, the most spectacular
building in the bathing complex at Bath*

train runs by the Kennet and Avon Canal, with views of Rennie's great Avoncliff and Limpley Stoke aqueducts.

Bradford-on-Avon
The train follows canal and river to Bradford, a lovely old cloth town with a Saxon chapel, medieval church, great tithe barn, 17th-century bridge with circular lock-up, many 17th- and 18th-century buildings and elegant 19th-century riverside mills.

Trowbridge
Though small, this is the county town of Wiltshire and another former cloth town, with riverside mills and large 18th-century houses.

Westbury
At Westbury, a major junction with marshalling yards for stone-laden trains from the quarries to the north, the train joins the main London–West Country line. Look south for the distant, 18th-century white horse cut in the chalk.

Frome
On a loop off the main line, Frome's covered station of 1850 is the oldest through-trainshed still in use in England. Stop here for Longleat House and Safari Park, four miles east

SS GREAT BRITAIN

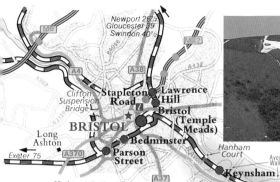

The 18th-century White Horse of Westbury may have its origins back in King Alfred's time

off the A362. The train then follows the River Frome, with a distant view to the south of Alfred's Tower, a folly. (On the other side is Stourhead.) At Cranmore, on the former line to Wells and Cheddar, is the preserved East Somerset Railway, eight miles west of Frome off the A361.

Bruton
Spread above the valley of the Brue, Bruton is dominated by the church with its magnificent 15th-century tower, 102ft high. Soon after Bruton, the train passes an embankment of the disused Somerset and Dorset line from Bath to the Dorset coast. It was famous for its steep inclines and viaducts, one of which is at Pitcombe, beside the A359 south of Bruton.

Castle Cary
The train then follows the Brue through hilly country. At Castle Cary the train leaves the main line to branch south towards Yeovil. Castle Cary, largely hidden from view, is a pleasant, tranquil place.

Yeovil
Leaving Castle Cary, the train joins a single track line through flat moorland to the west with increasingly powerful hills to the east. In a few minutes at Sparkford, which is on the A303 and has a motor museum, look east for Cadbury Castle, a mighty Iron Age hillfort thought by many to be King Arthur's Camelot. This is a remote region, with the distant villages of Queen Camel, Marston Magna and Mudford marked by their

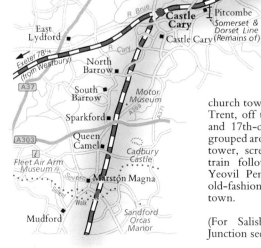

Transport history comes to life on the East Somerset Railway at Cranmore

church towers. Come back by car for Trent, off the B3148, with its 16th- and 17th-century houses and farms grouped around a church with delicate tower, screen and bench ends. The train follows the River Yeo into Yeovil Pen Mill station, pleasantly old-fashioned and convenient for the town.

(For Salisbury–Exeter via Yeovil Junction see pages 24–25)

LOOK OUT FOR
Between Bristol and Frome are fine examples of **19th-century industry and engineering.** First, the Great Western Railway itself, with its tunnels, rock cuttings, viaducts and stations, at Bristol and Bath, testifying to Brunel's extraordinary skills. Second, the great stone mills of the cloth trade, at Bradford, Trowbridge, Frome and near Bruton. Third, Rennie's Kennet and Avon Canal, opened in 1810 to link Bristol and London, and recently restored after years of decay. The most dramatic features are the great stone aqueducts that cross the Avon. At Avoncliff and near Trowbridge, aqueducts also carry the canal over the railway. A good walk is to follow the canal through Bath and along the Avon valley.

**Tourist Information
Centres** (*summer only)
Dorchester 7 Acland Rd
(0305) 67992
Minehead The Parade
(0643) 2624
Taunton Corporation St
(0823) 274785
Weymouth Pavilion,
Theatre Complex, The
Esplanade (0305) 785747
Yeovil see page 20
Yeovilton★ Fleet Air Arm
Museum, (0935) 75272

Walks
Bridport branch line ask at
Dorchester TIC
Maiden Castle and downs
walk/bus from Dorchester
*Radipole Lake, RSPB
reserve,* Weymouth
*South West Peninsula Coast
Path* from Minehead or
by car from Weymouth

Places to Visit
Dorchester County
Museum; Dinosaur
Museum; Maiden Castle
hillfort. *By car* Hardy's
Cottage, Higher
Bockhampton, NT
Dunster Castle and Mill,
NT (Apr–Oct)
Maiden Newton By car to
Cerne Abbas, Cerne
Giant; Abbey ruins
(Apr–Oct)
Washford Cleeve Abbey,
EH; Railway Museum
(Etr–Sep Sun, B.Hols)
Weymouth Sea Life Centre
(Feb–Nov). *By car*
Abbotsbury Swannery
(May–Sep)
Yeovil By car/bus
Montacute House, NT
(Apr–Oct). *By car*
Brympton d'Evercy
(May–Sep); Tintinhull
House Gdn, NT (Apr–
Sep); Worldwide
Butterflies & Lullingstone
Silk Farm (Apr–Oct);
Yeovilton, Fleet Air Arm
Museum

The harbour and quayside at Weymouth, a busy resort made popular by George III

BRISTOL – WEYMOUTH   *Yeovil – Weymouth*   27½ miles

Yeovil
Near Yeovil are the Fleet Air Arm Museum at Yeovilton and Ilchester (a Roman town) off the A303 to the north, Worldwide Butterflies and Lullingstone Silk Farm at Compton House off the A30 to the east, and a range of country houses, Brympton d'Evercy, Montacute, Tintinhull and Sandford Orcas Manor.

Peacock butterfly at Worldwide Butterflies

Yetminster
The stretch to Dorchester shows the English rural railway at its best. After Yeovil, the train passes under the Salisbury–Exeter line, still with the Yeo alongside, and then runs through an open landscape to Yetminster, which has a 16th- and 17th-century main street in soft golden stone. The next stop is **Chetnole**, a scattered village half hidden in woods. Red-brick Chetnole House of 1760 is now a police training college. To the west is Hardy's Melbury Bubb, with church tower standing out among the trees. A steep gradient leads to the short Holywell tunnel and then the line winds among the hills which rise steeply to the east. A wealth of pre-historic earthworks can be seen, and explored by car off the A37; further east, off the A352, is the 180ft Cerne Abbas Giant, cut into the hillside.

Maiden Newton
Approaching Maiden Newton the train passes Chantmarle to the west, a splendid early 17th-century manor in the trees, and Cattistock to the east, with tall church tower dominating the winding streets of old stone houses. Maiden Newton station has a traditional feeling, complete with signal box, and the track of the former branch line to Bridport can be seen swinging away to the west. Part of this is now a footpath. Leaving the station the train follows the Frome as it winds past Frampton. To the east a landscape dotted with earthworks is dominated by Grimstone Down.

WEST SOMERSET RAILWAY

Bishops Lydeard–Minehead   20 miles
(Some bus connections from Taunton BR Station to Bishops Lydeard)
Operates: Etr–Oct
(phone for details
(0643) 4996)
Single journey: 1½
hours

See above for **Tourist Information Centres, Walks, Places to Visit**

Along its 20-mile route from **Bishops Lydeard**, the West Somerset Railway runs between the Quantocks and the Brendon Hills. The line climbs steeply to **Crowcombe**, where the station lies in wooded country, with wildlife in abundance, and then runs through the widening valley past the single platform at **Stogumber**, and on to **Williton**, where the attractive stone station buildings date from the opening of the line in 1862.

There is a first glimpse of the sea after **Doniford Beach** station before the railway squeezes round the end of the bright-red cliffs at **Watchet**, and turns inland to **Washford**. Here are the ruins of the Cistercian Cleeve Abbey, within easy walking distance. At **Blue Anchor** the train regains the coast, with its magnificent views of the Bristol Channel with Steepholm Island and the South Wales coast from Cardiff to the Gower stretching along the horizon. Inland from **Dunster** are the stone towers of

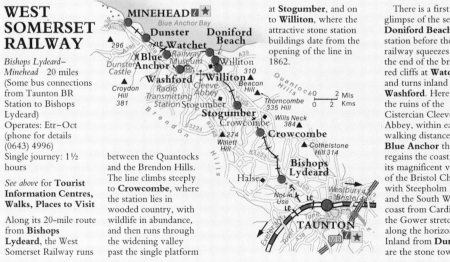

Yeovil – Weymouth
See pages 22-23

Salisbury – Exeter
From Yeovil Junction
(no rail connection)
See pages 24-25

Dorchester

The approach to Dorchester is rather grand. The train is raised on an embankment above the Frome, with the spire of Bradford Peverell Church to the west. The short Poundbury tunnel was cut in 1857 at Brunel's insistence to preserve the Iron Age hillfort above. Dorchester, Dorset's county town and the home of Thomas Hardy, still boasts two railway stations, a few minutes' walk apart past the decorative Victorian brewery. It is a fine stone town: walk along the high street to see the County Museum with its pretty cast iron interior and Judge Jeffreys' timbered lodgings, as well as good, old hotels and pretty shop fronts.

GWR 0-6-0 Collett goods locomotive on the West Somerset Railway. The engine dates from 1946

Dunster Castle, inhabited by the Lutterell family since 1376, set on the hillside above the village. There is a brief glimpse of Dunkery Beacon, the highest point on Exmoor, before the railway finishes at **Minehead**, with a fine view along the coast to North Hill, the starting point for the Somerset and North Devon Coast Path.

Weymouth

South of Dorchester the train joins the main line from London and then starts the gradual descent towards Weymouth, with the sea ahead. To the west is the enormous hillfort of Maiden Castle. This area is particularly rich in ancient sites, best explored by paths off the B3159. After the Gothic façade of Herringston House to the east, and Winterborne Monkton Church to the west, the train reaches **Upwey**, and enters Weymouth alongside Radipole Lake. The new station is the terminus of the line which formerly went on to the Isle of Portland.

One of England's most appealing resorts, Weymouth was made popular by George III whose colourful statue is on the esplanade, and whose huge figure on horseback is cut into the Downs about Osmington. Traditional Regency terraces look out over the great curve of the sandy beach, and the enclosed harbour is busy with fishing boats, coasters, yachts and the ferries to Cherbourg and the Channel Islands. In between are narrow streets of shops and cafés, crowded in the summer, and delightfully empty out of season.

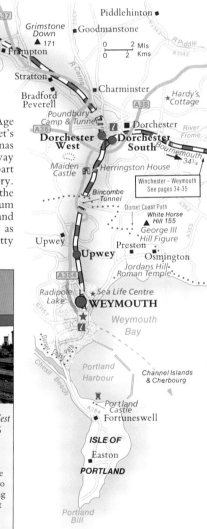

LOOK OUT FOR

Numerous **hillforts, barrows and other earthworks** associated with Iron Age and earlier cultures can be seen from the train. Notable examples are Cadbury Castle, east of Sparkford; Castle Hill and Cross Hill, east of Cattistock; Grimstone Hill east of Frampton; Poundbury Fort north of Dorchester and Maiden Castle south of Dorchester. In between, those with sharp eyes can spot numerous barrows, ditches and terraces formed by early cultivation. Other major monuments near by, such as Eggardon Hill, off the A35 west of Dorchester, and the Cerne Abbas Giant, can be explored by car.

Thomas Hardy's statue in Dorchester

GET OFF FOR

The line from Yeovil to Weymouth crosses the heart of **Hardy country**, and many of the settings for Hardy's novels can be explored on foot or by car. Start at Max Gate (not open), Hardy's own house in Dorchester or at his birthplace near Higher Bockhampton, 3 miles to the east, then discover the *Mayor of Casterbridge* in Dorchester. Next is Cerne Abbas and Melbury for *The Woodlanders*, followed by the Frome valley and Bere Regis for *Tess of the D'Urbervilles*. See Egdon Heath and Puddletown, off the A35 for *Far From the Madding Crowd*, and then Weymouth for *The Trumpet Major* and Isle of Portland for *The Well-Beloved*.

The soaring spire of Salisbury Cathedral. At 404 feet, this 14th-century steeple is the highest in England

TRAINS
(2 hours)
Mon–Sat 10; Sun 8
Refreshments: usually

**Tourist Information
Centres** (*summer only)
Axminster★ Church St
(0297) 34386
Exeter Civic Centre, Paris
St (0392) 265297
Honiton★ High Street
(0404) 3716
Salisbury Fish Row
(0722) 334956
Sherborne★ Hound St
(0935) 815341
Yeovil Johnson Hall,
Hendford (0935) 22884

**For all information on
Exeter and Yeovil see
pages 12 and 22**

Walks
Cranborne Chase reached
by car from Tisbury
*South West Peninsula Coast
Path* Dorset and South
Devon, reached by car or
bus from Axminster.

Cycling (see pages 5–7)
Salisbury – Stonehenge
– Salisbury

Places to Visit
Axminster By car Shute
Barton Manor; NT
(Apr–Oct)
Crewkerne By car Clapton
Court Gdns (Feb–Nov);
Cricket St Thomas
Wildlife Park; Forde
Abbey (Apr–Oct) &
Gdns
Feniton Cadhay House
(Spr BH, Jul–Aug)
Honiton Allhallows
Museum (Etr, May–Oct)
Salisbury Cathedral; Duke
of Edinburgh's Royal
Regiment Museum;
Mompesson House, NT
(Apr–Oct); Salisbury &
South Wiltshire Museum.
By car/bus Old Sarum,
EH; Wilton House
(Apr–Oct); Wilton Royal
Carpet Factory (tours
and museum)
Sherborne; Abbey; Castle
(Etr–Sep); Old Castle,
EH; Museum. *By car/bus*
Purse Caundle Manor
(Etr–Sep); Worldwide
Butterflies &
Lullingstone Silk Farm
(Apr–).
Tisbury By car Philipps
House, NT (by
appointment); Pythouse
(May–Sep); Wardour
Castle (summer school
holidays); Wardour Old
Castle, EH.

Rivers and Cathedrals

SALISBURY – EXETER *88¾ miles*

There are two routes from London to Exeter, a legacy of the days of rival railway companies. High speed Intercity trains from Paddington take the former Great Western line, while the slower trains from Waterloo follow the old London and South Western route. The best part of this journey is described here, from one cathedral city to another, past rolling hills, old stone villages and farms, thatched cottages and handsome churches. Above all it is a journey of rivers, from the winding Nadder to the Yeo, the Axe, the Otter and finally the Exe.

Salisbury

With its 404ft spire, the Early English cathedral was the centrepiece of a 13th-century new town laid out to replace the fortified hill of Old Sarum, and many of the streets still follow the medieval grid pattern. Starting with the cathedral and cathedral close, this is an interesting city to explore on foot. Old inns and pretty shop fronts add to the appeal, but Salisbury's best view is still that favoured by Constable and many other painters, the cathedral seen across the water meadows of the Avon.

Leaving Salisbury with the cathedral spire to the south, the train passes Wilton where the River Nadder meets the Wylye. Famous for its carpets and Inigo Jones's magnificent 1647 Wilton House, the town once had 12 but now has two parish churches, one a confection of mosaics, marble and medieval stained glass.

Among the Nadder valley's stone villages, look out for the fine arched bridge at Burcombe, to the south, with its distant view of Salisbury cathedral, and Dinton to the north where the church forms a pretty group with 18th-century Hyde House. Come back by car to see Teffont Evias and Teffont Magna, one

with a stream along the main street, and numerous prehistoric sites like Chiselbury Camp, the Ridgeway, Grim's Ditch and a wealth of burial mounds, all near the A30 or B3089. Also just off the A30, above the village of Fovant, are the Regimental badges cut into the chalk hillside by World War I soldiers.

Tisbury

Approaching Tisbury through the chalk downs, the train passes England's largest thatched tithe barn, just east of the station. Also dominant is St John's Church, with wagon roof supported inside by lively carved angels. After Tisbury look out for classical Pythouse, on a hill to the north. This can be visited by car, along with the two Wardour Castles, one a ruined fortified manor of the 14th century, the other built by James Paine in 1771 and now a school.

Gillingham

Gillingham (with a hard G) has a large church, 1769 silk mill and pleasant atmosphere. Mounds mark the site of a hunting lodge built by King John to the south, just east of the station. West are views across the Stour, with early terracing on the hillsides.

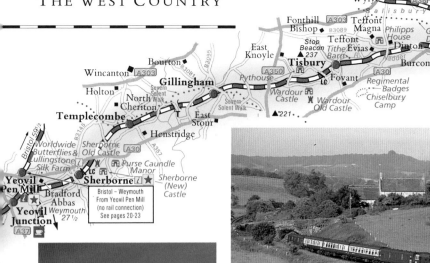

Rural stretch near Tisbury with one of the stone bridges typical of this line

Sherborne Castle, built by Sir Walter Raleigh in 1594 to replace the 12th-century castle

Templecombe
The approach to the town (named after the Knights Templars), is dominated by the church, on a mound to the north. In the old days, famous trains such as the Pines Express from Manchester to Bournemouth used to connect here with west country services from London.

Sherborne
This is the most enjoyable place to break the journey: the pretty station is well placed, and there is plenty to see. The ruins of the 12th-century castle rise by the line to the south. Beyond the lake, part of a Capability Brown park, is the 'new' castle, built for Sir Walter Raleigh in the 1590s. In the town proper are the abbey, the school, Roman remains, a museum, and plenty of shops and restaurants.

Yeovil Junction
Between Sherborne and Crewkerne are rolling hills, woods and traditional fields, with the River Yeo to the south. Look out for Bradford Abbas, about a mile east of Yeovil Junction, with the magnificent tower of St Mary's Church right by the line. Yeovil itself is well to the north, a bus ride from Yeovil Junction, a grand station

marking the point where the line from London meets the former Great Western's route to Weymouth. (For Bristol–Weymouth via Yeovil Pen Mill station see pages 20–23.) West is Sutton Bingham reservoir, used for water sports; to the north lies East Coker, where T S Eliot is buried.

Crewkerne
After passing Pendomer church and manor, on top of a hill to the north, the train reaches Crewkerne's tall stone station, designed by Sir William Tite. A mile north is the town, with its market square, handsome 15th-century church and coaching inns. West of Crewkerne the train follows the River Axe. To the south is Forde Abbey and to the north is Chard, which once boasted three railway stations but now has none.

Axminster
Famous for its carpets, markets and 18th-century buildings, Axminster is a short walk from the station. Stop here for the Devon and Dorset coast and for the traditional resorts of Lyme Regis and Seaton, easily reached by car or bus. West of Axminster the train winds along river valleys and between steep hills, with distant views of Kilmington Church and Elizabethan Shute Barton Manor.

Honiton
Flanked by the River Otter and the railway, this is an 18th-century town, rebuilt after a fire in 1765. Honiton lace can be seen in the museum. Come back by car for Gittisham, a remarkably undeveloped village of cob, stone and thatch in the hills to the southwest. There is a good church at **Feniton**, near the station and at **Whimple** the line passes the extensive Whiteways cider orchards. The train then passes Exeter airport, the M5 and suburban **Pinhoe** station before reaching **Exeter Central**, the best placed station for exploring the city. For **Exeter**, see page 12.

LOOK OUT FOR
Railway reminders The line from Salisbury to Exeter is largely single track and has every appearance of a country railway. However, this is misleading, for the route was once the main line from London to the Devon resorts and the West Country. There are plenty of reminders of the great days of the Southern Railway, the large rough stone bridges, the elegant and sometimes quite substantial stations, the big embankments and the impressive signal boxes. Also to be seen are the overgrown traces of long disused branches and interconnecting lines, at Templecombe, Chard Junction and Axminster. At Feniton, formerly called Sidmouth Junction, the main line used to branch southwards to Ottery St Mary, Sidmouth and Budleigh Salterton. Those with sharp eyes will be able to spot many other reminders of the steam-hauled West Country expresses, for example the old trackside signs saying Whistle, the semaphore signals and the turntable at Yeovil Junction.

Days of steam revived at Yeovil Junction

Severn and Cotswolds

Gloucester is the starting point for two classic, but very different journeys. One follows the Severn to Newport in South Wales as England's longest river becomes a mighty estuary; the other travels through the heart of the Cotswolds to join the Thames valley near Swindon, home of the Great Western Railway.

GLOUCESTER – NEWPORT *44¾ miles*

Gloucester

The cathedral, its cloisters and close, and the surrounding streets are the city of Gloucester's heart, and not far away are the revitalised docks, home of the National Waterways Museum.

As it leaves the station, the train passes close to the cathedral and then crosses the Severn. Churcham Church stands to the north, with its eccentric spire built in 1878 in an 11th-century style. An open landscape leads to Westbury, where the large church stands by the line, close to the formal water gardens of Westbury Court, laid out from 1698. To the north are distant views of Flaxley Abbey. The train then joins the Severn, and passes below Newnham, an old coaching town with, from the south, the 14th-century church prominent above the river.

Lydney

As the train approaches Lydney there are views across to Sharpness and the docks. The old track leading to a former rail bridge over the Severn is to the north. South of the station are the Victorian canal and harbour. Stop here for the Forest of Dean, part of whose once-extensive railway network is preserved by the Dean Forest Railway. The train continues beside the Severn, now over a mile wide, with views across to Berkeley and Oldbury power stations.

Chepstow

The train comes out of a steep cutting directly on to the bridge over the Wye, and Chepstow is suddenly spread out around the battered walls of the massive castle. This is the perfect introduction to the town with its 13th-century walls and fine old buildings. The stone station was designed by Brunel in 1850. Chepstow is the stop for the Wye valley, where parts of the former Chepstow–Monmouth railway can be walked. Now in Wales, the train follows the Wye to meet the Severn, below the M4 bridge.

Chepstow's great castle, begun in Norman times, was still inhabited up to the present century

Shrewsbury – Newport
See pages 64-65

Sidebar

TRAINS
Gloucester–Newport
(48 mins approx)
Mon–Sat 8; Sun 5
Refreshments: some

Gloucester–Swindon
(45 mins approx)
Mon–Fri 12; Sat 11;
Sun 7
Refreshments: some

Tourist Information
Centres (*summer only)
Chepstow★ High St
(02912) 37727
Gloucester St Michael's
Tower, The Cross
(0452) 421188
Newport John Frost Sq
(0633) 842962
Stroud Kendrick St
(04536) 5768
Swindon Brunel Centre
(0793) 30328/26161

Walks
Cotswolds paths around
Kemble
*Forest of Dean and Wye
Valley* Offa's Dyke and
Wye Valley Walk start at
Chepstow. For other
walks see Chepstow TIC
and Forestry Commission
pages 5–7
*Monmouthshire and Brecon
Canal* starts at Newport
Ridgeway by car from
Swindon.
R. Thames Path starts near
Kemble
Usk Valley Walk from
Newport

Places to Visit
Caldicot Castle. *By car*
Caerwent Roman Town
Chepstow Castle. *By car*
Goodrich, Monmouth
and many other border
castles; Tintern Abbey
Gloucester Cathedral;
Museum of Packaging &
Advertising; National
Waterways Museum
Kemble/Stroud By car
Cirencester, Cirencester
Park; Corinium Museum
Newport Tredegar House
(Etr–Sep) and Country
Park. *By car* Caerleon
Roman Amphitheatre
Stonehouse By car
Slimbridge Wildfowl
Trust
Swindon GWR Museum.
By car Avebury, Silbury
Hill, West Kennet Long
Barrow

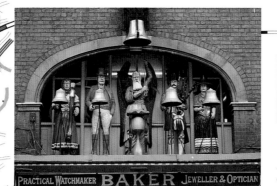

Figures on a chiming clock adorn Southgate Street in Gloucester

Mural painted 1976 in Henry Street, Swindon: King class locomotive

Caldicot

Continuing beside the Severn the train passes Portskewett Church to the north and the extensive sidings that serve the Severn tunnel. Caldicot Castle, the birthplace of Henry VII, can be seen to the north. The Severn tunnel, 4½ miles long, was completed in 1885 after many years of struggling with the 'Great Spring', whose output of 20 million gallons a day is controlled by continuous pumping. Two miles north is the Roman town of Caerwent.

Newport

From Caldicot to Newport the landscape is more remote, with marshland to the south. The line goes by churches at Rogiet, at Magor beside a ruined manor and below the hillfort on Willcrick Hill, at Bishton, right by the track and at Llanwern, facing the vast bulk of the steelworks. The train enters Newport, crossing the Usk below the castle, and with a view of the 1906 transporter bridge to the south. A Victorian town of some style, Newport has a well-restored shopping centre, a good covered market, a museum and art gallery.

GLOUCESTER – SWINDON
36½ miles

Gloucester

Most trains from Gloucester depart from its remarkably long Platform One. Sit on the left for this journey.

Stonehouse

The tower of Gloucester Cathedral remains in sight for some while as the line curves southwards. Look out for the splendid spire of the 14th-century church at Standish among the trees to the west. The train swings round the golden-capped Maiden Hill to Stonehouse. This is the stop for visiting Slimbridge Wildfowl Trust (by car).

Stroud

The train enters Stroud on a high embankment, with the stone town spread over the hills to the north. The pleasantly old-fashioned station still has a stone goods shed with GWR lettering.

A cloth town since the Middle Ages, Stroud had over 150 mills in 1824, and a handful still operate. After Stroud, the train enters the narrow Frome Valley and from here to Kemble the train is high on the southern side, overlooking the river, mills, golden stone houses and the winding A419, as well as the locks and bridges of the long-closed Thames and Severn Canal. The best section is the Golden Valley that leads to Chalford with its steep terraces of excellent 18th- and 19th-century houses overlooking the large church.

Kemble

After Chalford the valley is more wooded and remote until a long tunnel takes the train into the rolling Cotswolds. The isolated church at Coates is to the north, with wooded Cirencester Park beyond, and then, shortly before Kemble, the train passes close to Thames Head, the source of the Thames in a field to the north. Stop at Kemble's pretty stone station for walks in the lovely countryside of the Cotswolds.

Swindon

After Kemble the train crosses a flatter landscape before reaching the handsome, stone former railway workshops around Swindon station. Swindon was the historical base of the Great Western Railway, and the best part is the New Town, built by the GWR from 1842. Now the GWR Museum is here. Swindon is also a good base for the ancient sites around Avebury to the south, and for Ridgeway walks.

LOOK OUT FOR

Waterways At the heart of the region is the Severn, a great navigation that still carries large ships to Sharpness and occasionally as far as Gloucester, whose elegant docks are linked to the Severn by a ship canal. The smaller and more rural Monmouthshire & Brecon Canal used to join the Usk in Newport, and is still open north of Pontypool. Much more significant is the Thames & Severn Canal, built in the early 19th century to link the two rivers but now long closed. Locks and bridges mark its course along the Frome valley from Stonehouse to north of Swindon, and one of the typical circular lock-keeper's houses can be seen near Chalford. The major feature of the canal was the 2½-mile long Sapperton Tunnel, to the north of the railway tunnel, and best visited by car, or on foot. Much of the canal's towpath has been restored as a walkway.

SOUTH
&
SOUTH EAST
ENGLAND

Passing through Little Bedwyn on the Reading–Great Bedwyn route.
The train follows the Kennet & Avon Canal whose towpath
makes an easy and pleasant walk at the end of the journey

THE COMMUTER
AND THE
CROSS CHANNEL
TRADE

RAILWAY HISTORY AND ARCHITECTURE

RAILWAYS CAME EARLY to the south of England. The first steam line in the south, the Canterbury and Whitstable, opened in 1830, but London was the main impetus for railway building in the 1830s and early 1840s. The first main lines, to Southampton, Brighton and Dover were in use by 1844, and from then on a network of lines was constructed from London. Fierce competition between several companies resulted in many routes being duplicated, and few parts of Kent, Surrey and Sussex were without a railway service by the end of the century. The London and South Western Railway also drove its lines into Dorset, Devon and Cornwall, competing with the Great Western Railway for the growing holiday traffic. Many routes opened specifically to take people to and from work; commuter trains from Brighton, for example, were running as early as 1844.

In 1923 all the companies were merged into one, the Southern Railway. However, there are many legacies of the days of competition still to be seen, especially the diverse styles of stations promoted to capture custom. Notable examples include medieval at Battle, Italianate classical at Rye, Tudor at Etchingham and wooden rural at Plumpton.

An 1844 engraving of the London and Brighton Railway terminus at Brighton

NEAR HERE WAS THE TERMINUS
OF THE
CANTERBURY AND WHITSTABLE
RAILWAY, 1830
(GEORGE STEPHENSON, ENGINEER)
THE WORLD'S FIRST RAILWAY
SEASON TICKETS ISSUED HERE 1834

Railway style: Battle's 'medieval' station . . .

. . . and the Italianate look, at Rye

In the 1930s, the Southern Railway instigated a modernisation programme and stations and lineside buildings were reconstructed in contemporary styles, with the result that Art Deco and modernism are a railway feature only in the south. The best example is Surbiton station, but minor touches can be seen all over the place, in platform lights, seats and other station fittings.

The glories of the Southern Railway – seen at Surbiton's Art Deco station (left) and extolled in posters from the 1930s and 1940s (above)

Another reflection of company rivalry was the proliferation of boat trains serving the Channel Ports. The eclipse of Liverpool by Southampton was entirely due to the efforts of the London & South Western Railway. While many of the cross-channel ports are still served by special trains, the era of the grand Boat Train is now gone. From the 1880s Pullman and other de luxe trains linked London with the capitals of Europe via the channel ports. The most famous was the Golden Arrow service to Paris, but more romantic perhaps was the Night Ferry, whose blue and gold Wagons-Lits carriages were actually taken onto the ship. But a new era in cross-channel train services will come with the Channel Tunnel, and trains running from London to Paris in under three hours will fulfil some of the most ambitious dreams of Victorian railway companies.

WALKING IN THE REGION

The train is an easy way to reach some of the best walks in the South and South East, notably in the New Forest and along the Dorset, Hampshire and Sussex coastline, through the Weald of Kent and along the South Downs, and along Constable's Stour Valley. For further information on the Walks suggested on each route in the following pages, contact the local Tourist Information Centres. See also page 7.

Railway walks highlight some of the prettiest and least known parts of southern England. A selection of the closed railways now designated official footpaths is given below:

East Grinstead to Groombridge (9 miles), a part of the former Three Bridges to Tunbridge Wells line. Also Three Bridges to East Grinstead (6 miles)

Heathfield to Polegate (10 miles), part of the former Edenbridge to Eastbourne line

Highgate to Alexandra Palace (2 miles), former branch line off the Finsbury Park to East Finchley line

Knowle Junction to West Meon (9 miles), part of the former Alton to Fareham line

Litchfield to Highclere (3 miles), part of the former Whitchurch to Newbury line

Yarmouth to Freshwater (2½ miles), part of the former Newport to Freshwater line. Other Isle of Wight footpaths include Shanklin to Wroxall (2 miles)

Shoreham to Baynards (18 miles), part of the former Shoreham to Guildford line

THE END OF THE LINE

LONDON'S RAILWAY STATIONS

A new age for London: the coming of the railways meant easy travel to and from the country

Right: detail of Sir George Gilbert Scott's former Midland Grand Hotel, the frontage to St Pancras station, spectacular in its opulence inside and out

Brunel's Paddington: above, the oriel window over platform one. Left, the glazed trainshed – with its nave and transepts a cathedral of the railway age

Waterloo station: recent restoration has highlighted its Edwardian qualities. Right, detail of decorative ironwork on the platforms. Below, the arms of the London and South Western Railway in stained glass

Right: clock tower of St Pancras station's gothic façade, elevated above the Euston Road

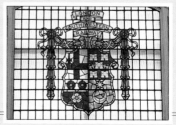

THE ARCHITECTURAL DIVERSITY of London's stations, a reflection of the varied ambitions of the railway companies that built them, makes them visually exciting and worth while to explore. The best, Paddington, St Pancras and Waterloo, featured below, are among the most important Victorian and Edwardian buildings in Britain, but many lesser stations are still full of interest. Much individuality and period detail has survived the process of reconstruction and amalgamation that culminated in the formation of British Railways in 1948 and stations can be an entertaining adjunct to catching trains.

Over the years London has had at least 20 railway termini. The first, Euston, Nine Elms, London Bridge, Bishopsgate and Paddington (a temporary building), were built in the late 1830s. Others opened in the 1850s and 1860s, notably King's Cross, St Pancras, Victoria, Charing Cross, Fenchurch Street and the present Paddington, while Marylebone dates from the end of the Victorian period. Some stations have subsequently been closed or adapted for other uses, but London can still boast 14 termini and the completion of the Channel Tunnel may well increase this grand total.

PADDINGTON

For journeys to Cornwall, Devon, the West Country, South Wales and the Welsh Borders, the Cotswolds and the South Midlands.

Paddington is one of London's most exciting stations, visually and historically, and it stands as a memorial to the Great Western Railway and its engineer, Isambard Kingdom Brunel. Completed in 1854, Paddington is in two parts, a hotel and a trainshed. The Great Western Royal Hotel, facing on to Praed Street, is the public front of the station, although the entrances to the platforms are actually from adjacent side streets. Designed by P C Hardwick in a style, pioneering for its time, that combined French Renaissance and baroque elements, the hotel was, at its opening, the largest in London and it established a pattern for luxury hotel building by railway companies throughout Britain. The façade was partly rebuilt in the early 1930s.

Behind the hotel is Brunel's great trainshed, a glazed three-bay cover for the platforms and concourse supported by a mass of decorative cast iron. Inspired partly by the Crystal Palace, it is a marvellous reflection of the Victorian love for decoration combined with adventurous engineering. A variety of styles, including gothic and Moorish, were freely used in the decoration, and much of this can still be enjoyed, thanks to careful restoration and to the fact that Brunel's original structure was little affected by later alterations and enlargements to the station.

LOOK OUT FOR
The hotel façade, with its pediment of Victorian virtues sculpted by John Thomas, and its stylish Art Deco GWR monogram
The oriel window above platform one, installed to allow GWR directors to keep an eye on things
The delicate wrought iron screens separating the station from the hotel
The excellent war memorial with its powerful soldier figure by C S Jagger
The former Royal waiting room on platform one

ST PANCRAS

For journeys to Bedford, Leicester, Derby, the Midlands and South Yorkshire

St Pancras is London's most distinctive station, and was by far the most remarkable architecturally. The Midland Railway, after many years of using other companies' stations, finally built their own London terminus in 1868 and they did it in the grandest manner possible. Like Paddington, St Pancras is both a hotel and a trainshed, separate parts that together reflect the extraordinary dynamism of Victorian architects and engineers. The trainshed, designed by W H Barlow, is a great soaring single span arch of glass and iron extending over the platforms and concourse. The space created is like no other, for it is uninterrupted by internal structures or columns. It remains very much as Barlow built it, its bold scale and rich detailing a fitting memorial to the railway age.

The more familiar feature of St Pancras is Sir George Gilbert Scott's great hotel, whose façade has dominated its surroundings since its opening in 1873. Scott's major commercial building and a structure that shows the Victorian gothic style at its best, the Midland Grand Hotel is a riot of colour and decorative detail. The interior is even more splendid than the exterior and its original fittings included ten grand pianos along with 500 rooms, gas lighting and hydraulic lifts. As it is no longer a hotel, the interior cannot be seen, but its Victorian magnificence largely survives.

LOOK OUT FOR
The booking hall, also designed by Scott, with its linenfold panelling and the corbels carved as railwaymen
Decorative tiling along the side walls of the trainshed
The intricacy of the iron roof, and the name of its maker, the Butterley Company of Derbyshire, cast into its ribs
The covered carriage entrance at the west end
The roofline, with its forest of pinnacles, spires and chimneys

WATERLOO

For journeys to Hampshire, Dorset, the South Coast and the Isle of Wight

With its spacious concourse, its direct platform access and the great curve of its powerful Edwardian architecture, Waterloo is London's grandest station. The first Waterloo station was opened in 1848 but continuous piecemeal enlargement by the London & South Western Railway resulted in a building that had become confusing and almost unworkable by the end of the century. A programme of complete reconstruction started in 1899. Completed in 1922, the present station is a monument to the space and grace of the Edwardian era, and the great curving brick and stone screen wall that encloses the concourse is richly embellished with classical motifs and sculpture both inside and out. The massive glazed roof, while not remarkable architecturally, gives the whole station a feeling of light and order. The best way to arrive at Waterloo is on foot, through the raised ornamental arch that faces the Thames.

LOOK OUT FOR
The great Victory arch and war memorial that forms the main entrance, with its sculptures of War, Peace and Britannia, and its winged clock
The Edwardian decoration of the former Windsor Bar, now the information centre, with its pretty domed pay boxes
The stained glass window featuring the arms of the London & South Western Railway
Decorative ironwork on the platforms, featuring lions and other motifs, which have recently been repainted in red and gold

Royal Wessex

WINCHESTER – WEYMOUTH   *77 miles*

TRAINS
(Stopping train 2 hrs approx)
Mon–Fri 14; Sat 12; Sun 13
Refreshments: usually

Tourist Information Centres (*summer only)
Bournemouth Westover Rd (0202) 291715/290883
Christchurch Saxon Sq (0202) 471780
Dorchester Acland Rd (0305) 67992
Eastleigh Leigh Rd (0703) 614646
Poole The Quay (0202) 673322
Southampton Above Bar Precinct (0703) 221106
Wareham Town Hall, East St (09295) 2740
Winchester The Guildhall, Broadway (0962) 840500

For all information on Weymouth & Dorchester see pages 22–23

Walks
Dorset Coast Path from Bournemouth, Poole, Weymouth
New Forest from Ashurst, Brockenhurst
Solent Way from Lymington
Wayfarers Walk from Alresford

Places to visit
Ashurst New Forest Butterfly Farm (Mar–Oct)
Bournemouth Big Four Railway Museum; Russell-Cotes Art Gallery
Brockenhurst By car Beaulieu
Christchurch Castle & Norman House, EH
Poole Compton Acres Gdn (Etr–Oct); Model Railway; Pottery
Southampton Art Gallery; Tudor House Museum
Wareham By car/bus Corfe Castle, NT (Feb–Nov)
Winchester Cathedral Great Hall; Hospital of St Cross. *Bus* to Alresford for Mid Hants Railway (page 35)
Wool By car Clouds Hill, NT; Tank Museum

The Royal Wessex was the original name for this line running across southern England, linking rural river valleys, great harbours and estuaries, the traditional seaside and the royal hunting grounds of the New Forest. It takes in a great diversity of towns and cities, from medieval Winchester to 18th-century Weymouth, via Southampton, Bournemouth, Poole and Dorchester. Take the hourly train which stops at the principal stations *en route* – change at Poole for the hourly service to Weymouth. Sit on the left.

Winchester

The capital of England from 829 to 1066, Winchester is easily accessible from the station and is a city of great architectural and historical wealth. The train proceeds along the Itchen valley with good views to the east. By the river at **Shawford** is a fine 17th-century mansion, and beyond it Twyford's Victorian church. At **Eastleigh** the train passes the huge 1840s railway works which brought the town into being. South of Eastleigh is Southampton airport, served by **Southampton Parkway**.

Southampton

Passing the decorative stations at **Swaythling** and **St Denys** the train runs briefly beside the Itchen estuary before entering Southampton. A major port since the Norman period, Southampton's heyday was between the wars, during the great days of the transatlantic liners. Between **Totton** and **Redbridge** the train crosses the Test estuary before entering the New Forest, with isolated stations at **Lyndhurst Road** and **Beaulieu Road**. Five miles to the south-east, along the B3056, is Beaulieu Abbey and the National Motor Museum.

Brockenhurst

The line through the New Forest is attractively remote, with plenty of wild flowers and ponies. At Brockenhurst station you can change for the Lymington branch and Isle of Wight ferries (see page 35). The New Forest towns, **Brockenhurst, Sway** and **New Milton**, owe their development largely to the railway.

Christchurch

After **Hinton Admiral** the New

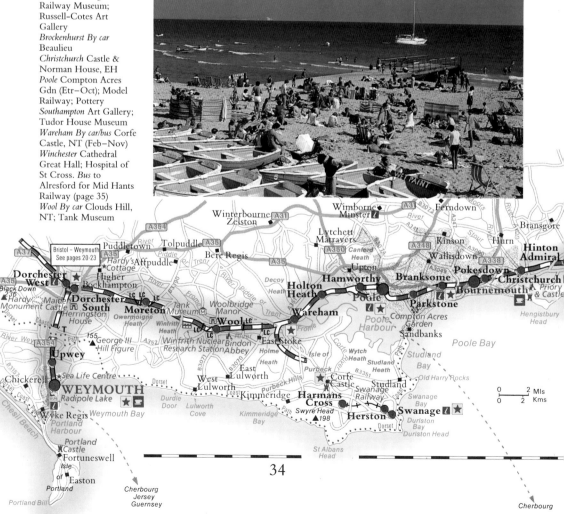

Bournemouth beach: the resort's mild climate has attracted holidaymakers since Victorian times

Forest is left behind and there are views along the Avon valley to Christchurch Priory and castle.

Bournemouth

West of Christchurch the train passes **Pokesdown** before it reaches the rather grand red-brick station with its glazed trainshed roof. Bournemouth is full of discreet seaside charms, not the least of which is the splendid Russell-Cotes Museum. The spread of Bournemouth continues westward into Dorset through the leafy suburbs of **Branksome** and **Parkstone**. From Parkstone there are good views across Poole harbour to Brownsea Island.

Poole

The train runs along beside Poole Harbour before entering Poole station through the centre of the new shopping precinct. The old town and the harbour are easily accessible to the south. West of Poole the train curves across Hole Bay on a causeway, and then reaches **Hamworthy**.

Wareham

After Hamworthy the train crosses Lychett Bay, with Rockley Sands to the south, and runs on, through **Holton Heath**, beside the Wareham Channel of Poole Harbour. Wareham station is well to the north of the town. Wareham has considerable character, particularly around its harbour on the Frome. Part of the old branch line to Corfe Castle and Swanage has now been reopened by the Swanage Steam Railway.

Wool

West of Wareham the train runs through a landscape of woods and heathland, with East Stoke Church right by the line. East of Wool it crosses the Frome, with the remains of Bindon Abbey in woods to the south. Near by is the pretty 17th-century Woolbridge Manor. This is the station for Bovington Camp, the Tank Museum and Lawrence of Arabia's cottage at Clouds Hill, to the north, and Lulworth Cove to the south. West of Wool is the nuclear research station at Winfrith Heath. The line crosses a wooded landscape to **Moreton**, then follows the Frome valley to the new **Dorchester South Station**.

Weymouth

West of Dorchester the train turns south and joins the line from Bath and Bristol for the journey into Weymouth. See page 23.

MID HANTS RAILWAY/ WATERCRESS LINE

The Watercress Line runs over the downs to the north-east of Winchester. When opened in 1865, it formed a slightly shorter route between London and Southampton than the main line via Basingstoke, but had

The Atlantic Coast Express diverts to the Watercress Line

much steeper gradients. Closed in 1973, the line was reopened by the Preservation Society in 1977.

From **Alton** there is a continuous climb for the first 4½ miles to **Medstead and Four Marks**, passing through Chawton Park Wood. To the south lies Chawton, home of Jane Austen. At **Ropley** visitors can watch the locomotive restoration work.

The descent continues to **Alresford**, ponds and streams reminding us that watercress is still grown here – during the season it is sold on the trains.

Alton (BR station) – Alresford 10 miles (0962) 734200/733810 (Phone for details). Single journey: 35 mins

A railway backwater: the branch line train between Lymington's stations

THE LYMINGTON BRANCH

TRAINS
Brockenhurst–Lymington Pier 5¼ miles
½ hourly service
No refreshments

Tourist Information Centre
Lymington Waitrose Car Park, St Thomas St

After leaving Brockenhurst, the train follows the main line for about a mile before branching south across Setley Plain, a typical New Forest landscape of heathland backed by trees. As it approaches the river, the country becomes more wooded, partly concealing

Buckland Rings, an Iron Age earthwork. To the east is the village of Boldre, whose rector in the late 18th century was the picturesque author William Gilpin. The line then follows the river into Lymington, pausing at **Lymington Town** before crossing the river to its terminus at the **Pier** station where the Isle of Wight ferry stands waiting. Lymington, best approached from the **Town** station, is excellent, the narrow streets around the busy harbour leading up to the wide and handsome main street.

Arun Valley and South Coast

HORSHAM – PORTSMOUTH & ISLE OF WIGHT via Barnham *49 miles*

TRAINS
Horsham–Bognor Regis
via Barnham
(40 mins approx)
Mon–Fri 17; Sat/Sun 12
Refreshments: some

Barnham–Portsmouth
Harbour
(40 mins approx)
Frequent services
Refreshments: some

Portsmouth
Harbour–Ryde Pier
Head
Sealink British Ferries
Tel (0705) 827744
(15 mins approx)
Frequent services

Ryde Pier
Head–Shanklin
(25 mins approx)
Frequent services

Tourist Information
Centres (*summer only)
Arundel High St
(0903) 882268
Chichester St Peter's Mkt,
West St (0243) 775888
Havant★ Park Rd South
(0705) 480024
Portsmouth The Hard
(0705) 826722
Ryde★ Western Esplanade
(0983) 62905
Sandown The Esplanade
(0983) 403886
Shanklin High St
(0983) 862942

Walks
*South Downs Way/Wey
South Path* from
Amberley
Isle of Wight Coast Path
Bembridge and Culver
Downs, IOW access from
Sandown or Brading

Places to visit
Amberley Chalk Pits
Museum
Arundel Castle
(Apr–Oct); Cathedral;
Museum of Curiosity
(Mar–Oct); Toy and
Military Museum
(Feb–Dec); Wildfowl
Trust
Chichester Cathedral;
Mechanical Music &
Doll Collection; Pallant
House Gallery. *By car/bus*
Weald & Downland
Open Air Museum
Fishbourne Roman Palace
Portsmouth & Southsea
Charles Dickens'
Birthplace (Mar–Oct);
D-Day Museum &
Overlord Embroidery;
historic ships
Pulborough By car Bignor
Roman Villa; Parham
House & Gdns
(Apr–Sep); Petworth
House & Park, NT
(Apr–Oct)
Ryde By car/bus
Carisbrooke Castle, EH;
Osborne House, EH
(Mar–Oct)
Shanklin Chine

To travel from Horsham to Portsmouth involves a change of trains at Barnham, a natural break in a journey that falls into two distinct parts. The first part is a delightfully rural ride through the Weald of Sussex and along the Arun valley, with splendid castles at Amberley and Arundel, and the chance to enjoy the traditional English seaside at Bognor and Littlehampton. The second part is a coastal journey with plenty of sea and ships, from little sailing harbours to the naval dockyards at Portsmouth, plus a great cathedral and a chance to explore the Isle of Wight.

Horsham
Little of Horsham can be seen from the station. This is a rather muddled town, but the best part is the Causeway – a pretty Wealden village in the middle of the town.

Christ's Hospital
The train quickly reaches Christ's Hospital with the famous Blue Coat school to the west. This was formerly a junction with branches to Shoreham and Guildford, but little remains and the station buildings have been demolished. The train passes fields and paddocks, enclosed by wooded hedges.

Billingshurst
This town, too, is rather hidden from the train. The main street still has the air of an old coaching town, and includes a 16th-century inn. The line now enters the Arun valley, running parallel to Roman Stane Street, now the A29. The towers of Beedings House can be seen to the east.

Pulborough
Roads, the river and the railway come together at Pulborough, but the best parts are by the river. Just south of the station, the train crosses the Arun with excellent views along the valley. Pulborough was once a busy port, where boats transferred their cargoes to the Wey and Arun Canal. To the west is Stopham, with its 15th-century bridge. The train follows the Arun southwards, with the valley narrowing towards the dramatic gap through the chalk cliffs at Amberley.

Amberley
Amberley Castle is a magnificent sight, protecting the village behind its walls. This great view continues as the river winds between towering chalk cliffs. Amberley is the stop for the Chalk Pits Museum and the South Downs Way. The train criss-crosses the river, passing South Stoke's flint cottages around the 11th-century church, and the hilltop village of Burpham. Arundel now comes into view, the castle towering over the valley to Ford.

Arundel
Arundel station, with its delicate iron-work, is the starting point for any visit to Arundel: the town's riches unroll as

Amberley Chalk Pits: industrial history breaks a predominantly rural journey

you cross the Arun and climb the steep streets to the castle. Despite its fairy-tale appearance, Arundel castle is largely Victorian. The train now continues along the Arun valley, passing Lyminster church, to the junction with the Portsmouth or Worthing line, and to **Ford** and **Barnham**.

Barnham
At Barnham you either continue to the end of the line at Bognor Regis, with its traditional seaside

atmosphere, or you change either to the local service for Little-hampton and its harbour and beaches, or to the coastal service to Chichester and Portsmouth.

Chichester

From Barnham the train follows the coastal plain to Chichester, passing the flint village of Aldingbourne and the Battle of Britain airfield at Tangmere. Dating from the 1080s, the cathedral is the most exciting part of Chichester, but the city has plenty to offer, including the market cross of 1501 and a wealth of 18th-century buildings. West from Chichester the train passes some of the harbour's intriguing channels but little can be seen because of the flat landscape.

Havant

Between Chichester and Havant the train passes **Fishbourne**, where the Roman villa has excellent mosaics, **Bosham**, a popular sailing centre, **Nutbourne** and **Southbourne**, with Thorney Island and the remote moorings at Prinsted to the south, and **Emsworth**, an 18th-century port now given over to pleasure boating. West of Emsworth is **Warblington**, where the remains of the 16th-century castle stand in a remote spot overlooking the water. To the south is Hayling Island. These treats, despite being close by, are hidden by the trees that surround the harbour and are best explored on bicycles, or by car. The route from Havant to Portsmouth is largely urban, but there is plenty to see. Between **Bedhampton** and **Hilsea** there are views to the north to Portsdown Hill and its 19th-century forts, and to the south towards Hayling Island. The train crosses the Broom Channel onto Portsea Island, passes through **Fratton** and reaches

Portsmouth & Southsea station. This is well placed for the civic centre, a blend of Edwardian and modern architecture. For Old Portsmouth, Southsea and the harbour, go on to **Portsmouth Harbour** station, built on a pier. Here are wonderful views of the sea, and every type of boat and ship. The Isle of Wight passenger ferry leaves from the railway pier, and the hovercraft from Clarence Pier.

The Isle of Wight

Only one Isle of Wight railway survives today, from Ryde to Shanklin – the first to have been opened, in 1864. It is a highly eccentric journey, which starts at **Ryde Pier Head** station. The trains are former London 'tubes', sent out to a seaside retirement. After a ride along the pier to **Ryde Esplanade**, the train burrows beneath the town to emerge at **Ryde St John's Road**. From here it is a rural journey to **Brading** and then along the Yar valley to **Sandown**, with views of Culver Cliff to the east. The train then runs by the sea to end at **Shanklin**.

LOOK OUT FOR

Water is at the heart of this journey: the River Arun from Pulborough to Littlehampton, then the seaside at Bognor, the inland channels and saltmarshes of Chichester and finally the great harbour at Portsmouth. The importance of these waterways and coastal reaches is reflected by the Roman civilisation of the region, the mighty castles at Amberley, Arundel and Southsea and the later 18th- and 19th-century fortifications that surround Portsmouth; and Chichester Cathedral shows a measure of the wealth of the area derived from sea and river-borne trade. Many traces of this maritime past can be seen, including the Arun navigation and the former canal that linked it to London, the many isolated harbours and moorings as well as the Victorian development of the seaside. This is a journey through the history of the Royal Navy, from the *Mary Rose*, the *Victory* and the *Warrior*, to modern frigates, destroyers and submarines, all to be seen in and around Portsmouth harbour.

Nelson figurehead in Portsmouth Naval Base

Picturesque Old Shanklin, Isle of Wight

The Garden of England
TONBRIDGE – HASTINGS – ASHFORD   *60 miles*

TRAINS
Tonbridge–Hastings
(55 mins approx)
Mon–Sun 15 approx
Refreshments: some

Hastings–Ashford
(48 mins approx)
Mon–Sat 14; Sun 10
No refreshments

Tourist Information Centres
Ashford Lower High St
(0233) 37311
Battle High St
(04246) 3721
Hastings Robertson Terr
(0424) 722022
Rye Cinque Ports St
(0797) 222293
Tunbridge Wells Town
Hall (0892) 26121

Walks
Saxon Shore Way from
Rye to Hamstreet
Wealdway from Tonbridge

A journey through the rolling hills and woodland of the Weald of Kent and into rural Sussex leads to the seaside at Hastings, a satisfyingly old-fashioned resort. Change at Hastings for a more local train to Ashford which crosses the flat and rather mysterious marshlands.

TONBRIDGE – HASTINGS
33 miles

Tonbridge
A typical Kentish town, Tonbridge still has only one main street. Dominating the River Medway are the ruins of the Norman castle. From Tonbridge the train crosses a rather suburban landscape, with Southborough to the east, and then passes **High Brooms** before entering the tunnel that leads to Tunbridge Wells.

Royal Tunbridge Wells
Tunbridge Wells has managed to retain its original spa town character. Nothing of the town can be seen from the train but the curving station is good, the Italianate up side dating from 1846 and the grander down side designed by Sir Reginald Blomfield in 1911. After Tunbridge Wells, the train passes through a landscape of hills and woods with stations at **Frant**, **Wadhurst**, **Stonegate** and **Etchingham**, some built in the Tudor style. Etchingham has a good 14th-century church, near the station.

Robertsbridge
From Etchingham the train follows the Rother valley to Robertsbridge, the former junction with the Kent and East Sussex Light Railway, part of which has now been reopened as a steam railway. Bodiam Castle, best approached via the A229, is four miles to the east.

Battle
Taking its name, and its foundation, from the Battle of Hastings in 1066, the pretty town is dominated by the massive remains of the abbey. Even the station is in the medieval style, with a splendid vaulted waiting room.

St Leonards Warrior Square
After leaving **West St Leonards** the train quickly reaches Warrior Square, the main station and an impressive classical building that reflects the style of St Leonard's as a whole.

Hastings
Hastings' 1930s station is well placed with good views of the castle and the old town, and with the seaside not far away. The train from Tonbridge terminates here. Change platforms for the Ashford service.

The site of the Battle of Hastings and Battle Abbey, where King Harold fell

Places to visit
Ashford Godinton
House (Etr–Sep).
By rail to
Folkestone and *bus* to
Hythe for Romsey,
Hythe & Dymchurch
Railway. *By car/bus*
Tenterden for Kent &
East Sussex Railway
Battle Abbey, EH;
Museum (Etr–Oct)
Hastings Castle
(Mar–Oct); Hastings
Embroidery; St Clements
Caves; Shipwreck
Heritage Centre
Robertsbridge Aeronautical
Museum (Jan–Nov). *By
car* Bateman's, NT
(Apr–Oct); Bodiam
Castle, NT
Rye Lamb House
(Apr–Oct); Ypres Tower
Museum (Apr–Oct)
Tonbridge Castle. *By car*
Penshurst Place
(Apr–Oct)
Tunbridge Wells Pantiles.
By car Bayham Abbey,
EH (Apr–Sep); Scotney
Castle Gdns, NT
(Apr–Nov)

The attractive lime-fringed Pantiles at Tunbridge Wells

HASTINGS – ASHFORD
27 miles

Leaving Hastings the train swings inland to **Ore** and then a long tunnel leads into the open country. After the somewhat remote stations of **Three Oaks** and **Doleham** the line follows the River Brede through farmland with the occasional oast house.

Winchelsea
The station is well to the north of this medieval town. Planned in the 13th century as a port for the French wine trade, Winchelsea lost its harbour, closed by silting in the 16th century. The grid pattern of little streets filled with picturesque houses is enjoyable to explore. After Winchelsea the ruins of Camber Castle can be seen out in the marshes to the south.

Rye
Rye's appeal is apparent from the train. The hill town rises from the marshland, a windmill stands outside the station, and the River Rother is full of boats. The town's narrow streets are charming out of season; a nightmare at any other time.

Appledore
From Rye the line runs across a strange, haunting landscape of open marshland. In the distance are the towers of Dungeness lighthouse and power station. The village of Appledore is well west of its station.

Hamstreet
South of Hamstreet, look west for the churches of Kenardington and Warehorne and the Royal Military Canal.

Ashford
The train enters past the remains of the once substantial railway works that gave Ashford its character. A busy railway junction, Ashford offers routes in five directions, but Canterbury, 14 miles north, is the best bet.

Charming Rye, once a prosperous Sussex port

Stringing hop poles

LOOK OUT FOR
Traditional and varied types of farming are a feature of Sussex and Kent and many of these can be seen from the train, including the hop fields with their distinctive forests of poles, orchards of fruit trees, oast houses with their conical spires, timber-framed farm buildings and, above all, the characteristic sheep of the Romney Marsh and the surrounding levels. The marshes are also rich in wild flowers and birds.

THE CHANNEL TUNNEL

Scheduled to open on 15 May 1993, the Channel Tunnel complex, described as the largest and most important engineering feat ever undertaken in the world, will be designed, built and operated under a joint concession of the British and French governments by an Anglo–French consortium of construction companies and banks from both sides of the English Channel, known as Eurotunnel. The cost of construction will be £3.65 billion. It will consist of twin-bored rail tunnels of 7.6-metre diameter running some 15 metres either side of a 4.8-metre service tunnel, all lying some 40 metres beneath the sea bed. The tunnels will run 50 kilometres from a terminal at Folkestone in Kent to Cocquelles near Calais in France. The running tunnels will be connected at 375-metre intervals by cross-passages via the central service tunnel to allow access for maintenance and emergency evacuation.

There will also be two cross-over rail tunnels approximately one-third and two-thirds down the length of the sea portion of the tunnels.

The running tunnels will allow the passage of large shuttle trains capable of carrying cars, coaches, caravans and heavy duty lorries between the two terminals and the whole complex will be linked to the national railway networks of British Rail and the SNCF French Railways, carrying both passengers and freight.

Work on the English end of the Tunnel may be viewed from passenger trains running between Folkestone and Dover and at Folkestone, about a mile from the Central Station, is the Eurotunnel Information Centre, an exciting place to visit, with models, videos etc covering all aspects of the design, construction and use of the Tunnel.

The English Seaside
LEWES – HASTINGS *32 miles*

This is a journey through the magnificent landscape of the South Downs to the English seaside, from the Regency raciness of Brighton, to the west of Lewes, to the beach huts and fishing boats of Hastings via the genteel elegance of Eastbourne.

TRAINS
(1 hr approx)
Mon–Sat 24; Sun 12
Refreshments: some

Tourist Information Centres (*summer only)
Bexhill De Warr Pavilion
(0424) 212023
Hastings Robertson Terr
(0424) 722022
Lewes High St
(0273) 471600
Pevensey★ Castle Car
Park (0323) 761444

For information on Hastings see page 38

Walks/Cycling
South Downs Way, Weald Way from Eastbourne

Places to visit
Berwick Charleston
Manor; Drusillas Zoo
Park (2½m)
Eastbourne Butterfly
Centre (Mar–Oct);
Martello Tower 73
(Apr–end Oct); Towner
Art Gallery. *By car* Seven
Sisters Country Park
Glynde Glynde Place
(Jun–Sep)
Lewes Castle; Barbican
House Museum. *By car*
Firle Place (Jun–Sep). *By rail* Brighton Aquarium
& Dolphinarium; Royal
Pavilion
Pevensey Castle, EH; Old
Minthouse
Polegate Filching Manor
Motor Museum. *By car/bus* Alfriston Clergy
House NT (Apr–Oct)

GET OFF FOR
South of Berwick is the
Cuckmere River valley,
cutting through the
Downs in dramatic
serpentine curves. At its
estuary is Seven Sisters
Country Park.

Lewes
Lewes station is rather grand, a legacy of the days when five railway lines met here. The steam-hauled Bluebell Line, a preserved railway at Sheffield Park to the north, was once connected to Lewes. The town covers the steep hillside in a splendidly picturesque manner with the castle at the top.

The train follows the River Ouse as it leaves the town behind, before swinging east past great white scars of the old chalk quarries. Not far from **Glynde** station are 16th-century Glynde Place, the opera house at Glyndebourne and Firle Place.

Berwick
Berwick village is worth a visit for the paintings by Vanessa Bell and Duncan Grant in the church. This is very much Bloomsbury territory, with Charleston 2½ miles to the west.

Eastbourne
With Folkington Manor visible to the south the train passes **Polegate** and turns south before entering Eastbourne's extravagant station. Some trains divide at Eastbourne and, where they do, passengers should ensure they travel in the correct portion of the train.

Although the station is central, there is no atmosphere of the seaside,

Entertainment on the Eastbourne seafront

and you need to walk to the end of Terminus Road to find the familiar 19th-century bow-fronted houses.

The train leaves Eastbourne as it came in, and then swings east across flat marshland. Sit on the right.

Pevensey & Westham
An excellent sight, with the ruins of both the Roman fort and the Norman

Pevensey Castle, Roman and Norman fortress

castle visible from the train. Pevensey is one of the original Cinque ports although the sea is well to the south. As the train passes **Pevensey Bay** and **Norman's Bay** Martello towers dominate the foreshore. At **Cooden Beach** there is a traditional view of groynes and beach huts.

Bexhill
The Victorian seaside town is barely visible from the big old-fashioned station, but east of the town the seaside atmosphere returns, before the outskirts of **St Leonards**.

Hastings
The vista of Hastings old town comes as an enjoyable surprise as the train pulls in. With its fishing boats, tall black net stores and early 19th-century architecture, Hastings is the south coast seaside town *par excellence*.

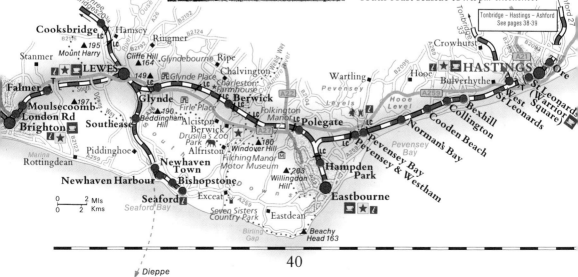

Along the Stour

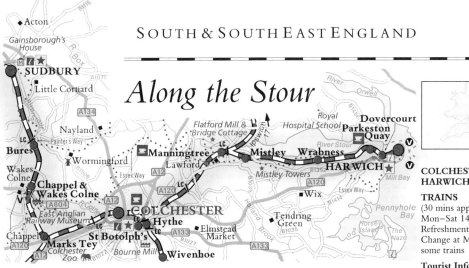

The best way to see the Stour valley is by train and these two journeys from Colchester show the different faces of this famous river. The line to Harwich, with its wonderful views over the Stour estuary, is actually a main route to the Continental ferry port at Parkeston Quay. The line to Sudbury follows the meanderings of the upper Stour through the lush landscape painted by Constable.

COLCHESTER – HARWICH
19 miles

Colchester
Sit on the left for this journey from the main station. The skyline of Colchester is a series of Victorian spires and the massive water tower, not a fair representation of Britain's oldest recorded town, with its extensive Roman remains, huge Norman keep, medieval churches and wealth of 18th-century buildings. Near **Manningtree** the train comes into the open, passing Lawford Hall and church as it approaches the wide expanse of the Stour estuary. The line joins the Stour at **Mistley**, where Robert Adam's church and his two lodge gates can be seen. The Stour can be seen through the trees, its northern shore dominated by the tall tower of the Royal Hospital School. After **Wrabness** the line drops down to the edge of the mudflats before it reaches the international port at **Parkeston Quay**. Sidings full of cars and containers, and ships in the harbour make this an exciting sight. The train then curves round the bay and passes **Dovercourt**, the seaside just a short walk away. The journey ends at **Harwich Town**. Outside the station is the high lighthouse of 1818, a good introduction to a fine old seaport.

COLCHESTER – SUDBURY
16¾ miles

The best way to start this delightful journey is from **St Botolph's**, the little-used terminus station in the heart of Colchester. The branch, however, actually leaves the main line at **Marks Tey**. The train comes out high above the Colne valley as it approaches the great Chappel viaduct of 1849, with its 32 arches. Below to the west is Chappel village. North of the viaduct is **Chappel and Wakes Colne** station, home of the East Anglian Railway Museum. The station is in the old LNER style, a visual timeswitch for the unwary. As the train goes into Suffolk look along the Stour valley to the east towards the windmill at Wormingford for a typical Constable scene. The next station is **Bures**, set high above the village, and then the train follows the lush Stour valley with its traditional pink coloured timber-framed farms, distant views of church towers emphasising the Constable atmosphere. **Sudbury**, an excellent small market town with its Gainsborough museum, in the house where the painter was born, is now the end of the line but it used to continue northwards and some of it is now a footpath.

Constable's Valley of the Stour and Dedham, *landscape typical of the Sudbury line*

COLCHESTER–HARWICH

TRAINS
(30 mins approx)
Mon–Sat 14; Sun 7
Refreshments: some
Change at Manningtree
some trains

Tourist Information Centres
Colchester Queen St
(0206) 712233
Harwich Parkeston Quay
(0255) 506139

Walks
Essex Way access
Harwich/Mistley
Painter's Way
Manningtree to Sudbury

Places to visit
Colchester Bourne Mill, NT (Apr–Oct); Colchester & Essex Museum (Castle); St Botolph's Priory, EH; Zoo
Harwich Maritime Museum (Apr–Sep); Redoubt (Etr–Oct)
Manningtree 1¾m or bus & walk ¾m Flatford Mill/Bridge Cottage, NT (Apr–Aug)
Mistley Towers, EH

Colchester Castle's Norman Keep, built on a Roman temple

COLCHESTER–SUDBURY

TRAINS
(35 mins approx)
Mon–Fri 9; Sat 7; Sun 5
No refreshments
Change at Marks Tey
some trains

Tourist Information Centre
Sudbury Library, Market Hill (0787) 72092

Walks
Sudbury Walk along disused railway line – information from TIC

Places to visit
Chappel East Anglian Railway Museum
Sudbury Gainsborough's House

READING–BEDWYN

TRAINS
(55 mins approx)
Mon–Sat 11; Sun 1
No refreshments

Tourist Information Centres
Newbury The Wharf
(0635) 30267
Reading Civic Centre
(0734) 592388

Walks
Kennet & Avon Canal
follows rail line

Places to visit
Aldermaston By car
Silchester Roman town
Bedwyn Stone Museum;
Crofton Beam Engines
(Apr–Oct) 2m south
Hungerford By car
Littlecote House
(Apr–Oct)
Newbury Cloth Hall
(Museum); Donnington
Castle ruins
Reading Abbey ruins;
Blake's Lock Museum.
By car Basildon Park
(Apr–Oct); Childe Beale
Wildlife Trust (Etr–Sep);
Mapledurham House
(Etr–Sep)

TWYFORD–HENLEY

TRAINS
(15 mins approx)
Mon–Fri 15; Sat 13;
Sun (summer only) 10
No refreshments

Tourist Information Centre
Henley Town Hall
(0491) 578034

Walks
Oxfordshire Way from
Henley

Places to visit
Henley The Chantry
House; Kenton Theatre

MAIDENHEAD–MARLOW

TRAINS
(20 mins approx)
Mon–Sat 13
Sun (summer only) 11
No refreshments

Tourist Information Centres (*summer only)
Maidenhead St Ives Rd
(0628) 781110
*Marlow** Higginson Pk
(02684) 3597

Walks
Thameside paths from
Bourne End or Marlow
and between Cookham
and Maidenhead

Places to visit
Cookham Stanley Spencer
Gallery
Maidenhead Courage
Shire Horse Centre
(Mar–Oct).
By car/bus Cliveden
(Apr–Oct)

Thames and Kennet

READING – BEDWYN   *30 miles*
and HENLEY AND MARLOW BRANCHES

Although this route is a main line for high speed trains, it is best seen from the stopping train to Bedwyn, a pretty journey along the valley of the River Kennet. The branch lines to Henley and Marlow are delightful excursions through parts of the Thames Valley.

Reading
Reading's new station is well placed for the town, whose chief virtues are its fine 19th-century buildings. The train leaves through **Reading West** station, and then comes quickly into open country as it crosses the Kennet. The line passes under the M4 and **Theale** appears.

Aldermaston
Between Theale and Aldermaston the valley narrows, and the Kennet and Avon Canal runs parallel to the south. Aldermaston village, with its brick cottages, is over a mile south. Approaching **Midgham**, the spire of Woolhampton Church can be seen and, beyond, Douai Abbey.

Newbury
As the train passes **Thatcham** there is a good view of the canal lock to the south. Outside Newbury is the race course, with its own station. At one time Newbury had a number of connecting lines; a reminder of these is an old bridge in a field west of the station.

Kintbury
The line between Newbury and Kintbury is attractively wooded, particularly around Hamstead Marshall. To the north is Benham House (1772) in its Capability Brown park.

Hungerford
West of Kintbury, the train crosses to the south of the canal, with fine views to the north. Look backwards as the train leaves Hungerford station to enjoy the best view of the town. It has a good variety of 18th- and 19th-century buildings, and old shops. West of Hungerford the train crosses the canal again, into Wiltshire. Littlecote House lies two miles north-west, off the B4192.

Bedwyn
The spire of Little Bedwyn church can now be seen ahead. Walk from Bedwyn station into Great Bedwyn village to enjoy the eccentric Stone Museum with its fossilised dinosaur's footprint. Two miles to the south is Crofton Beam Engines and to the north-west is Savernake Forest.

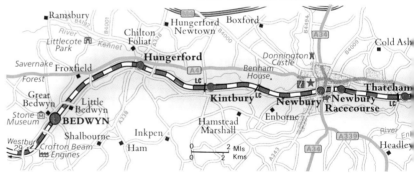

Littlecote House near Hungerford, later a Cromwellian stronghold

THE HENLEY BRANCH

TWYFORD – HENLEY
4½ miles

The Henley branch starts from Twyford, a typical Thames valley station in coloured brick, but there are some through trains from Reading. The train curves round the village and then runs straight to **Wargrave**, well to the east of its minimal station, but worth a visit for its surprising Arts and Crafts and Art Nouveau buildings. The train crosses the Thames, allowing plenty of time to enjoy the views of the river. Up in the wooded hills further east can be seen the white bulk of Wargrave Manor, dominant early 19th-century classicism. Now in Oxfordshire, the train crosses the Thames water meadows to **Shiplake**. Little of the village, which is well to the south, can be seen but its fine Edwardian and Art Nouveau riverside mansions should not be missed. After a lovely stretch of river, the train reaches its terminus at Henley's new station. The delightful town is close at hand. Cross the 18th-century bridge over the river, and then turn back to see the town's wealth of decorative 18th- and 19th-century architecture and the pretty Gothic church.

Ornamental detail – Henley bridge

LOOK OUT FOR

The **Thames** from Maidenhead to Reading and the **Kennet** from Reading westwards dominate this journey. The Thames is at its best as it winds its way around Marlow, Henley and Cookham. The Kennet branches south from the Thames just north of Reading station, and then is never far

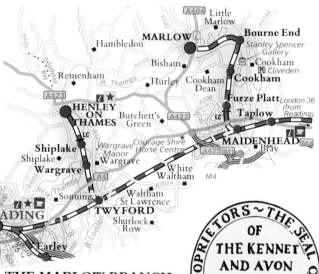

Springtime view of Cliveden. The former home of the Astors is now a luxury hotel

THE MARLOW BRANCH

MAIDENHEAD – MARLOW
7 miles

The Marlow branch starts from Maidenhead, an enjoyably decorative station. The train curves round the town and then reaches **Furze Platt** station. The landscape then opens out, with good views towards the Thames to the east. Barry's great mansion at Cliveden can be seen above the trees all the way to **Cookham**. The village, with its 13th-century church, decorative iron bridge, pretty riverside cottages and Stanley Spencer Gallery is well to the east of the station. After Cookham the train drops down towards the Thames and crosses the river into Buckinghamshire before coming to a dead end at **Bourne End**, where it now reverses and sets off along the branch to Marlow, a slow and pretty riverside journey. The riverside setting of Marlow is particularly enjoyable and there is plenty to see, including the splendid suspension bridge of 1831, three Victorian churches, Marlow Place and other Georgian houses. Both Marlow and Henley are good bases for explorations of the Thames valley, which is notably attractive between the two towns.

from the line to Bedwyn. Far more noticeable, however, particularly west of Newbury, is the canal, part of the waterway that connects Reading and the Thames with Bristol. The Kennet was made navigable between Reading and Newbury by 1723, involving 18 locks, but the canal to link Newbury with the River Avon near Bath was not completed until 1810, to the designs of the engineer John Rennie. The Kennet and Avon Canal was at its peak in the mid-19th century but then declined, becoming unnavigable and derelict by the 1950s. Since then the canal has gradually been restored and in 1989 it should be possible to travel by boat once again between London and Bristol.

WALES

The Cambrian Coast line is one of Wales's most scenic routes,
much of it running beside the sea against a dramatic mountain backdrop:
the Pwllheli train at Friog with the Barmouth bridge ahead

THE GREAT LITTLE TRAINS

SINCE THE EARLY 19TH CENTURY narrow gauge lines have been a notable feature of the railway network in Wales. Like the main lines, most were built as industrial lines to transport stone from the mines and quarries in the mountains down to the main line railways and the ports and harbours of North Wales, and the narrow gauge was chosen to minimise construction and operating costs. Many passed through spectacular mountain scenery.

Wagons were hauled initially by horses or ropes powered by stationary engines but from the 1860s small steam locomotives were increasingly used. By the end of the 19th century, some lines began to carry more passengers than freight, while one or two, such as the Snowdon Mountain Railway, were built entirely with tourism in mind.

During the early part of this century many narrow gauge lines closed down. Many of the mines and quarries that had brought them into existence were reaching the end of their life, and by the 1940s only a handful of lines were operating. More recently, the pattern of decline has been reversed. The first railway to be taken over by the preservation society and operated by volunteers was the Talyllyn, in 1950, and since then others have been restored and reopened.

Today, there are ten little railways, and others are planned. Their routes range from ¾ mile to over 13 miles.

Each railway is privately owned and operated and so each one issues its own tickets. However, joint British Rail tickets are available for some lines, while eight lines, marketed together under the Great Little Trains of Wales title, issue a combined Wanderer ticket.

Bala Lake Railway
Yr Orsaf, Llanuwchllyn, Bala, Gwynedd LL23 7DD, tel: 06784 666
Nearest stations: Barmouth, Ruabon

Opened in 1972, the railway follows 4½ miles of the former standard gauge Ruabon to Barmouth line, which was closed in 1963. The route is from Bala to Llanuwchllyn beside Lake Bala in the Snowdonia National Park, beneath the Aran and Arenig mountains. Locomotives used worked formerly in the North Wales slate quarries.

Brecon Mountain Railway
Pant Station, Merthyr Tydfil, Mid Glamorgan CF48 2UP, tel: 0685 4854
Nearest station: Merthyr Tydfil

Opened in 1980 as the only narrow gauge railway in South Wales, the line will ultimately follow 5½ miles of the former standard gauge Brecon to Merthyr Tydfil route. Climbing high into the mountains, the line has fine views of the Brecon Beacons. Locomotives used come from South Africa and East Germany as well as Wales.

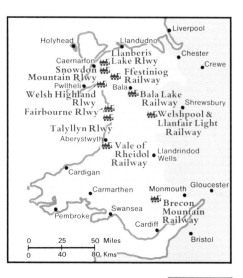

Great little engines – Dolbadarn, which operates on the Llanberis Lake Railway . . .

. . . and The Earl, owned by The Welshpool and Llanfair Light Railway, currently on static display at Didcot Railway Centre

Fairbourne Railway
Beach Road, Fairbourne, Dolgellau, Gwynedd LL38 2PZ, tel: 0341 250362
Nearest station: Fairbourne (direct connection)

Built in 1890 to transport building materials, the line runs for 1¼ miles from Fairbourne to the end of the peninsula and the ferry for Barmouth. It passes one of the finest beaches in Wales and there are splendid views along the coast and the Mawddach estuary.

Ffestiniog Railway   see page 55

WALES

Llanberis Lake Railway
Padarn, Llanberis, Gwynedd LL55 4TY,
tel: 0286 870549
Nearest station: Bangor

Built originally in the 19th century to transport slate from the Dinorwic quarries to Port Dinorwic on the Menai Straits, the line now runs for two miles from Gilfach Ddu near the Welsh Slate Museum to Pen-y-llyn along the shore of Lake Padarn. Fine lakeside scenery and the views of Snowdon add to the attractions of the Padarn Country Park.

Snowdon Mountain Railway
Llanberis, Gwynedd LL55 4TY, tel: 0286 870223
Nearest station: Bangor

Opened in 1896 and built for passenger carrying, the line is Britain's only rack and pinion railway. It climbs from Llanberis to the summit of Snowdon in under five miles, with spectacular views.

Talyllyn Railway   see page 57

The Snowdon Mountain Railway climbs 3,000 feet (914 metres) to Snowdon's summit, with magnificent views all the way

Welsh Highland Railway
Gelert's Farm Works, Madoc Street West, Porthmadog,
Gwynedd LL49 9DY, tel: 0766 513402
Nearest station: Porthmadog

The original Welsh Highland Railway, opened in 1923, ran from Porthmadog, where it connected with the Ffestiniog for 22 miles to Dinas, near Caernarfon, via the Aberglaslyn Pass and Beddgelert. Always short of passengers and freight, the line closed in 1937. A short ¾-mile section from Porthmadog to Pen y Mount was reopened in 1980, with the eventual aim of restoring the whole route with its spectacular scenery.

Vale of Rheidol   see page 58

Welshpool & Llanfair Light Railway
The Station, Llanfair Caereinion, Powys SY21 0SF,
tel: 0938 810441
Nearest station: Welshpool

Opened in 1903 to serve the agricultural community between the market towns of Welshpool and Llanfair Caereinion, the line existed quietly until its final closure in 1956. Reopened in stages from 1963, the 8-mile route follows a wandering course through the Welsh borders. Locomotives used came from West Africa, the West Indies and Finland as well as those built for the original line.

WALKING IN THE REGION

Wales is a country made for walkers, and the best areas for walking can be reached by train. These include the Snowdonia National Park, the Brecon Beacons and the Pembroke Coast Path. Railway walks are a good way to discover the lesser known parts of the country, particularly the valleys of South Wales and along the river estuaries of the north.

A selection of the closed railways now designated as official footpaths:

Arthog to Penmaenpool (4 miles) along part of the former Barmouth to Bala line, beside the Mawddach estuary

Dinas to Porthmadog, the former Welsh Highland Railway

Gilwern to Llanfoist (3 miles), part of the former Merthyr to Abergavenny line (see pages 64–65)

For further information about the Walks suggested on each of the routes in the following pages, contact the local Tourist Information Centre. See also page 7.

Ports and Castles of Dyfed

SWANSEA – PEMBROKE DOCK   73 miles

TRAINS
(2hrs 10mins approx)
Mon–Fri 8; Sat 7; Sun 4
No refreshments

**Tourist Information
Centres** (*summer only)
Carmarthen Lammas St
(0267) 231557
Kilgetty Kingsmoor
Common (0834) 813672
Swansea Singleton St
(0792) 468321
Whitland Canolfan
Hywel Dda
(0994) 240867

Walks
Pembrokeshire Coast Path
join at Tenby, Penally or
Pembroke

Places to Visit
Carmarthen Castle;
Roman fort. *By car/bus*
Gwili Steam Railway
(details from TIC)
Kidwelly Castle, Cadw;
Museum (Etr–Sep)
Lamphey Palace, Cadw
Llanelli Parc Howard Art
Gallery & Museum
Manorbier Castle, 1m
(May–Sep)
Pembrey & Burry Port
Pembrey Country Park
Pembroke Castle; Castle
Hill Museum (Etr–Oct);
National Museum of
Gypsy Caravans
(Etr–Sep)
Swansea New Castle;
Glyn Vivian Art Gallery
& Museum; Maritime &
Industrial Museum;
University College of
Swansea & Royal
Institution of South
Wales Museum
Tenby Museum; Town
Walls; Tudor Merchant's
House, NT (Etr–Sep).
Whitland Abbey ruins

A n exploration of the varied landscape of south Wales, this journey is a tour through the old counties of Carmarthen and Pembroke, linking fine hill and coastal scenery, echoes of industrial and naval history and old-fashioned market towns and resorts.

Swansea
Swansea station, which is a terminus, stands to the east of the city centre, near the River Tawe. The best view of the town is from the Pembroke Dock train as it climbs up the valley with the bulk of Kilvey Hill to the east, and then swings to the west. A tunnel marks the end of Swansea's suburbs and then the train enters the hilly landscape of the Gower peninsula. At **Gowerton** the hills recede and the line drops down to cross the marshes that surround the estuary of the Loughor. A long viaduct takes the train across the river, with good views to the south, and then the sprawl of **Llanelli** appears ahead. The station is near the old port, well to the south of the town centre, with the remains of old industries all around.

Kidwelly
West of Llanelli the line runs right along the shore, with excellent views across to the Gower. A huge power station has several types of wind generator in use and beyond is **Pembrey and Burry Port**, a rather uneasy blend of old houses and the relics of former industries, particularly around the once busy harbour. The train now enters the vast area of coastal marshland known as Pembrey Burrow and then swings north into woodland. Pembrey Forest lies to the west and

ahead and to the east are powerful hills. Kidwelly comes into view, announced by the distinctive steeple of the 13th-century church, formerly a Benedictine priory, and the remains of the great castle, started about 1275. The station is well to the west, surrounded by the later, industrial heart of Kidwelly. Leaving Kidwelly, the train runs along the edge of the Gwendraeth estuary and then curves round towards the mouth of the Tywi. **Ferryside**, a village of pleasant terraces round a big Victorian church, stands by the riverside, but much better is the view across to Llanstephan where the ruined castle stands romantically on the headland, and the rows of colourwashed cottages face out over the water.

Carmarthen
The River Tywi narrows quickly through a landscape of rolling hills broken into small fields. Carmarthen comes into sight, its skyline formed by church towers and the great mass of the French-style County Hall. A busy market town since the Middle Ages, Carmarthen still has plenty of 18th- and 19th-century buildings. The station is now a terminus, and the train reverses, but it was formerly a junction of some importance, with connections north to Aberystwyth via Lampeter and east to Shrewsbury via Llandeilo. Leaving Carmarthen the train crosses the Tywi, the old lifting bridge a reminder of the former port, and then it runs away from the river into a landscape of hilly farmland. As

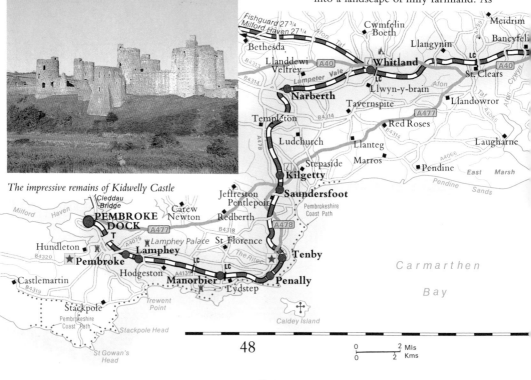

The impressive remains of Kidwelly Castle

A jumble of colourful houses in Tenby – a seaside resort with a long history

the line crosses the River Cywyn there is a view of St Clears to the south, and then a pretty wooded stretch takes the train through the hills to the valley of the Taf. At **Whitland** the Pembroke branch swings away to the south from the main line to Fishguard.

Tenby

The train climbs up Lampeter Vale to **Narberth** through a landscape rich in hillforts and other reminders of earlier civilisations, and then from **Kilgetty** it winds its way down towards the coast. **Saundersfoot** station is over a mile inland, and there are only glimpses of the town as the train makes its rather private way through the woods towards Tenby. Here the line curves round the town on a big stone viaduct that leads directly to the pretty 1866 station. Tenby, with its castle, Norman church, medieval streets and busy harbour, is to the east and then suddenly the seaside comes into view as the train runs along the dunes to **Penally**. Big stone houses and a church on the

hillside face out to sea and over Caldey Island, with its Cistercian abbey. The line then leaves the coast to run through hilly farmland to **Manorbier**. The village and its imposing castle are situated well to the south and out of sight.

Pembroke

Just east of **Lamphey** station the ruins of the 13th-century Bishop's palace stand by the track, with the tall church near by. The train then completes its crossing of the peninsula in a dramatic way, making a triumphal entry to Pembroke high above the town. As the train crosses the river all the town comes into view, spread along the southern shore with its great castle at its heart. There is an excellent view of the town from the west as the line curves up into the hills, so look back. After a short tunnel, it reaches the terminus at Pembroke Dock. The station is high above the old naval town with its 18th-century grid pattern of streets, and overlooks the docks where so many famous ships were built, including the first Royal Yacht. To the north Neyland and Milford Haven can be seen across the estuary.

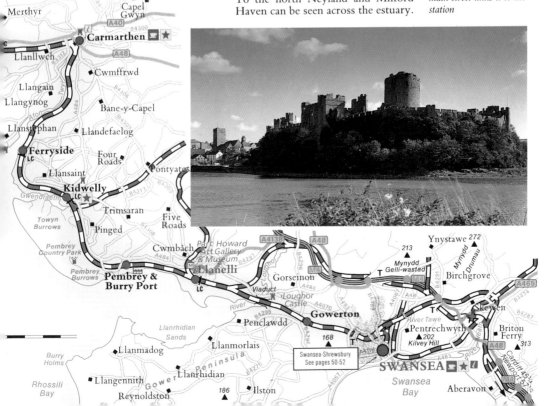

Heart of Wales

SWANSEA – SHREWSBURY *121½ miles*

TRAINS
Swansea–Shrewsbury
(3hrs 37mins approx)
Mon–Sat 5; Sun 1
Refreshments: some Sats

**Tourist Information
Centres** (*summer only)
Builth Wells★ Groe Car
Park (0982) 553307
Llandovery★ Central Car
Park, Broad St
(0550) 20693
Llanwrtyd Wells The
Bookshop (0591) 3391
Swansea Singleton St
(0792) 468321

**For all information on
Llanelli and Swansea
see pages 48–49**

Walks
*Breacon Beacons National
Park* walks and trails
information from
National Park
Information Centre,
Broad St, Llandovery
(Mar–Sep)
Cwm Irfon Forestry
Commission walks near
Llanwrtyd Wells
*Golden Grove Country
Park* Countryside
Commission walks near
Llandeilo
Sugar Loaf Walk from
Cynghordy
Swansea industrial,
archaeological and
historical walks (details
from Tourist Information
Centres)
The Wye Valley Walk
passes Builth Wells

Pony Trekking
Llandybie to Pontarddulais
pony trekking is
available in the Irfon and
Loughor valleys and
throughout central Wales

Places to Visit
Ammanford By car Carn
Ilecharth stone circle;
Dan-yr-Ogof Caves and
tourist complex
(Etr–Oct)
Builth Wells (2m from
Builth Road station)
Castle. *By car* Llewelyn's
Cave at Aberedw
Cilmeri Llewelyn
Monument
Gowerton By car Loughor
Castle
Llandeilo Dynevor Castle.
By car Carreg Cennen
Castle, Cadw; Dryslwyn
Castle, Cadw; Paxton's
Tower
Llandovery Castle; St
Dingat's Church
Llangadog By car Carn
Goch hillfort
Llanwrda By car Talley
Abbey; Dolaucothi Gold
Mines, NT (Etr–Oct)
Llanwrtyd Wells Cambrian
Tweed and Wool
Factory. *By car* Strata
Florida Abbey, Cadw

*Only ruins now remain
of 12th-century Talley
Abbey*

This journey through the heart of Wales is a delightful anachronism, a real country railway whose trains meander very slowly through an attractive and varied landscape. The line was originally built to enable the London and North Western Railway to compete with the Great Western for the south Wales coal traffic, but today buzzards and wild flowers are more common than coal trucks. Passengers should note that most stops are by request.

SWANSEA–BUILTH WELLS *64 miles*

Swansea–Llanelli
See Swansea–Pembroke route
page 48

Llanelli
At one time the trains from Swansea to Shrewsbury followed a direct route from Pontarddulais but since 1964 they have travelled via Llanelli, necessitating a reversal. Leaving Llanelli the way it arrived, the train quickly reaches the junction and swings north east along the Loughor estuary. Initially it passes the remains of old industries, some now romantically ivy-clad, but after **Bynea** the surroundings become more rural. The line follows the river valley past Llangennech, where the church looks good against a backdrop of hills and then it becomes much more like a branch line, with flowers brushing the carriage sides. The little tunnel just south of **Pontarddulais** looks too small for the train, but somehow it squeezes through. Following the twisting Loughor, the line continues north, the narrowing hillsides scattered with farms. At **Pantyffynnon** the station still has its Brunel-type hipped roof and the branch lines are busy with coal traffic. Then, with rabbits running across the track, **Ammanford** comes into view, with the Black Mountain to the east. The next stop is **Llandybie**, a village of stone houses grouped round the big church. To the north is a huge quarry, and a range of old lime kilns by the track.

Llandeilo
The line now follows the River Cennen, and from **Ffairfach**, where old mills stand by the river, there is a good view of Llandeilo, with its colour-washed houses and big Victorian church set on the hillside above the River Tywi. To the west, just off the A40, is Dynevor Castle on its crag. Leaving Llandeilo the train swings east along the Tywi valley with attractive hills to north and south, and past **Llangadog** and **Llanwrda** stations. Five miles west of Llangadog, and off the B4302 are the ruins of Talley Abbey, while about nine miles north of Llanwrda, up the Dulais valley and off the A482 are the Roman gold mines at Dolaucothi.

Llandovery
West of Llandovery the Tywi is joined by the Bran and these two rivers enclose this old drovers' and market town. The two churches, both outside the town centre, stand by the line. Particularly attractive is the sturdy one to the north, sitting on a mound

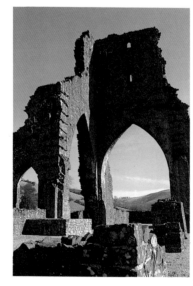

Dynevor Castle can be seen from the train near Llandeilo

The rare Red Kite: its numbers are increasing

that was once a Roman fort. Also visible are the remains of the castle. The train continues along the Bran valley, climbing steadily through a landscape of woods and farmland. At **Cynghordy** the hills begin to dominate, adding drama to a pastoral countryside, and these pave the way for the great viaduct of 1868 north of the station, eighteen stone and brick curving arches that carry the train 100ft above the river. Ahead now is the distinctive Sugar Loaf hill, its flanks defaced by somewhat monotonous forestry plantations, and the train climbs steeply up to pass through the Sugar Loaf in a rather damp tunnel. The hills then gradually open out, with good views along the Irfon valley as the train drops down to **Llanwrtyd Wells**. One of several old spa towns along the line, Llanwrtyd owed its success in the late Victorian period to the railway. Now it has turned to other things, to become a centre for pony trekking, walking and mountain bike riding.

Builth Wells

The train continues its descent along the Irfon valley, a remote and attractive landscape rich in buzzards. At **Llangammarch Wells**, another former spa now noted for its fishing, the church stands in a pretty graveyard by the track. The next stations are **Garth** and **Cilmeri** and all along this stretch are fine views of the Eppynt ranges to the south.

West of Cilmeri is the monument to Llewelyn, the last native Prince of Wales, and east of Cilmeri the train crosses the Wye, high above the river, with Builth Wells visible to the south. Another former spa town full of Victorian buildings, Builth is known now for livestock shows and sales. The station, **Builth Road**, well to the west, was once a busy junction where the central Wales line was crossed by the line from Brecon to Llanidloes.

LOOK OUT FOR

One of the most delightful features of this journey is the **wildlife** to be observed from the train as it makes its leisurely way through the countryside of mid Wales. Buzzards, not a common sight in most of Britain, are plentiful on the more remote sections of the route, soaring on rising air currents, or even perching on posts beside the line. Ravens too may sometimes be seen, distinctive by their large size and aerobatic skill. One of Britain's rarest birds, the red kite, also occurs in these parts. Reduced to just a few breeding pairs not many years ago, the revival of the red kite is a success story for local conservationists. This country train holds no fears for rabbits, which may be seen crossing the track near remote stations, and foxes too are not an uncommon sight for rail travellers.

A massive 19th-century viaduct towers over the village of Cynghordy

LOOK OUT FOR

Although it is now among the most rural of all Britain's country railways, the line from Swansea to Shrewsbury was built largely for **commerce**. Opened in 1868, it was used extensively by coal and mineral trains for the first part of its life. Many of the stations still have their old goods sheds, often now standing disused in fields. Examples can be seen at Llanbister Road, Knighton and Bucknell. The transport of livestock was also important, with the train taking over the traditional role of the drover in getting the sheep and cattle to and from the many busy markets along the route. Several stations still have the ramps used to load the livestock into the trucks. It is hard to imagine this sleepy line busy with passengers, yet in the late Victorian and Edwardian eras the trains carried hundreds of thousands of people each year, mostly visitors taking the waters at the **spas** along the route. Towns such as Builth and Llandrindod owed their existence to the railway and today, even though most of the wells are now disused, these places are still full of echoes of the great days of rural railways.

TRAINS
see page 50

Tourist Information Centres (★summer only)
Llandrindod Wells Rock Park Spa (0597) 2600
Church Stretton★ Church St (0694) 723133
Shrewsbury The Square (0743) 50761/2

For information on Church Stretton, Craven Arms and Shrewsbury see page 64

Walks
Offa's Dyke Path and *Glyndwr's Way* can be joined at Knighton

Place to Visit
Llandrindod Wells Castell Collen Roman fort (2m)

LLANDRINDOD WELLS – SHREWSBURY *57½ miles*

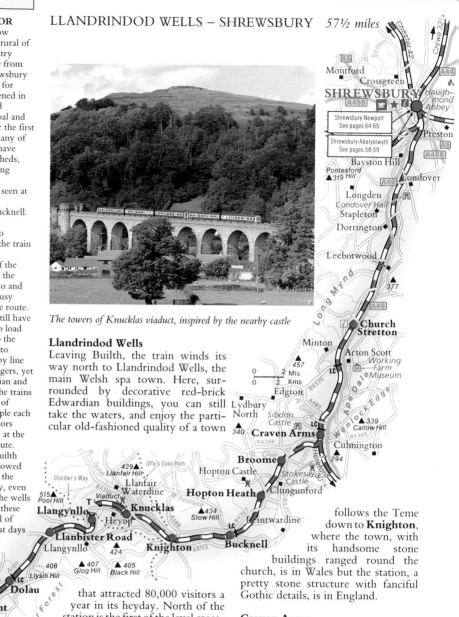

The towers of Knucklas viaduct, inspired by the nearby castle

Llandrindod Wells

Leaving Builth, the train winds its way north to Llandrindod Wells, the main Welsh spa town. Here, surrounded by decorative red-brick Edwardian buildings, you can still take the waters, and enjoy the particular old-fashioned quality of a town that attracted 80,000 visitors a year in its heyday. North of the station is the first of the level crossings operated by the guard, and the old Roman fort at Castell Collen stands by the river to the west. With views of big bare hills in the distance, the train passes a little church set in the fields to the south and then reaches **Penybont**.

Knighton

The line follows the River Aran, passing **Dolau** with its pretty flowers and benches. Ahead is Llysin Hill, distinctively rounded with an old hillfort visible on top. At **Llanbister Road**, a remote halt far from anywhere, hills surround the line again, with handsome farms set in valleys. The next station, **Llangynllo**, is equally remote and then the train passes through a tightly curving tunnel and down through the hills to **Knucklas**. West of the station is the great viaduct, all rough stone and crenellations, with excellent views ahead to the Teme valley. To the north are the remains of Knucklas Castle, the inspiration for the viaduct's unusual style. The train

follows the Teme down to **Knighton**, where the town, with its handsome stone buildings ranged round the church, is in Wales but the station, a pretty stone structure with fanciful Gothic details, is in England.

Craven Arms

With hills all around, the line stays close to the meandering Teme to **Bucknell**, where there is another substantial stone station, now a private house. The train now swings north to enter the wider valley of the Clun. This is Marches country, and all around are the sites of the great castles built to defend the border from Roman to medieval times. A good example is Hopton, a mile west of **Hoptonheath** station, where the Norman keep still stands proudly. Three miles to the south east, off the B4385, is the Roman town of Leintwardine. With the hills of the Long Mynd now visible in the distance ahead, the train passes Clungunford, to the east, with its 14th-century church and crenellated Broadwood Hall. The next station is **Broome**, and then 18th-century Sibdon Castle stands by the line as it comes to Craven Arms, and the junction with the main Shrewsbury to Newport route.

For Craven Arms to Shrewsbury, see page 64

The North Coast and Anglesey
LLANDUDNO JUNCTION – HOLYHEAD   40 miles

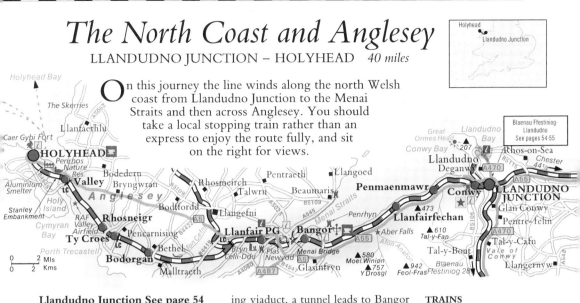

On this journey the line winds along the north Welsh coast from Llandudno Junction to the Menai Straits and then across Anglesey. You should take a local stopping train rather than an express to enjoy the route fully, and sit on the right for views.

Llandudno Junction See page 54

Conwy
Set on the corner of the Conwy estuary, this fine town is one of the few in Britain still to have its walls virtually intact, and a walk along the walls is the best way to see it. The major element, both historically and visually, is Edward I's great castle, built from 1283. Beside the castle are the bridges across the river, the best being Telford's suspension bridge of 1826, and alongside it Stephenson's tubular railway bridge of 1849.

The train continues along the rocky shore, against a dramatic backdrop of mighty hills. At **Penmaenmawr** the little Victorian resort enjoys excellent views of Puffin Island and the eastern tip of Anglesey. The next stop is **Llanfairfechan**, another pleasantly old-fashioned resort.

Bangor
The train swings away from the shore with views across to the Anglesey coast and then the battlements and pinnacles of Penrhyn Castle come into view above the trees. After a big curv-ing viaduct, a tunnel leads to Bangor station. Bangor is a city of some style and its decorative stone station is well placed. The train now runs along the Menai Straits. Telford's great suspension bridge can clearly be seen, and then the line crosses into Anglesey.

Holyhead
The station commonly known as **Llanfair PG** reopened in 1973 after a period of closure and so its 58-letter name, Llanfairpwllgwyngyllgogery-chwyndrobwllllantysiliogogogoch, again greets arriving passengers. The train runs through a typical Anglesey landscape of small fields, stone walls and white houses set in rolling hills, then the line crosses the marshes to run inland again to **Bodorgan**. The next station is **Ty Croes**, with big windmill towers near by, and then the train comes to the little resort of **Rhosneigr**. **Valley** station is to the north of Valley airfield and then the train crosses on to the Holy Island peninsula at the water's edge. The line swings past the aluminium works, and then the train runs slowly through Holyhead to the harbour terminus.

TRAINS
(1hr 5mins approx)
Mon–Sat 10; Sun 4
Refreshments: some

For Llandudno Junction take main line from Chester, or Conwy valley line from Blaenau Ffestiniog

Tourist Information Centres (★summer only)
Bangor★ Theatr Gwynedd (0248) 352786
Conwy★ Castle St (0492) 592248
Holyhead★ Marine Sq, Salt Island App (0407) 2622
Llanfairpwll Station Site (0248) 713177

For all information on Llandudno see pages 54–55

Walks
Holyhead Mountain
Penrhos Nature Reserve, 2m from Holyhead

Cycling
Llanfair PG, to Rhosneigr see pages 5–7

Places to Visit
Bangor Cathedral. *By car/bus* Penrhyn Castle, NT (Apr–Oct)
Conwy Aberconwy, NT (Mar–Sep); Castle, Cadw; Plas Mawr (Apr–Oct); Smallest House (Apr–Sep)
Holyhead Caer Gybi Fort. *By car* (2m) South Stack Lighthouse. *By boat* The Skerries
Llanfairfechan history trail to standing stones and Aber Falls
Llanfair PG By car/bus Anglesey Sea Zoo at Brynsiencyn (Mar–Oct); Bryn Celli Ddu burial chamber, Cadw; Plas Newydd, NT (May–Sep)
Penmaenmawr history trails to Bronze and Iron Age sites
Prestatyn Graig Fawr viewpoint, NT

Ancient stone circles, possibly used for Celtic worship, adorn the hills above Penmaenmawr

The Conwy Valley
BLAENAU FFESTINIOG – LLANDUDNO *31 miles*

TRAINS
(67mins approx)
Mon–Sat 6; Sun 3
(summer only)
No refreshments except
summer Sundays

**Tourist Information
Centres** (*summer only)
Betws-y-Coed* Royal Oak
Stables (06902) 426/665
Blaenau Ffestiniog* Isallt,
High St (0766) 830360
Llandudno Chapel St
(0492) 76413

Walks
Forestry Commission walks
and nature trails from
Betws-y-Coed/Llanrwst
Great Orme coast and
nature trails from
Llandudno
Snowdonia National Park
walks and trails –
information from Tourist
Centres

Places to Visit
Betws-y-Coed Conwy
Valley Railway Museum
(Etr–Oct): Gallery. *By
car/bus* Swallow Falls
Blaenau Ffestiniog Gloddfa
Ganol Slate Mine
(Etr–Sep); Llechwedd
Slate Caverns (Apr–Oct)
Deganwy Castle ruins
Dolwyddelan Castle,
Cadw
Glan Conwy Felin Isaf
Watermill
Llandudno Cabin lift from
Happy Valley
(May–Oct); Doll
Museum and Model
Railway (Etr–Sep); Great
Orme Tramway
(May–Oct); Rapallo
House Museum and Art
Gallery
Llanrwst Gwydir Castle
(Etr–Oct); Gwydir
Uchaf Chapel, Cadw;
Gwydir Uchaf Forestry
Exhibition
Pont-y-Pant By car/bus Ty
Mawr, NT (Apr–Sep)
Tal-y-Cafn By car/bus
Bodnant Garden, NT
(Mar–Oct)

LOOK OUT FOR
The railways of north
Wales were developed in
the middle of the 19th
century largely to serve
the **stone trade**. Today
many of the quarries
have closed, along with
many of the railway
routes, but there is still
plenty to see, and the
remains of this once great
industry can be explored
by train. (See Ffestiniog
Railway panel, opposite.)
The range and quality of
north Wales stone can be
seen, above all, in
buildings: the chunky
stone terraces, the
powerful churches, the
bridges and viaducts
with their rough finish
and the great tunnels and
cuttings carved through
the solid rock.

The stone quarries of north Wales make this a journey through industrial history. Both the Conwy valley line and the Ffestiniog Railway were built to carry slate to the ports. The route carves its way from the mountainous heart of the country to follow the Conwy river to its estuary through excitingly varied scenery.

The slate quarries of Blaenau Ffestiniog form a dramatic backdrop for the preserved narrow gauge railway

Blaenau Ffestiniog
Overshadowed by great grey mountains of slate, Blaenau's new station, shared by the narrow-gauge Ffestiniog Railway, is a fitting starting point for a journey of drama and excitement. At one time the town had two stations, but the old GWR route south to Bala was closed long ago, leaving only a short branch to serve the nuclear power station at Trawsfynydd. Leaving the station, the train is quickly at the heart of the old slate industry, with the old inclined planes running steeply up the mountains of broken slate. To the·east are the Llechwedd caverns and museum. A long tunnel takes the line through the mountains and then it follows the twisting route of the River Lledr, with dramatic views across the valley. After **Roman Bridge** the ruins of 12th-century Dolwyddelan Castle come into view, set on a mound to the west. On **Dolwyddelan** station there is an old quarry locomotive, a reminder of the great mineral wealth that justified the building of such expensive and heavily engineered routes.

Betws-y-Coed
The line continues its downward descent, winding its way through rocky cuttings and under rough stone bridges. The landscape is increasingly wooded past **Pont-y-Pant** and then the train leaves the woods briefly to cross Cethin's Bridge, a splendid viaduct made from great lumps of rough-cut stone. The line swings north as the Lledr joins the Conwy which it then follows to Betws-y-Coed. This Victorian town, at the heart of the Gwydir Forest, and served by the A5 as well as the railway, is the natural starting point for visits to north Wales. It is a town of bridges, the best being Telford's cast iron Waterloo Bridge. By the station is a railway museum, with old carriages in a siding and an extensive garden railway. The 14th-century church is near by. From here the train continues northwards along the widening Conwy valley, thickly wooded to the west.

Llanrwst
The line skirts round this little market town and the station is well to the north, so Llanrwst's best features, the 17th-century bridge and chapel and the Tudor Gwydir Castle, cannot be seen. The train then returns to the Conwy, with good views across the now wide valley to the white houses of Trefriw, to the west. Also visible across the river is **Dolgarrog**, rather dwarfed by its aluminium works. The station is connected to the town by an elaborate steel footbridge. The next station is **Tal-y-Cafn**, beside the big road bridge, and then the line follows the sweeping curves of the Conwy as it flows towards its estuary. This is the stop for Bodnant Garden, to the east of the A470. It is worth looking back for the views up the valley to the south.

Llandudno
Curving round a great bay, a vast expanse of mudflats and saltmarsh at low tide, the train comes to **Glan Conwy** and the first view of Conwy Castle with the ornamental rail and road bridges that stand adjacent to it. After **Llandudno Junction**, a big station where the Conwy branch crosses the main Chester–Holyhead line, the train rejoins the eastern shore of the estuary, with a clear view of Conwy's bridges. (See page 53 for Llandudno Junction to Holyhead.) After **Deganwy** the line swings inland with the mound of Great Ormes Head dominating the view. Ahead are the spires of Llandudno, north Wales's top resort, which makes the most of its two

beaches, quieter Conwy Bay to the west and Ormes Bay to the east. The station is near the beach, the museum and the Great Orme Tramway.

Great Orme, whose cliffs rise to the north-west of Llandudno, can be enjoyed from the local Tramway

FFESTINIOG RAILWAY

Linda, who runs on the Ffestiniog Railway

The Ffestiniog Railway is the longest and most spectacular of the preserved Welsh narrow-gauge railways. It runs from the harbour-side at **Porthmadog** to **Blaenau Ffestiniog**, where the quarries remind us of the vast quantities of slate it transported to the ships that carried it all over the world.

When the line was opened by the Festiniog Railway Company in 1836, horses were used uphill, and the loaded waggons returned to the port by gravity. Then in 1863 came a breakthrough, when steam locomotives were introduced to run on a gauge of only 1ft 11½ins. Six years later the first of the double-ended Fairlie locomotives appeared, which have been a unique feature of the line ever since.

After World War II the line became derelict, but was rescued in 1954. Since then the original company, supported by the voluntary Festiniog Railway Society, has reopened it throughout, which involved building a new stretch, complete with a tunnel and spiral, around the old section flooded by a hydroelectric scheme. For much of its length the line clings to a narrow ledge on the mountain-side, with spectacular views of Harlech Castle

on the coast. There are countless walks to be made from the line, while at Blaenau Ffestiniog it is possible to go underground in two of the old slate mines (see panel left).

FFESTINIOG RAILWAY
Porthmadog–Blaenau Ffestiniog 12 miles (also direct interchange at Minffordd)
Operates: weekends Mar; daily Apr–Oct (phone for details (0766) 512340)
Single journey: 65 mins

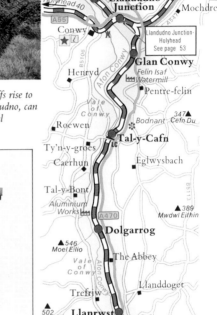

Dovey Junction-Pwllheli See pages 56-57

Llandudno Junction-Holyhead See page 53

Professor Codman's Punch and Judy shows continue a long Llandudno tradition

The Cambrian Coast

DOVEY JUNCTION – PWLLHELI *57½ miles*

TRAINS
(1hr 54mins approx)
Mon–Sat 6; Sun 3
(summer only)
No refreshments

**Tourist Information
Centres** (*summer only)
Aberdovey★ The Wharf
(065472) 321
Barmouth★ Station Rd
(0341) 280787
Criccieth★ The Square
(076671) 2489
Harlech★ High St
(0766) 780658
Porthmadog★ High St
(0766) 512981
Pwllheli★ Y Maes
(0758) 613000
Tywyn★ High St
(0654) 710070

Walks
Dinas Oleu, NT from
Barmouth
Mawddach Estuary walks,
trails and birdwatching –
information from Tourist
Centres
Snowdonia National Park
walks and trails –
information from Tourist
Centres

Places to Visit
Aberdovey birdwatching
in the Dovey estuary
Criccieth Castle, Cadw.
By car/bus Lloyd George
Museum at
Llanystumdwy
(May–Sep)
Fairbourne Fairbourne
Railway and Butterfly
Safari (Etr–Sep)
Harlech Castle, Cadw
Llanbedr Maes Artro
Tourist Village (Etr–Oct)
Minffordd Portmeirion
(Apr–Oct)
Porthmadog Ffestiniog
Railway Museum
(Mar–Nov); Porthmadog
Pottery (Etr–Oct); Welsh
Highland Railway
(Apr–Oct). *By car*
Aberglaslyn Pass, NT
Tonfanau birdwatching at
Broad Water
Tywyn Narrow-gauge
Railway Museum
(Apr–Oct)

*Italianate Portmeirion,
reached from Minfford*

This delightful journey explores the sandy beaches, old harbours and traditional resorts of the Cambrian coast, with highlights including Harlech Castle and the Italianate village of Portmeirion. Although the line starts at Dovey Junction, many trains do not stop there, so board at Machynlleth. Sit left and let the guard know in good time if you want to get off, as many of the stops are by request.

A Sprinter on its way to Barmouth after crossing the Mawddach estuary on a wooden viaduct

Aberdovey
From **Machynlleth** the train follows the River Dovey to **Dovey Junction**. After crossing the river the line runs beside a vast expanse of saltmarsh and sand. The train is right on the seashore, on a low embankment, passing through narrow, steep-sided tunnels to **Penhelig**, a little village of tall houses with splendid views over the estuary. Aberdovey soon comes into sight. A few sailing boats maintain the town's maritime tradition, but the harbour is now a quiet place, a far cry from its heyday in the 19th century as one of Wales's busiest ports. Now it is just old hotels, the traditional seaside and the golf course in the dunes.

Tywyn
Tywyn is announced by the terminus of the Talyllyn narrow-gauge steam railway, right by the line (see opposite page). It is a busy resort, with caravans and chalets, but the old-style seaside survives. In the church is the 7th-century St Cadfan's stone, inscribed with the earliest known example of Welsh writing. After Tywyn, the line crosses the Dysynni estuary, passing the old army camps that surround **Tonfanau** station.

Fairbourne
Steep rocky hills push the track right to the water's edge as the train runs north past **Llangelynin** and **Llwyngwril**, and then Fairbourne comes into view, with Barmouth Bay beyond. A resort on land reclaimed from the Mawddach estuary, **Fairbourne** makes the most of one of the best beaches in Wales.

Barmouth
The next station is **Morfa Mawddach** with its triangular platform, a legacy of the junction with the former line to the east. Part of the route along the Mawddach is now a footpath. Then the train crosses the great expanse of the Mawddach estuary on the famous 1867 wooden viaduct. At the end are two steel arches, one of which used to open for ships. **Barmouth** lies ahead, a pretty town with plenty of old seaside atmosphere. To the east is Cader Idris. From Barmouth the train runs north along the beach to the village of **Llanaber**.

Harlech
The train now runs inland, over saltmarshes and then through a landscape of little fields divided by rough stone walls, to **Tal-y-bont** and then to **Dyffryn Ardudwy**, with its prehistoric settlements. After **Llanbedr** and its airfield the train returns to the seashore at **Llandanwg**. Soon Harlech Castle comes into view on its rock high above the town. Look back after **Harlech** for another view of this mighty 13th-century fortress. The line now runs well inland. From **Tygwyn** and **Talsarnau** there are views across the Dwyryd estuary to the Italianate towers of Portmeirion.

Harlech Castle, set on a crag 200ft above sea level

395 ▲

Ffestiniog Railway
See page 55

LOOK OUT FOR

The sea and its history dominate this route. The great medieval castles show how Edward I had to fortify his coastline, while the many old harbours are a legacy of the trade that was for centuries the backbone of the Welsh economy. As this trade declined, many of the old seaports turned themselves into resorts to exploit the new enthusiasm for sea and sand. The transition from trade to tourism is above all reflected by the **narrow-gauge steam railways**. Built as mineral railways, their resurrection as tourist steam railways is a recent phenomenon.

Porthmadog

After **Llandecwyn** the train crosses the Dwyryd on a curving wooden viaduct, with excellent views west and east. From **Penrhyndeudraeth** the line curves up to **Minffordd** where there is a connection with the Ffestiniog Railway (see page 55). This is also the stop for Portmeirion. The train now curves round across the saltmarshes to **Porthmadog**.

Criccieth

The train now runs inland, through a cliff-lined valley and then up into the woods, before returning to the sea east of Criccieth, with the castle clearly in view, high above the town of traditional stone and white-painted terraces. **Penychain** is the station for the Butlin's Holiday Camp and then, after **Abererch**, the line terminates at the resort and market town of **Pwllheli** with its pretty wooden station.

TALYLLYN RAILWAY

The Talyllyn Railway, opened in 1866 to carry slate from the quarry above Abergynolwyn, was the first in the world to be operated by a preservation society. They took over the almost derelict line in 1951, turning it into the efficient railway we know today, still largely operated by volunteers. It runs inland from **Tywyn**, where the 2ft 3in narrow-gauge railway has two stations. **Wharf** is close to the one on the BR coast line, with **Pendre** only a short distance away. The other terminus is **Nant Gwernol**, where there used to be a rope-worked incline climbing to the former slate quarries. This is now a footpath forming one of the many forest walks that can be made from stations on the line.

The main inland railhead is **Abergynolwyn**, since Nant Gwernol cannot be reached by road. Another intermediate station, at **Dolgoch**, is situated close to the famous Falls,

and the ravine which the line spans by a viaduct. Many walks can be made from this point, with the Railway, Forestry Commission and Royal Society for the Protection of Birds all producing leaflets.

There is also the Narrow-Gauge Museum at Wharf, which gives insight into the railway's earlier years.

TRAINS

Tywyn (short walk from BR station)–Nant Gwernol (no road access) 7 miles
Operates: Daily Apr–Oct (phone for details (0654) 710472)
Journey time: 51 mins Tywyn–Nant Gwernol; 60 mins opposite direction with wait at Abergynolwyn

Walks

Dolgoch Waterfalls from Dolgoch station
Nant Gwernol forest walks from Abergynolwyn

Places to Visit

Abergynolwyn Castell y Bere ruins (2m); Village Museum (summer only)

Sir Haydn (below), one of Talyllyn Railway's engines

Land of Diversity

SHREWSBURY – ABERYSTWYTH 81½ miles

TRAINS
(2hrs 7mins approx)
Mon–Sat 7; Sun 2
Refreshments: some

Tourist Information Centres (*summer only)
Aberystwyth Eastgate
(0970) 612125/611955
Machynlleth Owain
Glyndwr Centre
(0654) 2401
Newtown★ Central Car
Park (0686) 25580
Shrewsbury The Square
(0743) 50761/2
Welshpool Vicarage
Garden Car Park
(0938) 2043/4038

For all information on Shrewsbury see page 64

Walks
Glyndwr's Way passes
Welshpool and
Machynlleth
Offa's Dyke Path passes
2m west of Welshpool

Places to Visit
Aberystwyth Ceredigion
Museum; Constitution
Hill cliff railway
(Etr–Oct); National
Library of Wales
Borth Twyn Bach Nature
Reserve, 3m north of
station
Caersws Roman fort
Machynlleth Owain
Glyndwr Centre
(summer only). *By car*
Corris Railway Museum
(summer only)
Newtown W H Smith
(1920s shop replica)
Welshpool Powis Castle,
NT (Etr–Oct);
Powisland Museum;
Welshpool and Llanfair
Light Railway (Jun–Sep)

To cross Wales by train from east to west is to sample every aspect of that country's very diverse landscape, for the line explores river valleys, forests, great bare hills and rocky mountains, seaside and estuary, small market towns, remote villages and farms, and rolling green hills broken up by small fields. It is a journey of quiet pleasures and occasional excitements, at an enjoyably restful pace. For the best views, sit on the right.

Shrewsbury See page 64

Leaving the spires of Shrewsbury behind as it crosses the Severn, the train swings west from the main line at Sutton Bridge, and runs through flowery cuttings to a rolling landscape distinguished by typical tall houses and red brick farms. The hills increasingly dominate the horizon as the line crosses into Wales and the train takes a winding route towards Welshpool.

Welshpool
Passing the site of the former branch north to Oswestry, the train follows the Severn, crossing it by the fine cast-iron road bridge. The decorative brick and stone station is a good introduction to this Georgian market town. The terminus of the Welshpool and Llanfair steam railway is near by,

while the Montgomery branch of the Shropshire Union Canal passes through the town centre. Leaving Welshpool the train turns south, with the tall spire of Leighton Church to the east and Powis Castle dominating the hills to the west.

Newtown
The train approaches Newtown through a lovely landscape of rolling hills dotted with white-painted farms, and the Severn never far away. The station has attractive details in wood and stone and a fine old stone goods shed, but the town looks best when seen from the west, with the big Victorian church predominant.

Caersws
Still following the winding course of the Severn, the train passes the former

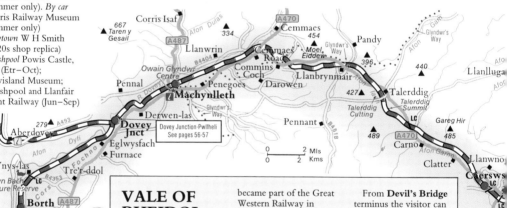

VALE OF RHEIDOL RAILWAY

The Vale of Rheidol Railway, with its 1ft 11½in gauge, was opened in 1902 to run from the seaside resort of Aberystwyth to the local beauty spot of Devil's

VALE OF RHEIDOL RAILWAY
Aberystwyth (BR station)–Devil's Bridge
11½ miles
Operates: Daily
Apr–Oct (tel
(0970) 612378 for
information)
Single journey: 1hr
approx

Bridge. It also served the mines in the valley. Business boomed, with new halts being opened, and special trains run for Revival meetings and summer army camps. After World War I, the line's tourist potential was developed and it

became part of the Great Western Railway in 1922. From 1948 British Rail continued to run it as a tourist line, retaining steam power 20 years after it had disappeared from the rest of their system. It was offered for sale to the private sector in 1988.

Aberystwyth also boasts a cliff railway opened in 1896, but the Rheidol line leaves from its own platforms in the BR station. For the first five miles to beyond **Capel Bangor** it runs close to the river, and then climbs the southern side of the valley, concluding with four spectacular miles on a continuous gradient of 1 in 50 after **Aberffrwd**. The views are best seen from the Vista Car.

From **Devil's Bridge** terminus the visitor can walk around the Mynach Falls, climb Jacob's Ladder and peer down from the three-tiered bridge into the Devil's Punchbowl, hundreds of feet below.

Walks
Cwmrheidol Nature Trail can be joined at Capel Bangor
Vale of Rheidol Railway Nature Trail from all stations – particularly good at Devil's Bridge.

Places to Visit
Aberystwyth see main panel left
Devil's Bridge Mynach Falls; three bridges
Rheidol Falls Rheidol Power Station and Information Centre
(Etr–Oct); waterfall

junction with the line south to Builth Wells. There was also once a narrow-gauge line serving the mines in the hills to the west and both can be explored on foot. Caersws, set attractively where the Rivers Garno and Trannon meet the Severn, is still visibly a Roman town, with its grid street pattern and the remains of the fort standing by the line to the west.

Machynlleth

Leaving Caersws the train climbs steadily up the Garno valley to Carno where another Roman fort can be seen, and then it crosses a more open landscape before winding its way through the dramatic rock walls of the Talerddig cutting. At 120ft, this was the deepest cutting in the world when the route was carved in 1863. The line then begins its descent, following first the River Iaen and then criss-crossing the wooded Twymyn west from Llanbrynmair. Machynlleth's pretty stone station of 1863, set north of the market town, is typical of the line. You change here for Cambrian coast trains to Pwllheli, *not* at Dovey Junction. Formerly a branch line ran north from Machynlleth, to link with the narrow-gauge Corris Railway, whose history is commemorated by a small museum at Corris. West of Machynlleth, the train follows the widening Dovey estuary to the isolated wooden station at **Dovey Junction**, where the Cambrian coast line branches west.

Aberystwyth

The dunes and flat saltmarsh of the Dovey estuary dominate the line on its way to the coast, and then it swings south to the Victorian resort of **Borth**. The train then turns inland to climb through the hills before dropping down again to the Rheidol valley and into Aberystwyth, with the Vale of Rheidol steam railway (see box left) near by. The large 1920s station is a reminder that another long-closed line used to link Aberystwyth with Carmarthen. Aberystwyth is the home of the National Library of Wales, while the ruined castle of 1277 is an echo of former glories.

LOOK OUT FOR
The physical nature of the Welsh landscape must have posed a serious challenge to the **Victorian railway builders** who for reasons of finance had to create the most direct route with a minimum of major engineering features. By and large they followed the many river valleys that carved their way through the hills, and the line from Shrewsbury to Aberystwyth is the most typical example of this.

Joan, a locomotive of the Welshpool & Llanfair Light Railway, Welshpool

For most of its 81 miles the line follows closely one river or another, first the Severn, then the Garno, the Iaen, the Twymyn and finally the Dovey. Although there are many bridges, the only major engineering involved was in cutting the route through the mountains near Talerddig. A railway across central Wales with no tunnels or major viaducts must stand as a great monument to Victorian enterprise. In its heyday the line to Machynlleth was the backbone of the central Wales railway network, connecting with other lines at Buttington, near Welshpool, at Caersws and at Dovey Junction north and south along the coast. It also served at least six smaller branch lines. Traces of many of these can be seen from the train, or fully explored on foot or by car, useful reminders of the extent of the network and the extraordinary ingenuity of its builders from the 1860s.

Near Machynlleth: a Sprinter on its way along the Dovey valley

CENTRAL ENGLAND & EAST ANGLIA

The journey from Ely, cathedral city on the River Ouse (below), to Leicester is one that links the Fens of East Anglia with the ancient heart of England

A CERTAIN STYLE

RAILWAY HISTORY AND ARCHITECTURE

THE RAILWAYS OF EAST ANGLIA have always had a distinctive character of their own, reflecting the region's landscape and the diversity of the many companies that built its network. Constructed in a piecemeal fashion by companies like the Eastern Union, Stour Valley, Lynn & Ely, Ipswich and Bury, the Eastern Counties and the Norfolk Railway, mostly during the 1840s, the network was amalgamated in 1862 to form the Great Eastern Railway. In 1923 this became a part of the LNER but the system, with its mass of meandering rural routes, remained largely unaltered until the 1950s, approaching the Beeching era. Apart from the suburban services near London, East Anglian traffic was predominantly agricultural, with the railway carrying livestock, vegetables and sugar beet. Market towns such as Swaffham, Beccles or Sudbury were dependent on the railway. Also important was fish, and Grimsby and Lowestoft owed their existence to the railway. The harbours of East Anglia were particularly well served, with lines to major ports and minor local harbours like Snape or Wells. Some coastal lines were built to encourage tourism, and the railway played its part in the development of the Norfolk Broads.

The proliferation of East Anglian lines resulted in a degree of duplication, and both large towns such as Norwich and Wisbech (which now has no passenger service) and small villages, like Maldon, Cromer or Haddiscoe, sometimes ended up with more than one station.

Although many of the rural railways of East Anglia have disappeared, there are still reminders of the scale of the original network, and the character of the companies that created it.

Berney Arms, reached only by train or boat, is notable of the delightful rural stations, and many others exhibit unexpected architectural individuality. The most popular mid-

19th-century style was Tudor or Jacobean, with elaborate decoration in brick or stone and frequently high stepped Dutch gables. Good examples can be seen at Thetford, Stowmarket, Maldon East (closed), Wansford, Louth (closed) and Stamford. Other interesting styles are Renaissance, at Bury St Edmunds, the French chateau at Norwich, and plain classicism, used to great effect at Cambridge and Audley End.

The railway buildings of Central England also reflected local styles. Examples include the gothic station at Hereford, the extraordinary Tudor façade of Shrewsbury, looking like an Oxford college, and the simple style of Abergavenny. More unusual perhaps are the highly ornamental stations at Malvern, the simple timber style of Charlbury, the decorative tiling of Worcester Shrub Hill and finally the chunky GWR Art Deco of Leamington Spa.

Tourism by rail in the Norfolk Broads

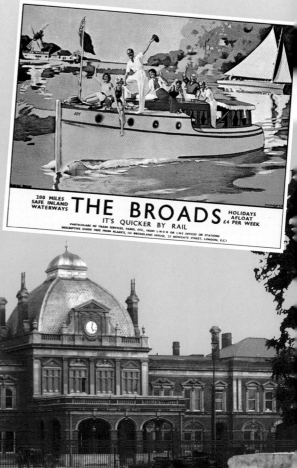

Thorpe Station at Norwich, where East Anglian lines had more than one terminus

Examples of the decorative style of the mid-19th century: at Thetford (above), built of flint, with brick dressings and pointed Jacobean gables; and Malvern (below right), with its ornamental woodwork and cast iron. Right: multi-coloured glazed tiling at Worcester Shrub Hill. Below: appropriate detail on a Yarmouth South Town bench (now in the National Railway Museum, York)

WALKING IN THE REGION

The best walking in Central England is to be found in the Malverns and Cotswolds, along the valley of the Wye and round the coast of East Anglia. Access by train is easy to all these regions, while the railway walks give ample opportunity for exploring the lesser known landscape of the region.

A selection of the closed railways now designated as official footpaths is given below:

Coalport to Ironbridge (3 miles), part of the Shrewsbury to Kidderminster line

Haverhill (3 miles through the town), part of the former lines from Halstead and Long Melford to Cambridge

Hellesdon to Drayton (2 miles), part of the former Norwich to Melton Constable line

Hertford to Cole Green (2 miles) and Welwyn Garden City to Wheathampstead (2 miles), former Hertford to Dunstable line

Horncastle to Woodhall Spa (7 miles), part of the former Horncastle branch line, now incorporated in the Viking Way

Lavenham to Long Melford (4 miles) and other parts of the former Sudbury to Bury St Edmunds line

Southwold to Blythburgh (3½ miles), part of the former Southwold Railway

Wivenhoe to Brightlingsea (3 miles), part of the former Colchester to Brightlingsea branch line

Wolverton to Newport Pagnell (3 miles), the former Newport Pagnell branch line

For further information on the Walks suggested on each route in the following pages, contact the local Tourist Information Centres. Also, see page 7.

TRAINS
(1hr 50mins approx)
Mon–Sat 12; Sun 3
Refreshments: some

**Tourist Information
Centres** (*summer only)
*Abergavenny** Lower
Monk St (0873) 3254
*Church Stretton** Church
St (0694) 723133
Hereford St Owens St
(0432) 268430
Leominster School Lane
(0568) 611100/6460
*Ludlow** Castle Street
(0584) 3857
Newport John Frost Sq
(0633) 842962
Shrewsbury The Square
(0743) 50761/2

**For all information on
Newport see page 26**

Walks
The Long Mynd access
from Church Stretton
*Monmouthshire & Brecon
Canal* access from
Abergavenny, Pontypool
Offa's Dyke Path access
from Abergavenny
Wye Valley Walk access
from Hereford

Cycling
Shrewsbury–Ludlow
(see pages 5–7)

Places to Visit
Abergavenny Castle;
Museum (Mar–Oct). *By
bus* Llanfihangel Court
(Jun–Aug). *By car* White
Castle
Church Stretton By car
Acton Scott Working
Farm Museum
(Apr–Oct); Wilderhope
Manor, NT
Craven Arms Stokesay
Castle (Mar–Oct)
Hereford Bulmer Railway
Centre (Apr–Sep);
Cathedral; Churchill
Gdns Museum; Cider
Museum (Apr–Oct); The
Old House; St John &
Coningsby Museum
(Etr–Sep). *By car* The
Weir Gdns, NT
(Apr–Oct)
Leominster By bus
Berrington Hall, NT
(Apr–Oct); Burton
Court (May–Sep); Croft
Castle, NT (Apr–Oct).
By car Dinmore Manor
Ludlow Castle
(Feb–Nov); Museum
(Apr–Sep); Reader's
House (on application)
Pontypool The Valley
Inheritance, Park House
Shrewsbury Abbey (by
arrangement); Castle;
Clive House Museum;
Rowley's House
Museum. *By bus/car*
Attingham Park, NT
(Apr–Oct); Haughmond
Abbey, EH; Shropshire
Country & Butterfly
World (Etr–Oct);
Wroxeter for
Viroconium Roman City,
EH. *By car* Condover
Hall (by appointment)

The Marches Line

SHREWSBURY – NEWPORT   *94 miles*

This journey is an exploration of the Marches, the borderlands that traditionally separate Wales from England. Rich in history from Roman times to the 19th century, the route is dominated by the great castles and fortresses, monuments to centuries of border disputes.

For stations other than Hereford and Ludlow, take the stopping train.

Old ways and winding streets survive in Shrewsbury – here Fish Street and Bear Steps

Shrewsbury

Shrewsbury station, with its extravagant façade, could not be more central. Above it towers the castle and the church spire, and below is the old town, contained by the loop of the Severn. Shrewsbury is particularly rich in the traditional black and white architecture of the region, but the fine 18th-century mansions, reflecting the town's wealth from the textile trade, should not be overlooked. As the train leaves Shrewsbury it crosses the Severn, and this is the best point to look back for a view of the town centre. It then enters a landscape of wide open fields with a line of distant hills to the west; to the east is the hillfort at Bayston Hill and a distant view of the church at Condover with its fine monuments. Near by is Condover Hall, the best Elizabethan house in Shropshire. Continuing south past Leebotwood Church the landscape becomes more dramatic, with pockets of woodland as the line enters a narrow valley framed by the Long Mynd to the west and the gaunt summit of Caer Caradoc with its Roman fort to the east. On the hillsides are old farms, some in red stone, others typically black and white.

Church Stretton

The A49, a Roman road, follows the line closely through the wooded valley to Church Stretton, a popular inland resort in late Victorian times. To the south, just off the A49, is Acton Scott with its farm museum, and, beyond, Wenlock Edge.

Craven Arms

This little town grew up around a major road junction and the railway

followed the pattern, with the Heart of Wales line (see pages 50–52) branching westwards here. The train follows the wooded Onny valley to Stokesay, where the 13th-century fortified house and church form one of the highlights of the journey, right beside the track. Look out for Telford's cast-iron bridge over the Onny. To the south is the tower of Onibury Church, also by the line, which follows the Onny to its junction with the Teme.

Ludlow

Ludlow is announced by its racecourse, well to the north. One of the best small towns in England, with a fine castle and a diversity of excellent buildings, it is easy to explore on foot. Ludlow also looks good from the south, with the River Teme beside the line. The train continues through a pretty landscape of old farms, fields and copses, with distant views of churches. Eye Church, with its powerful tower, stands beside the track, to the east, and beyond is Georgian Berrington Hall, with its Capability Brown park of 1780.

Leominster

This elegant wool town with its great medieval priory is to the west of the station, but easily accessible via a street lined with Georgian houses. From Leominster the line follows the River Lugg, passing through Dinmore Hill in a tunnel. There are good views of the river, and the churches at Hope and Bodenham at either end. Between Leominster and Hereford the landscape is more open, with views of the Victorian churches at Marden and Moreton and the Iron Age hillfort at Sutton Walls.

Hereford

For its size, Hereford makes little impression from the train, but the cathedral is clearly visible, its tower moving around confusingly as the line meanders. The best view is from the south, so look back. The handsome station, with its Gothic and Art Nouveau details, is east of the city centre, but all Hereford's main features are close together and easily accessible on foot. South of Hereford is initially agricultural and then the bare top of Orcop Hill dominates the view as the train passes St Devereux Church. At Pontrilas the former station marks the junction with the long-closed line up the Golden Valley to Hay-on-Wye, via Abbey Dore. As it crosses the River Monnow, the train enters Wales.

Looking across the Wye to Hereford Cathedral

Abergavenny

Following the Monnow along a valley lined with steeply wooded hills, the train passes Llanfihangel Church, with the Black Mountains filling the landscape to the west. Abergavenny, set to the west of the station, is a pleasant market town whose qualities are not apparent from the train. A former branch, whose route can still be seen, ran westwards from the town connecting with the huge Valleys network of mining and industrial lines. South of Abergavenny the line enters the Usk valley while across to the west, the Monmouthshire and Brecon Canal makes its way southwards towards Newport. Still navigable northwards from Pontypool, the canal makes an excellent walk through the foothills of the Black Mountains.

Pontypool

From Pontypool to Cwmbran the route is largely industrial while south of Cwmbran the line curves through a more rural landscape past the Roman town of Caerleon. Entering Newport from the north, the train then joins the main line from Bristol before crossing the Usk.

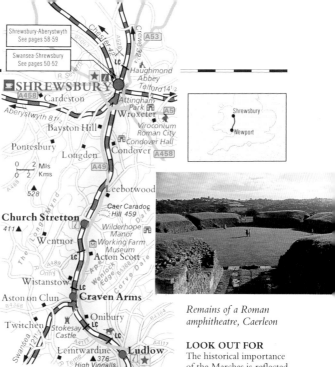

Remains of a Roman amphitheatre, Caerleon

LOOK OUT FOR

The historical importance of the Marches is reflected by the many **castles** along the route. The Romans were the first to fortify the border and there are notable examples of their work at Caer Caradoc and Caerleon. However, in many cases they made use of earlier Iron Age hillforts, of which some can be seen from the train, notably Sutton Walls near Hereford. The next wave of castle building came after the Norman conquest and through the Middle Ages. Castles still stand at Shrewsbury, Ludlow and Newport, but many more have disappeared. Often these are close to the line, and can be identified from the train. The most dramatic castle on the route is at Stokesay, one of the earliest in England to bring together domestic needs with conventional defensive requirements. Stokesay is the epitome of the turbulent history of the Marches.

Stokesay Castle, really a fortified house, is a romantic survival of medieval England

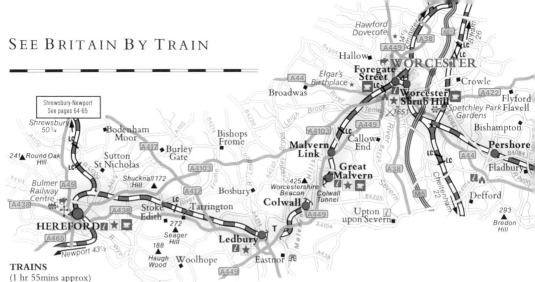

TRAINS
(1 hr 55mins approx)
Mon–Sat 7; Sun 2
Refreshments: some

Tourist Information Centres
Evesham Abbey Gate
(0386) 6944
Hereford St Owens St
(0432) 268430
Ledbury High St
(0531) 2461
Malvern Grange Rd
(0684) 892289
Oxford St Aldates
(0865) 726871
Pershore High St
(0386) 554711
Worcester High St
(0905) 723471

For all information on Hereford see page 64

Walks
Malvern Hills access from
Colwall/Malvern
Oxfordshire Way access
from Kingham/Shipton
Wychwood Forest access
from Finstock

Cycling
Oxford–Moreton-in-
Marsh (see pages 5–7)

Places to Visit
Evesham Almonry
Museum (Mar–Nov)
Hanborough Blenheim
Palace (Mar–Oct) & Park
Honeybourne By car
Hidcote Manor Gdn, NT
(Apr–Oct)
Ledbury Old Grammar
School Heritage Centre.
By car Eastnor Castle
(May–Aug)
Malvern Priory
Moreton-in-Marsh By car
Batsford Arboretum
(Apr–Oct); Sezincote
House (May–Jul, Sep) &
Garden (all year)
Oxford Ashmolean
Museum; Carfax Tower;
Christchurch Cathedral;
University Botanic Gdn;
University colleges
(quadrangles & chapels
usually open pm); other
museums
Worcester Cathedral; City
Museum & Art Gallery;
The Commandery;
Elgar's Birthplace; The
Greyfriars (Apr–Oct);
Royal Worcester factory;
Tudor House. *By bus/car*
Hawford Dovecote, NT
(Apr–Oct); Spetchley
Park Gdns (Apr–Sep)

The Malverns and Cotswolds

HEREFORD – OXFORD 86¼ *miles*

From Severn to Thames via the Malverns and the Cotswolds, this is a classic journey through the heart of England, a journey evocative of a particular period in English life and full of Edwardian echoes, from music in the Malverns to craftsmanship in the Cotswolds.

Hereford
Leaving Hereford and the cathedral tower behind, the train passes the sidings that lead to the Bulmer Railway Centre and then turns east to cross the River Lugg. To the south are hop fields and oast houses and then two village churches, Stoke Edith and Norman Tarrington.

Ledbury
The approach to Ledbury is across a big viaduct, with excellent views along the valley. After the station, the train plunges into a tunnel and then swings northwards, with Eastnor Castle, 1814, to the south. West of Colwall there are good views to the north. To the south are the Malverns. Just outside **Colwall** station, the train passes the factory where Malvern spring water is bottled, and then it burrows under the hills.

Malvern
The entry to Malvern is theatrical, and the train emerges from the tunnel onto a stage framed by the great backdrop of the wooded hills. Malvern station, built in 1862 in an elaborate style thought suitable for the town's developing reputation as a spa, is a delight. Richly painted in red, gold and black, it is a mass of Gothic woodwork, pretty cast iron, stained glass, old lights and benches. A rhododendron-lined cutting leads to **Malvern Link.** As the train crosses the Teme, look back to the scarp at the north end of the Malverns.

Worcester
The entry into Worcester is also dramatic, with the cathedral and all the city laid out to the south as the train crosses high over the Severn. Worcester has two stations. The first, **Foregate Street**, is the best for the cathedral, the museum and the city centre. Change here for trains to Kidderminster and the Severn Valley

Malvern station – the capitals of the columns are wonderful, each naturalistically modelled with different tree leaves

Railway (see opposite page). **Shrub Hill** station has decorative tiling on platform one. Leaving Worcester the line turns east, crossing the Cheltenham–Birmingham railway at Norton junction, with classical Spetchley Park to the north.

Pershore
The station is over a mile from the town, but the abbey can be seen to the south. The train now follows the Avon, crossing it at Fladbury, with good views of the church and mill.

The huge bulk of Worcester Cathedral rises up above the city on the banks of the Severn

LOOK OUT FOR

Much of the journey from Hereford to Oxford is through a landscape formed by the **great rivers of prehistory** as they carved their way through the hills. The modern descendants of many of these can be seen from the train. First there is the Wye and its tributaries the Lugg and the Frome. Then there is the Leddon, but far more significant is the Severn, Worcester's river. Another tributary of the Severn is the Avon, visible between Pershore and Evesham. Next is the Evenlode, one of the prettiest rivers of the Cotswolds, and finally the train comes to the Thames, just north of Oxford.

Evesham

This small town, with its abbey, its waterfront and its tree-lined streets can easily be explored on foot from the station. East of Evesham the train crosses a flat landscape to **Honeybourne.** The Cotswolds now dominate the view ahead and the train begins to climb towards Campden Tunnel. Hidcote Manor with its excellent gardens is to the north. After the tunnel, Chipping Campden can briefly be seen to the west and the train then runs through typical Cotswold scenery.

Moreton-in-Marsh

In the heart of the Cotswolds, Moreton is the best station for visits to Stow-on-the-Wold, Chipping Campden, Broadway and Bourton-on-the-Water. South of Moreton, with Sezincote visible on the hillside to the west, the train follows the River Evenlode, passing pretty stone villages, to **Kingham**, a little station with original GWR nameboards. South of Kingham is Bruern Abbey, in woods to the west, and then the train reaches **Shipton** (the stop for Burford) and **Ascott** both stations with pretty views.

Charlbury

The train continues along the Evenlode to Charlbury, an excellent, original weatherboarded station set in the valley. To the south is the mysterious forest of Wychwood and Cornbury House and park and then **Finstock** station, with the 17th-century manor on the hillside. To the north is Stonesfield, whose quarries produced the Cotswold stone roofing tiles over many centuries. The line cuts across the course of the Evenlode to **Combe**, and then to **Hanborough**, the station for Blenheim Palace. The line now leaves the Evenlode, crosses open farmland and follows the Oxford Canal into **Oxford**.

SEVERN VALLEY RAILWAY

For most of its route, the Severn Valley Railway closely follows the river as it threads its way through the hills from Bewdley to Bridgnorth. It is operated by Britain's largest preservation society, whose first scheduled train ran in 1970, on tracks that dated back to the opening of the first Severn Valley line in 1862.

Today the line starts from **Kidderminster Town** station, built by the Severn Valley Railway in Great Western Railway style, adjacent to the BR station. Trains run westwards to the river valley at **Bewdley**, which has been refurbished in GWR colours, complete with all the *bric-à-brac* from steam days. Beyond **Northwood** the railway crosses the Severn by the magnificent Victoria Bridge, its 200ft cast-iron span being the world's longest when it was completed in 1861.

Arley and **Highley** have both won awards in the Best Restored Station competitions, the former being an excellent centre for leisurely walking along the river. At **Hampton Loade** there is a small museum and anglers come here to fish in the nearby stretches of the river, which is crossed by a water-operated ferry.

Continuing northwards, there is a fine view of **Bridgnorth** where the castle crowns one hilltop and a cliff railway is needed to link parts of the town.

Severn Valley Railway
Kidderminster Town–Bridgnorth 16 miles
Operates: Mar–Oct (phone for details (0299) 403816)
Single journey: 1hr 10mins approx

Tourist Information Centres
Bewdley Load St (0299) 403303
Bridgnorth Listley St (07462) 3358

Walks
River walks from stations north of Bewdley
Wyre Forest access from Arley/Bewdley

Places to Visit
Bewdley West Midlands Safari Park (Apr–Oct)
Bridgnorth Midland Motor Museum. *By car* Ironbridge Gorge Museum, Ironbridge

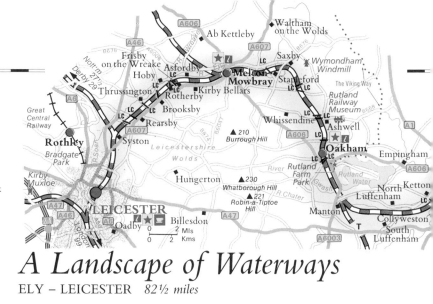

TRAINS
(1½ hrs approx)
Mon–Sat 13; Sun 5
Refreshments: some

Tourist Information Centres
Ely Palace Green
(0353) 662062
Leicester St Martin's Walk
(0533) 549922
Melton Mowbray Thorpe
End (0664) 69946
Oakham Catmos St
(0572) 2918
Peterborough Broadway
(0733) 48343/43146
Stamford Broad St
(0780) 55611

Walks
Viking Way access from
Oakham
For other walks contact
Tourist Information
Centres

Places to Visit
Ely Cathedral; Museum;
Stained Glass Museum
(Mar–Oct). *By car*
Stretham Beam Engine
Leicester Belgrave Hall;
Cathedral; Guildhall;
Hoskins Brewery
Museum; Jewry Wall
Museum & Site; John
Doran Museum;
Leicestershire Museum;
Museum of Technology;
Museum of Royal
Leicestershire Regiment;
Newarke Houses;
University Botanic
Gdns; Wygston's House
Museum of Costume. *By
car* Bradgate Park; Kirby
Muxloe Castle, EH;
Tropical Bird Gdns,
Desford
March March & District
Museum. *By bus/car* to
Wisbech: Peckover
House, NT (Apr–Oct);
Wisbech & Fenland
Museum
Melton Mowbray Melton
Carnegie Museum; St
Mary's Church. *By car*
Belvoir Castle
(Mar–Oct);
Wymondham Windmill
Oakham Castle; Rutland
County Museum;
Rutland Farm Park
(May–Sep). *By bus/car*
Rutland Water. *By car*
Rutland Railway
Museum
Peterborough Cathedral,
Flag Fen Bronze Age
Excavation (Apr–Oct);
Museum & Art Gallery;
Nene Valley Railway
(Apr–Oct, Dec). *By bus*
Elton Hall (May–Aug);
Longthorpe Tower, EH.
By car Wildfowl Trust
Waterfowl Gdns,
Peakirk
Stamford Brewery
Museum (Apr–Sep);
Browne's Hospital
(May–Sep); Burghley
House (Apr–Oct). *By car*
Careby Manor Gdns
(Apr–Sep); Tolethorpe
Hall (May–Aug)

A Landscape of Waterways
ELY – LEICESTER   *82½ miles*

This is a journey from the Fens to the ancient heart of England, from the great cathedrals of Ely and Peterborough that sail like ships across a flat landscape to the handsome market towns of Stamford, Oakham and Melton Mowbray whose names recall the forgotten shire counties of Rutland and Huntingdonshire.

Ely

Ely station, a mildly classical building of 1847, is beside the River Ouse, well to the south of the town. From it, there are magnificent views of the cathedral, set on its mound with the town clustered below. The best, but not the most direct, way into the town from the station is to walk along beside the river and then turn west straight up to the central market place. Ely is still a small town, easily explored, and the great cathedral is always dominant. The train leaves to the north, crossing the Ouse twice, and then the line branches away to the north-west and into the vast expanse of the Fens. It is a strange landscape that runs flat for miles to a horizon that is somehow made to seem high against the sky by the very flatness,

Ely Cathedral's unique 14th-century Octagon replaced a collapsed Norman crossing-tower

while close at hand all sorts of vegetables grow in huge fields broken only by drainage ditches. Ely Cathedral remains in view for miles, the only feature of significance.

March

After passing Downham to the south, with its church on a mound and near by the remains of the Bishop's Palace, the train crosses the two Bedford rivers, cut for drainage in the 17th century and running straight as dies to the horizon. Beyond is **Manea**, its station remote and isolated, and then **March** comes into view, its low skyline dominated by three spires. A pleasant town set on the old course of the Nene, March was once a major railway junction but although several routes still meet here, including the goods line to Wisbech, it is no longer a busy place, and the train is soon out in the Fens again. The next station is **Whittlesea**, serving a typical Fenland town with some good 17th-century houses and two good churches. The line now passes a series of huge brickfields, with great clay pits and tall chimneys, and then the long, low outline of Peterborough Cathedral comes into view.

Peterborough

The train joins the East Coast main line with Fletton Church to the south and then crosses the Nene. The Nene Valley steam railway terminates here and the station is well placed for the cathedral and the city centre. Leaving Peterborough to the south, the train follows the main line to Helpston and then branches west, where a handsome goods shed marks the site of the former station. The landscape is now different, smaller fields, a row of hills to the south and pockets of woodland. The line enters a region famous for its stone since the Middle Ages. Collyweston, Ketton and Barnack were the best known, with Barnack being used for both Peterborough and Ely Cathedrals.

Sculpture enhances the shoreline of man-made Rutland water

The Sixteen Foot Drain, seen from the train as the line crosses it north-east of Manea, is one of the dead straight man-made ditches typical of the Fens landscape of this route

Stamford

With Uffington to the north and the great park of Burghley House to the south, the train enters Lincolnshire, and comes to Stamford. The station, built in stone with plenty of Tudor details, is the perfect introduction to one of England's best small market towns, full of excellent stone buildings of the 17th and 18th centuries. West of Stamford, in a landscape that is suddenly rolling and wooded, the train winds its way along the valley of the Welland to Ketton, where a huge cement works maintains the quarry tradition. At Luffenham a signal box marks the site of a former junction and then the line follows the River Chater to another junction, at Manton, before swinging north to run beside Rutland Water, one of England's largest reservoirs, to **Oakham**, an attractive small town with a large church and a ruined castle.

Melton Mowbray

The line swings north from Oakham with 18th-century Burley on the Hill to the east, through a hilly landscape, with views of churches at Ashwell and Whissendine, and then it turns to the west round Stapleford Park. The bed of the former canal to Oakham can be seen here. From Stapleford the train follows the River Eye to Melton Mowbray, famous for cheese and pies. Here, the good station with its pretty ironwork and glazed canopies is right in the town centre, beside the river and near the great church. From Melton westwards the train follows the valley of the Wreake, an attractive journey whose progress is marked by a series of fine church spires well set among trees on the valley sides. Their villages, Kirby Bellars, Asfordby, Frisby, Hoby, Rotherby, Brooksby, Thrussington and Rearsby, capture the essence of traditional rural England. At Syston, amid encroaching suburbs, the train joins the main line for the last few miles into Leicester, a university and cathedral city at the heart of an agricultural county.

LOOK OUT FOR
The landscape of the Fens is largely man-made and it is no accident that it has a strong Dutch feeling. Until the 17th century, it was a region of inhospitable and remote marshland, with the few towns and villages linked by causeways, but in that century Dutch engineers transformed it. Under the guidance of Vermuyden, the marshes were drained and a vast acreage of rich arable land was reclaimed from the sea. This was a huge engineering achievement and its legacy can still be seen today in the network of drainage ditches and man-made rivers that separate the great vegetable fields and control the water levels. Being artificial waterways, these are mostly dead straight and their grid pattern is one of the typical features of the Fens. They range in size from little ditches to the massive Hundred Foot Drain, or New Bedford River. Some of the larger ones were constructed as navigations and so an unusual way to explore the Fens today is by boat, starting from the River Nene or the River Ouse.

Suffolk Branch Lines

Ipswich, a busy port at the head of the Orwell estuary, is the starting point for two contrasting rural journeys. One explores the heart of Suffolk and its old country towns before crossing the Newmarket plain to Cambridge, and the other wanders among the rivers and villages of the coast to its terminus at Lowestoft.

A training ride on the heath at Newmarket, for centuries England's premier horseracing centre

TRAINS

Ipswich–Cambridge
(1½ hrs approx)
Mon–Sat 9; Sun 7
No refreshments

Ipswich–Lowestoft
(1½ hrs approx)
Mon–Sat 10; Sun 6
No refreshments

Tourist Information

Centres (★summer only)
Beccles★ Fen Lane
(0502) 713196
Bury St Edmunds Angel
Hill (0284) 63233/64667
Cambridge Wheeler St
(0223) 322640
Ipswich Princes St
(0473) 58070
Lowestoft The Esplanade
(0502) 565989
Stowmarket Wilkes Way
(0449) 676800

Walks
Gipping Valley River Path
access from Ipswich or
Stowmarket
Harcamlow Way access
from Cambridge
Minsmere Nature Reserve
from Darsham

Places to Visit
Beccles Museum; Roos
Hall (Apr–Sep)
Bury St Edmunds Abbey,
EH; Angel Corner, NT;
Cathedral; Moyses Hall
Museum; Theatre Royal,
NT
Cambridge Fitzwilliam
Museum; Scott Polar
Research Institute;
University Botanic Gdn;
University colleges
Ipswich Ancient House;
Christchurch Mansion;
Museum. *By car*
Blackenham Woodland
Gdn (Apr–Sep);
Helmingham Hall Gdns
(May–Sep); The
Rosarium (May–Jul)
Lowestoft Maritime
Museum (May–Sep). *By
bus/car* Suffolk Wildlife &
Rare Breeds Park
(Apr–Oct); Transport
Museum (Etr–Sep)
Newmarket Horseracing
Museum (Apr–Nov)
Stowmarket Museum of E.
Anglian Life (Apr–Oct)
Wickham Market Museum
of Grocery Shop
Bygones
Woodbridge Kyson Hill
Park, NT; Tide Mill
(Jul–Sep)

IPSWICH – CAMBRIDGE
55½ miles

Leaving Ipswich northwards the train follows the valley of the Gipping, its route marked by a series of large weather-boarded mills, the first of which can be seen near Bramford. To the east is wooded Shrubland Park, with Barry's great mansion of 1852 visible above the trees. The river valley is open, with typical Suffolk colour-washed farms scattered among the small fields. **Needham Market** has a fine Tudor-style station of 1846 and a church with the best wooden hammer beam roof in England. **Stowmarket** has another splendid station, this time Jacobean. The church, with its strange 18th-century spire perched on the tower, stands among trees to the west. At Haughley Junction the train swings to the west, running past wild rose hedges and cuttings lined with daisies. Suffolk churches are now a feature of the rolling landscape, with glimpses of Haughley, Wetherden, Woolpit and Tostock to the south. One of the best is at **Elmswell**, with its rich flint decoration, while **Thurston**'s fine Victorian church is well to the east of the station. In summer, the elevated line gives wonderful views over wheat fields red with poppies. The scale and rich Renaissance decoration of **Bury St Edmunds** station indicates its former importance. The town, with its great abbey, Georgian streets, Adam town hall and 1819 theatre is well worth a visit. West of Bury the landscape changes, with wide views across prairie-like fields. Notable is the spire of Higham Church, and then the train reaches **Kennett.** West of Kennett is open heathland, with the rides and stud farms that announce **Newmarket**, entered via a tunnel. West of Newmarket the train passes the great embankment known as Devil's Ditch. **Dullingham** station is isolated and well to the north of its village, with its guildhall and interesting church. Where the line crosses the A11, there used to be a station with the unusual name of Six Mile Bottom. After a view of Great Wilbraham Church, to the north, the train makes a suburban entry to **Cambridge**, and ends beside the very long platform that is characteristic of the station.

IPSWICH – LOWESTOFT
49 miles

The centre of Ipswich, at its best around the 16th-century Christchurch Mansion, is some distance from the station. The local train for Lowestoft runs north before swinging eastwards and into a long cutting which leads to

Westerfield, with a pretty old timber goods shed. The Felixstowe branch turns south. The train then runs through typical Suffolk farmland. At Little Bealings the former station is now a restaurant and then the tower of Martlesham Church can be seen to the south as the Deben estuary comes into view. The line follows the Deben into **Woodbridge** with the tide mill clearly in sight. Woodbridge is a pretty station, right at the water's edge, a good introduction to an excellent small town. Across the river is Sutton Hoo, where the great Saxon ship burial was found in 1939. North of the town the train reaches **Melton** then follows the Deben, with village churches to west and east. The next station is **Wickham Market**, a long way from its village. The landscape now becomes more wooded, and the train crosses the River Alde, with a distant view of Snape and the Maltings concert hall to the east. **Saxmundham** is the station for Aldeburgh, Thorpeness and the coastal marshes which are noted for birds. To the east is Leiston, a town known for the ruins of its abbey, its eccentric church and the steam traction engines made by Garrett's. The track now undulates over the hills, with Kelsale and Yoxford Churches to the west. At **Darsham** the sea is only a few miles away, with excellent walks through

Woodbridge: restored tide mill on the Deben

the Minsmere Nature Reserve and along the coast to explore the few remains of medieval Dunwich, most of which is now under the water. Before reaching **Halesworth** the train crosses the Blyth, a river whose route to the sea between the excellent old resorts of Walberswick and Southwold shows rural Suffolk at its best. Halesworth's large church, and the windmill at Holton, to the east, are clearly visible. After passing the isolated **Brampton** station, with the moated 18th-century hall to the east, the train crosses a rolling wooded landscape to **Beccles**, once a busy junction. Little can be seen from the station, but it is a fine riverside town. The train now swings east across the marshes. The river is out of sight, but its route is marked by sails and cabin tops. At **Oulton Broad South** the marshes end, replaced by the back gardens and suburbs of **Lowestoft** as the train crosses the swing bridge over Lake Lothing.

Southwold in Suffolk, one of East Anglia's most pleasant old seaside resorts

LOOK OUT FOR

The line from Ipswich to Lowestoft illustrates **engineering economy**. Opened in 1859, it was built to serve Suffolk's rural heart and coast. As such, it had to be built cheaply and so its engineers chose a route that avoided the need for major cuttings, embankments or viaducts. The legacy of this economy can be seen today in its continual undulations. The route is a constant series of hills, some of which are quite steep gradients in railway terms. The line is straight, and so its switchback quality is all the more apparent ahead and behind. The way the train follows the contours of the landscape is also underlined by the many level crossings. There are 24 between Ipswich and Lowestoft. Many of the former crossing keepers' cottages still survive.

Norfolk Broadlands

Two journeys from Norwich explore the variety of the East Anglian landscape. The first makes its undulating way across north Norfolk farmland to the traditional seaside resorts of Cromer and Sheringham, and the second tours the rivers, marshland and holiday centres of the Broads on the way to Yarmouth and Lowestoft.

NORWICH – SHERINGHAM
30½ miles

With its great central dome and its French Renaissance façade looking proudly towards the city, **Norwich Thorpe** is a splendid terminus. The city centre, with its castle, cathedral, wealth of 18th-century buildings and open-air market, is only a short walk away. Norwich is above all a city to explore on foot. Trains for Sheringham leave Thorpe and then turn eastwards before branching north at Whitlingham Junction and climbing away from the busy River Yare. The first stop is **Salhouse**, a little station set among lilac bushes and a contrast to **Wroxham**, a Broads resort whose character can be clearly seen from the train as it makes its way over the River Bure with its mass of boats and chalets. The train then climbs through open fields again, passing Tunstead Church to the east and Sloley Church by the line to the west. The next stop is **Worstead.** The village lies to the east, its church, one of the grandest in Norfolk, reflecting the village's former wealth as a centre of weaving. After Worstead, the train passes wooded Westwick Park and, to the east, there is a distant view of Honing Church on Howard's Hill. **North Walsham**, an attractive station with platform canopies typical of this line, was once a busy junction. The church, the tower of which partly collapsed in 1724, dominates the town. The line now runs straight to

There is no harbour at Sheringham, but beaches offer fishing boats easy access to the sea

A medley of market awnings line up below the town and castle in Norwich

Gunton, passing under a series of handsome brick bridges. There are good views across the open landscape and to several village churches before the line reaches the woods that surround Cromer. **Roughton Road** station is almost hidden among trees, and then the train curves round a very sharp bend and drops down towards Cromer, with distant views of the sea. **Cromer** station, with the big church tower just beyond, is a terminus, and so the train now reverses for the short seaside journey to Sheringham. After **West Runton**, where the church stands almost on the beach, the line comes to an abrupt end at **Sheringham.** Originally it continued westwards, and part of it is now operated by the steam trains of the North Norfolk Railway.

NORWICH – LOWESTOFT
23½ miles

Trains for Lowestoft share the Yarmouth line as far as **Reedham**, and then they turn south-east, crossing the Waveney on a high swing bridge. The line runs beside the New Cut, a canal linking the Yare and the Waveney, to **Haddiscoe**. To the north is Herringfleet windmill. The train now follows the Waveney, crossing it at **Somerleyton** on another swing bridge. The elaborate station is a reflection of the tastes of the railway magnate, Sir Morton Peto, owner of Somerleyton Hall. The line then passes between the churches of Burgh St Peter and Oulton. **Oulton Broad North** is the station for boating on Oulton Broad and Lake Lothing. **Lowestoft Central** is the most easterly station in Britain, with docks, trawlers and seaside a few minutes' walk away.

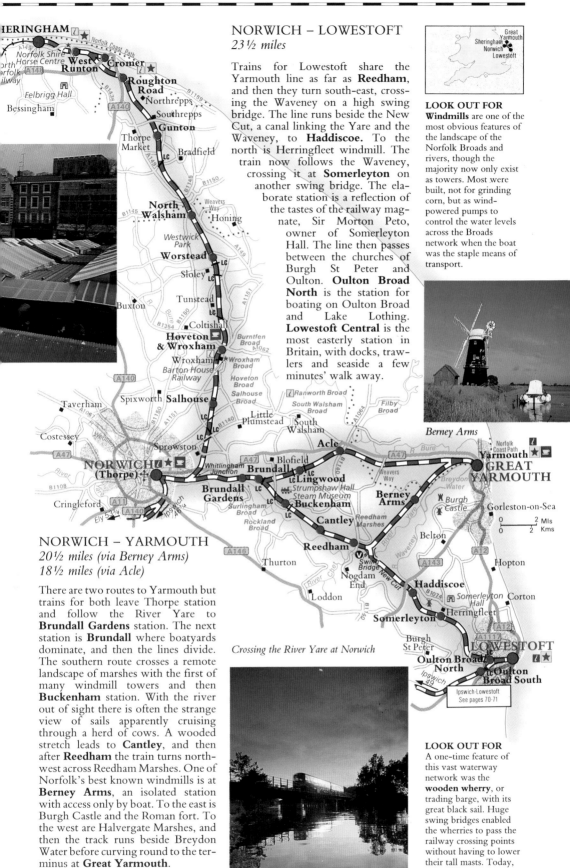

Crossing the River Yare at Norwich

LOOK OUT FOR
Windmills are one of the most obvious features of the landscape of the Norfolk Broads and rivers, though the majority now only exist as towers. Most were built, not for grinding corn, but as wind-powered pumps to control the water levels across the Broads network when the boat was the staple means of transport.

NORWICH – YARMOUTH
20½ miles (via Berney Arms)
18½ miles (via Acle)

There are two routes to Yarmouth but trains for both leave Thorpe station and follow the River Yare to **Brundall Gardens** station. The next station is **Brundall** where boatyards dominate, and then the lines divide. The southern route crosses a remote landscape of marshes with the first of many windmill towers and then **Buckenham** station. With the river out of sight there is often the strange view of sails apparently cruising through a herd of cows. A wooded stretch leads to **Cantley**, and then after **Reedham** the train turns northwest across Reedham Marshes. One of Norfolk's best known windmills is at **Berney Arms**, an isolated station with access only by boat. To the east is Burgh Castle and the Roman fort. To the west are Halvergate Marshes, and then the track runs beside Breydon Water before curving round to the terminus at **Great Yarmouth**.

The other route to Yarmouth swings north-east after **Brundall** and crosses farmland to **Lingwood**. After pausing at **Acle**, the train is back in a landscape of marshes, windmills and church towers. The line runs across Halvergate Marshes and then into **Yarmouth**.

LOOK OUT FOR
A one-time feature of this vast waterway network was the **wooden wherry**, or trading barge, with its great black sail. Huge swing bridges enabled the wherries to pass the railway crossing points without having to lower their tall masts. Today, sail still has a right of way over the train and so, if you are lucky, your train may be held at the signals while the bridge is swung to allow the passage of some large vessel.

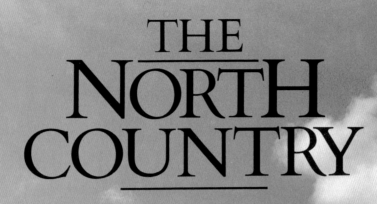

THE
NORTH
COUNTRY

Passing through Esk Dale at Houlsdyke, near Lealholm on North
Yorkshire's Middlesbrough–Whitby line

CRADLE OF THE RAILWAY NETWORK

RAILWAY HISTORY AND ARCHITECTURE

THE NORTH of England was the cradle of the British railway network. The world's first passenger-carrying steam railway, the Stockton and Darlington, was opened in 1825, but the previous century had already seen the growth of an extensive network of horse-drawn tramways built to transport coal from the pits to the ports. By 1750 over 100 miles of tramway were in use in Britain, most of which were in the north-east. Experimental steam locomotive engines built by Hackworth and Hedley were operating at Wylam by 1811. Three years later George Stephenson's first locomotive ran, the ancestor of all subsequent engines.

The opening of the Stockton & Darlington Railway as depicted by Terence Cuneo

Although coal and iron were the inspiration for the railway builders, passenger traffic was not overlooked. It was possible to travel by train from London to Liverpool and Manchester in 1838, and from London to Leeds by 1840, while the first coast to coast line, the Newcastle and Carlisle, was opened in 1838. Crossing the Pennines was a challenge readily accepted; the Leeds to Manchester line was completed in 1841 and two other trans-Pennine routes, via Woodhead and Standedge, were in use before 1850.

The legacy of these pioneering routes are the tunnels and viaducts which today stand as monuments to extraordinary endeavour.

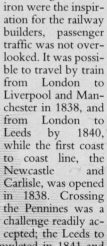

Shugborough Park is a fine example of a mid 19th-century crenellated railway tunnel

The greatest tunnels are those through the Pennines. Woodhead, completed in 1845 after six years of toil, and Standedge, opened in 1849, are both over three miles long and were cut entirely by hand. Further tunnels were later cut to meet increasing traffic demands and in the end there were three at Woodhead, all now closed, and four at Standedge. Totley, the longest Pennine tunnel, was not built until 1894. Tunnels often had decorative portals, to match the landscape or to celebrate the triumph of engineering.

Simple classicism was the usual style but some featured towers and crenellations. Among the best are Bramhope, Clay Cross and Shugborough Park, all dating from the 1840s.

More easily seen from the train are the viaducts that carry the line high above rivers and valleys. There are splendid examples all over the north: look out for Crimple near Harrogate, Knaresborough, Durham, Stockport, and Ribblehead. Finally, the high level bridges that carry the trains across the Tyne and into Newcastle, are one of Britain's great railway experiences.

The opening of the High Level Bridge across the Tyne at Newcastle, 1849

WALKING IN THE REGION

Some of the best scenery of the Peaks, Dales and Pennines can be explored by walking on disused railways.

A selection of the closed railways now designated as official footpaths is given below:

Ashbourne to Parsley Hay (13 miles), the Tissington Trail along part of the former Uttoxeter to Buxton line, also open to cyclists and horse riders

Buxton to Cromford (17½ miles), the High Peak Trail along the former Cromford and High Peak line, also open to cyclists and horse riders

Durham to Bishop Auckland (9½ miles), the Bishop Brandon Walk

Glasson Dock to Aldcliffe (3½ miles), the former Glasson Dock branch along the Lune estuary from Lancaster

Scarborough to Hawkser (13 miles), along part of the former Scarborough to Whitby line

For further information on the Walks suggested on each of the routes on the following pages, contact the local Tourist Information Centre. Also, see page 7.

Through the Peaks

These two highly enjoyable scenic journeys are both worthwhile in their own right, but a convenient bus service between Buxton and Matlock makes it relatively easy to complete the whole route from Manchester to Derby in half a day.

Buxton, the highest market town in England

TRAINS

Manchester–Buxton
(55mins approx)
Mon–Fri 24; Sat 16;
Sun 11
No refreshments

Matlock–Derby
(30mins approx)
Mon–Sat 14; Sun 7
No refreshments

Tourist Information Centres
Buxton The Crescent
(0298) 5106
Derby The Wardwick
(0332) 290664
Hazel Grove Civic Hall,
London Rd
(061) 4564195
Manchester Lloyd St
(061) 2343157/8
Matlock Bath The Pavilion
(0629) 55082
Stockport Princes St
(061) 4800315

For all information on Manchester see page 80

Walks
In Derbyshire, be sure to keep to the public paths.
High Peak Trail from Cromford
Peak District National Park details from TICs
Peak Forest Canal towpath at Whaley Bridge, Furness Vale and Newtown
Pennine Way starts 5m from Chapel-en-le-Frith

Cycling
Buxton circular route see page 5–7

Places to Visit
Buxton Country Park and Poole's Cavern
(Etr–Oct); Micrarium
(Apr–Oct)
Cromford Cromford Mill
Derby Cathedral;
Museum; Royal Crown Derby Porcelain Co. *By car* Kedleston Hall, NT
(Apr–Sep)
Disley Lyme Park, NT
(Apr–Sep)
Matlock Riber Castle Wildlife Park
Matlock Bath Heights of Abraham, cable car
(Etr–Oct)
Whatstandwell Crich Tramway Museum
(Apr–Oct)

MANCHESTER – BUXTON
25½ miles

Manchester
The Buxton train leaves from Manchester Piccadilly, making its elevated way through suburban Manchester to **Stockport**, pausing on the way at **Levenshulme** and **Heaton Chapel**. Just north of Stockport station the train crosses the immense 1842 viaduct with its 27 red brick arches, from which there are good views of the town in the valley. The suburbs continue through **Davenport** and **Hazel Grove**, and then the Peaks come into view.

New Mills Newtown
Woods now surround the track, particularly thick around the well-named **Middlewood** station. Just to the east an aqueduct carries the Macclesfield Canal over the line. The next stop is **Disley**, with the pleasant early 19th-century town centre near by. East of the station the line runs high above the Goyt valley, with the Peak Forest

Market day at Chapel-en-le-Frith

Canal alongside. From **New Mills Newtown**, with its pretty cast-iron footbridge, you can walk across the valley to New Mills Central.

Buxton
The train continues above the Goyt valley to **Furness Vale** station and then the line swings south to **Whaley Bridge**, a dramatic little town spread below the station. There are many good walks from here. South of Whaley Bridge the train climbs steeply into the hills and moors again, with fine views to the north. The line curves through great bare hills to **Chapel-en-le-Frith** station with its village to the north. The train then makes its way through tunnels and rocky cuttings to **Dove Holes**. From here the line runs south to Buxton, its handsome stone architecture filling the valley. Near the station are the workshops of the Peak Rail Centre, who plan to revive the Buxton–Matlock line.

Buxton to Matlock
Buses to Matlock depart regularly from Buxton's market square but the more energetic can walk. One route follows the old line of the railway via Monsal Dale, Bakewell and Rowsley, and the other the High Peak Trail via Parsley Hay and Wirksworth.

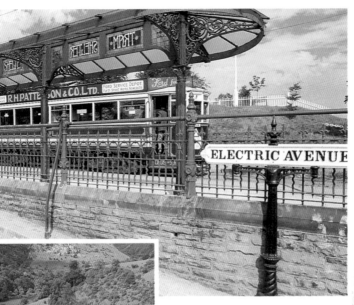

A fascinating museum of trams and tramway equipment is set in a disused limestone quarry in Crich (above). The five-arched Monsal Dale viaduct (left) which crosses the River Wye once carried the London Midland Region line

A British Railways London Midland Region poster depicts the attractions of Buxton, 'The Derbyshire Spa'

MATLOCK – DERBY
17¼ miles

Matlock

Matlock town, with its great Victorian hydropathic hotels, is to the north of the pretty station. At **Matlock Bath**, where there is a cable car to the Heights of Abraham, look back for views along the Derwent towards Matlock. After the ornate station of **Cromford**, the train follows the Derwent valley, with the Cromford canal near by. Look out for the iron aqueduct that carries the canal over the railway. Just to the east is the site of High Peak junction, where the old High Peak railway to Whaley Bridge joined the main line.

Belper

Continuing along the valley the train reaches **Whatstandwell**, the stop for the Crich Tramway Museum, and then at **Ambergate** joins the main line from Derby to Sheffield. The valley opens out, and there is a glimpse of Belper's famous textile mills. The station is approached by a long stone-lined cutting crossed by 10 handsome stone bridges which, along with two further south, near **Duffield**, are typical of George Stephenson's work.

Derby

After Duffield the best views are to the north. At Derby the locomotive works to the east are easily identified by the clock tower and office block of about 1851. The exteriors of the station and the Midland Hotel are imposing, and Derby centre, with its china works, cathedral and 17th-century county hall is close by.

LOOK OUT FOR
The mineral water springs of the Peak District, and the spas developed to exploit them are a characteristic feature of the Buxton and Matlock lines. The Buxton waters were used by the Romans and in the medieval and Elizabethan periods, but it was in the late 18th century that the town became a popular spa. From the 1780s the Duke of Devonshire employed the architect Carr of York to turn the town into a second Bath with a Crescent, Assembly Rooms and stables. A century later hotels, a pavilion and concert hall were added, followed by the opera house in 1903, this later development inspired by the arrival of the railway in 1867. At Matlock the waters were taken more for medicinal than fashionable purposes, with the first stone Bath being built in the 18th century. However the main growth was in the Victorian period, with the opening of Smedley's huge hydro and other similar establishments, treating thousands of patients each year.

Across the Pennines

MANCHESTER – SHEFFIELD *42 miles*

The most southerly of the three trans-Pennine routes that link Manchester with Yorkshire, the line to Sheffield is an exciting mixture of Victorian industrial architecture and splendid Peak District scenery. The train follows the Goyt, the Noe and the Derwent through the hills, and this is the line *par excellence* for walkers.

A journey through the rich, green Hope Valley between Hope and Edale

TRAINS
(1hr 20mins approx)
Mon–Sat 22; Sun 10
Refreshments: some

Tourist Information Centres
Manchester Town Hall
Extension, Lloyd St
(061) 234 3157/8
Sheffield Town Hall
Extension, Union St
(0742) 734671/2

Walks
In Derbyshire, keep to public paths to avoid unexpected visits to old mineshafts.
Peak District National Park stations from Chinley to Grindleford. Walks and trails information from local Tourist Centres
Pennine Way begins at Edale
Sett Valley Trail from New Mills

Places to Visit
Bamford By car or 2m walk to Ladybower Reservoir
Dore Abbeydale Industrial Hamlet
Grindleford Longshaw Estate. *By car* Chatsworth (Apr–Oct)
Hope By car to Castleton (3m): Blue John Cavern; Peak Cavern (Apr–mid Sep); Peveril Castle, EH; Speedwell Cavern; Treak Cliff Cavern and Mine
Manchester Cathedral; City Art Gallery; John Rylands University Library; various museums
Ryder Brow Belle Vue Leisure Park

Sheffield Bishop's House; Cathedral; City Museum and Mappin Art Gallery; Sheffield Industrial Museum; South Yorkshire Fire Service Museum (Apr–Oct); Sheffield Manor (May–Oct)
Note: For some places in Sheffield you may need to travel by car or bus. The bus station and a Tourist Information Centre are a short walk from the railway station.

Manchester
Leaving Piccadilly station, the train runs eastwards through **Ardwick**, **Ashburys** and **Belle Vue**, the track raised above an industrial landscape dotted with large Victorian churches. Belle Vue Leisure Park is best approached from **Ryder Brow**. After **Reddish North** the factories and mills give way to suburban housing and just before **Brinnington** there is the first sight of the country as the train crosses the River Tame. At **Bredbury** Elizabethan timber-framed mansions can be still found among the suburban villas but south-east of **Romiley**, where the church of 1864 with its tall spire stands beside the station, the suburbs end and the excitement begins.

Marple
The train emerges from a cutting to cross the wooded Goyt valley on a high viaduct, with the great stone arches of the canal aqueduct of 1801–1808 just to the south. The railway now follows the river and the Peak Forest Canal for some miles, with the latter often visible across the valley. Marple is a handsome mill town, made interesting by the canal with its flight of locks and the excellent Victorian church with Art Nouveau details. A branch line leads to **Rose Hill** station. From **Strines** there are views through the woods into the valley with its tall mill chimneys and then from **New Mills Central** you can see across the valley to Newtown and the Buxton line running parallel on the southern side. At this point there are three railways, a canal, a river and two 'A' roads squeezed into the valley, with dramatic results. From New Mills you can walk the Sett Valley Trail, along the former branch line to Hayfield. With the canal basin at Buxworth to the

Chatsworth House, a few miles south of Grindleford station

LOOK OUT FOR
The building of trans-Pennine railways in the Victorian period was inspired more by freight than passenger traffic, and the Manchester–Sheffield route is no exception. Several freight lines and branches are still to be seen, mostly used by stone trains from the Peak District quarries, while others, long closed, are now converted into footpaths. **This is one of the best lines in the country for walkers and ramblers**, with a great network of Peak and Pennine footpaths radiating out from New Mills, Edale, Hope, Castleton and Hathersage. Long distance walkers can attack the Pennine Way, while those with lesser ambitions can explore Kinder Scout, Mam Tor, Lose Hill or Tunstead Clough, all near the railway. Other walks lead along the Noe and Derwent valleys. The vast choice of walks in the region makes it easy to use the train as a basis for exploration of the Peaks, Pennines and their villages and river valleys.

south, the line swings east to **Chinley**. The High Peaks now dominate the horizon to the east as the train leaves the river and plunges into the long Cowburn tunnel.

Edale
Leaving the tunnel, the train is immediately in a splendid setting, with great hills all around the narrow Edale valley and a pretty pattern of fields and stone walls breaking up the steep valley sides. Edale village, where the Pennine Way long distance footpath starts, is spread to the north, over the foothills of Kinder Scout. The line now curves round Lose Hill to enter the Hope valley through a landscape of great bare hills broken by rock outcrops and stretches of moorland. **Hope** station, set above the village with its pretty church, is the stop for Castleton and the Peak caverns.

Hathersage
With Win Hill and Ladybower Reservoir to the north, the train follows the River Noe to its junction with the Derwent by **Bamford** station. Bamford church spire stands above the woods to the north, with a tall mill chimney near by. Hathersage looks good from the train, a stone village spread over the valley north of the line with the church high up at the end. Robin Hood's friend Little John is buried here. There are excellent views along the Derwent valley, with the hillsides scattered with old stone farms. East of Hathersage the hills are more wooded towards **Grindleford**, and then the train enters the great

Totley tunnel, 3 miles 950 yards and the second longest in Britain. Built in 1894, it is lined throughout with stone blocks.

Sheffield
East of the tunnel the train runs through a wooded cutting to **Dore** where it joins the main Sheffield–London line. This is the stop for Abbeydale Industrial Hamlet. The woods now give way to suburban and industrial surroundings as the train approaches Sheffield, with good views of the spires and towers of the city ahead. A long stone-lined cutting leads to the station, with its great arcaded entrance of 1904.

The starting point of the Pennine Way, which runs 250 miles from Edale in Derbyshire to Kirk Yetholm in Berwickshire, and was the first established long-distance walk

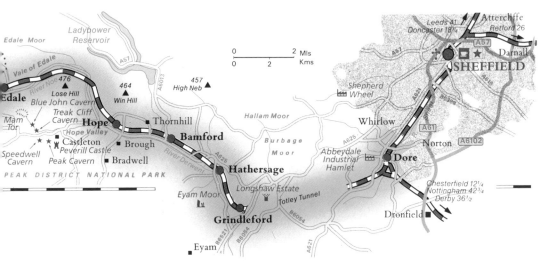

Into the Lake District

PRESTON – CARLISLE   *90 miles*

TRAINS
Preston–Carlisle
(1hr 20mins approx)
Mon–Sat 18; Sun 8
Refreshments: some

Oxenholme–Windermere
(25mins approx)
Mon–Sat 13; Sun 8
No refreshments

**Tourist Information
Centres**
Carlisle Old Town Hall,
Green Market
(0228) 25517
Kendal Town Hall,
Highgate (0539) 25758
Lancaster Dalton Sq
(0524) 32878
Penrith Robinson's
School, Middlegate
(0768) 67466
Preston The Guildhall,
Lancaster Rd
(0772) 53731
Windermere The Gateway
Centre, Victoria St
(09662) 6499

Walks
Cumbria Way passes
Windermere and Carlisle
Dales Way begins at
Bowness-on-
Windermere
Lake District National Park
walks and trails
information from local
Tourist Centres
Lancaster Canal towpath
from Preston to
Lancaster

Places to Visit
Carlisle Castle, EH;
Cathedral; Guildhall (mid
May–mid Sep, pm);
Hadrian's Wall; Museum
and Art Gallery; Prior's
Tower Museum
Kendal Abbot Hall Art
Gallery; Abbot Hall
Museum of Lakeland Life
and Industry; Castle
Lancaster Ashton
Memorial and
Williamson Park; Castle;
City Museum; Lune
Aqueduct
Oxenholme By car Levens
Hall (Etr–mid Oct);
Sizergh Castle, NT
(Apr–Oct)
Penrith Brougham Castle;
Castle. *By car* Acorn
Bank Garden, NT
(Apr–Oct); Dalemain
(Apr–mid Oct)
Preston Harris Museum
and Art Gallery; *The
Manxman* Isle of Man
steamboat. *By car/bus*
Commercial Vehicle
Museum, Leyland
(Apr–Sep)
Windermere National Park
Visitor Centre
(Apr–Oct); The Lakeland
Experience (Apr–Oct);
Steamboat Museum
(Apr–Oct). *At Bowness-
on-Windermere* (1½m):
Lake Windermere
Aquarium. *By boat* Belle
Isle (May–Sep). *By
car/bus* Stagshaw Garden,
NT (Apr–June)

O ne of the more spectacular of England's main line routes is the dramatic climb through the Lake District from Preston to Carlisle and the Scottish border. Modern locomotives have reduced the excitement of the labouring climb to Shap summit in steam days, but the landscape is as thrilling as ever. As a contrast, the rural Windermere branch wanders delightfully into the Lakes.

Preston

Well placed on the Ribble estuary, Preston is a 19th-century industrial town of surprising elegance and interest. The best part is the large central square, with Georgian streets and Victorian churches all around. The large stone station, still with its 1880 glazed roof, is a suitable starting point for an exciting journey. Leaving Preston, the train runs through open country, passing under the M55 and between two churches. The fells and moors to the north-east become more dominant as the line crosses the Rivers Brock and Calder. The M6 is never far away to the east, and to the west is the Lancaster Canal. Climbing steadily, the train crosses the Wyre, and soon the dark stone skyline of Lancaster comes into view, with the outline of castle and cathedral clearly visible.

Lancaster

Sir William Tite's 1846 station, a generous rough-stone Tudor-style building, is convenient for the city centre, with all its Georgian buildings and its views over the Lune estuary. The train crosses the Lune, with a splendid view of the city from the bridge, and then passes quickly through hills to run beside the sea at Hest Bank, with the Cumbrian hills to the north across the expanse of Morecambe Bay. The line swings inland again as the train passes through Carnforth, the home of Steamtown,

with its railway museum and mechanical coaling tower. (This train does not stop at Carnforth station. To do so, you have to change at Lancaster. Also, see Leeds–Morecambe route, pages 86–7.)

Oxenholme

The train now climbs continuously, with the M6 alongside, into an increasingly powerful landscape. Soon after passing Natland's Edwardian church it reaches Oxenholme, where the branch to Windermere leaves the main line. The line climbs steeply, twisting through cuttings and over the Dockray viaduct, with its fine views of the mountains, and then up the Lune valley, the river far below and the great fells all around. A fine sight is the viaduct that carried the former line to Sedbergh curving away to the south. The views are exciting in all directions. Shap summit, 279 metres (916ft) above sea level, surrounded by bleak windswept moorland, is quickly passed and the train now starts the long descent towards Penrith, leaving the hills behind as it enters a landscape of bleak farmland.

Penrith

The train curves round towards Penrith, crossing the River Eamont and the M6, with a good view of the red stone castle, which stands just by the station. A handsome stone market town with a fine early 18th-century

The Swan at Gummer's How on Windermere

church, Penrith looks best as the train continues northwards. From Penrith the line follows the Petterill valley through a more domestic landscape.

Carlisle

The train follows the River Petterill into Carlisle, passing over the M6 with the telecommunications tower dominating the skyline to the east. Always a busy railway junction, Carlisle is still the meeting point for five routes, and its importance is well reflected by Sir William Tite's grandiose Tudor-style station of 1847. The castle, the cathedral and the powerful classical streets of this stone border city are close at hand.

Carlisle-Lancaster
See pages 84-85

Settle-Carlisle
See pages 88-89

Carlisle-Newcastle
upon Tyne
See pages 94-95

Glasgow-Carlisle
See pages 102-103

Above: Cumbria's Lune Gorge, with the railway, the A685 and the M6 all squeezed in together.
Below: along the Windermere Branch

Carlisle-Lancaster
See pages 84-85

WINDERMERE BRANCH *10 miles*

The Windermere branch train takes a more leisurely pace after the fast Intercity express that leaves you at **Oxenholme**. The train follows the track that disappears into the bushes before curving gently down to **Kendal**. There are fine views of the castle, on its mound above the town and, beyond, the dramatic Lakeland skyline. The town is left behind as the train crosses the River Kent and runs through flowery cuttings to **Burneside**. To the north are the purple and green flanks of Potter Fell and Hugill Fell. The slate roofs of **Staveley** are spread below the track. Swinging in and out of cuttings, the train passes Ings Church, in a valley to the north, and then runs through a patchwork of fields and stone walls to **Windermere**. The station is set high above the town and there is no view of the lake, which is a mile away — a gentle stroll down through the town to catch the Windermere 'steamers' which connect with the Lakeside & Haverthwaite steam railway (see right).

LAKESIDE AND HAVERTHWAITE RAILWAY

A boat trip on Lake Windermere connects the Windermere branch line with the Lakeside and Haverthwaite Railway. The oldest lake ship, *Tern*, dates back to 1891. The transfer point between lake and rail is **Lakeside**.

The Lakeside and Haverthwaite Railway has a long tourist history, the branch from Lakeside to Ulverston having been completed in 1869 by the Furness Railway. They later bought the steamers operating on the lake. Passenger trains stopped in 1965 and the line closed after freight traffic ceased. The preservation society purchased the line and took over the most northerly 3½ miles, which reopened in 1973. Throughout the journey the River Leven runs to the east. Part way along the line is **Newby Bridge Halt** and the southern end of the line is now at **Haverthwaite**.

All aboard for Lakeside!

TRAINS
Lakeside–Haverthwaite (3½ miles approx)
Operates: Daily
May–Sep
(Tel (05395) 31594)
Single journey: 18mins

Walks
In Fell Foot Park, NT 1m from Newby Bridge

Places to Visit
Haverthwaite Artcrystal glass engraving workshop (mid Jan–Dec) *Lakeside* Stott Park Bobbin Mill, EH (Etr–Oct). *By car* Graythwaite Hall Gardens (Apr–July)

Unknown Cumbria

CARLISLE – LANCASTER   via Barrow *120 miles*

TRAINS
Carlisle–Barrow
(2½hrs approx)
Mon–Sat 5; Sun
(Carlisle–Whitehaven
only) 2
No refreshments

Barrow–Lancaster
(1hr 5mins approx)
Mon–Sat 17; Sun 6
No refreshments

Tourist Information
Centres (*summer only)
Barrow-in-Furness Duke St
(0229) 25795
Carlisle Old Town Hall,
Green Market
(0228) 25517
*Grange-over-Sands** Main
St (04484) 4026
Lancaster Dalton Sq
(0524) 32878
Maryport Senhouse St
(0900) 813738
*Millom** St George's Rd
(0657) 2555
*Ravenglass** Ravenglass &
Eskdale Rlwy Car Park
(06577) 278
Ulverston Coronation
Hall (0229) 57120
Whitehaven Lowther St
(0946) 5678

**For all information on
Carlisle and Lancaster
see pages 82–3**

Walks
Lake District National Park
walks and trails
information from local
Tourist Centres

Places to Visit
Barrow-in-Furness Abbey,
EH (1½m); Museum. *By
car and boat from Roa Island*
(3½m) Piel Castle
(Apr–Sep)
Cark Holker Hall and
Park (Etr–Oct)
Carnforth Steamtown
Railway Museum
(Apr–Oct, winter
wkends only)
Maryport Maritime
Museum. *By car/bus*
Wordsworth House, NT,
at Cockermouth
(Apr–Oct)
Millom Folk Museum
(June–mid Sep)
Ravenglass Railway
Museum (Apr–Oct)
St Bees St Bees Head
RSPB Reserve
Sellafield Nuclear Power
Exhibition Centre
Ulverston Cumbria
Crystal glassworks;
Swarthmoor Hall
(Mar–mid Oct). *By car*
Conishead Priory
(Etr–Sep wkends & BH)
Whitehaven Michael
Moon's Bookshop;
Museum
Workington Helena
Thompson Museum

*A glorious view south
from the slopes of Black
Coombe, Cumbria en
route to Millom*

This journey, which involves a change at Barrow, is a leisurely exploration of rural Cumbria and its remote coastline. An exciting and varied landscape forms a background to old ports and harbours, some in use since Roman times and still full of the atmosphere of the 18th and 19th centuries.

Leaving **Carlisle** (see page 83) quickly behind, the train runs through farmland beside the River Caldew to **Dalston**. The next stop is **Wigton**, an attractive market town with a good 18th-century church. **Aspatria**'s Tudor-style 1841 station is south of its town, and from here the train follows the River Ellen through a landscape marked by the remains of the mining industry, to **Maryport**, whose grid street pattern reveals its 18th-century development as a coal port.

Whitehaven
The line then runs along the beach to **Flimby**, where terraces of old houses look towards Scotland across the Solway Firth. The Victorian flavour of **Workington** can be felt as the train crosses the River Derwent, with a good view of the old harbour and docks. The big brick station with its ironwork and glazed canopies is in the centre of the town. **Harrington** is a cluster of colour-washed terraces, facing the little harbour, then the line reaches **Parton**. As the train rounds Redness Point, **Whitehaven**, one of Britain's earliest planned towns, comes into view, its 18th-century terraces, fine churches and old factories ranged round the old quays. The station is to the north, and then the line tunnels under the town to **Corkickle** before turning inland. The next stop is the little village of **St Bees**, and then the train is back beside the sea running along the shore past **Nethertown** and **Braystones** where old wooden beach huts have a pleasantly faded 1920s air.

Ravenglass
The nuclear processing plant at **Sellafield** is a dramatic interlude, its glittering structures seen against the background of distant hills. The train then reaches **Seascale**, a tired little resort, and swings inland to **Drigg**. The approach to Ravenglass is excellent, the line raised above salt-marshes. The pretty terraces of Ravenglass are ranged round the harbour and the miniature steam railway (see opposite) is beside the line, while just south of the station the train cuts through a Roman fort. The line now runs across farmland to **Bootle** and **Silecroft**, typically decorative Furness Railway stations. It then curves round to **Millom**, and the train crosses Millom Marsh to **Green Road. Foxfield** is at the head of Duddon estuary, and then from **Kirkby-in-Furness** and **Askam** there are fine views back towards Millom and Hadbarrow Point.

Barrow
South of Askam the line winds through lakes and then swings west towards the sea. Barrow was created by the Furness Railway from the 1840s as a centre for iron, steel and shipbuilding. **You have to change here and catch a train for Lancaster.** Leaving Barrow the line passes the docks and swings east through suburbs to **Roose**. The ruins of Furness Abbey can be seen before **Dalton** with its excellent station. The train now winds through hills and moorland to **Ulverston**'s extravagant stone station. Passing the junction

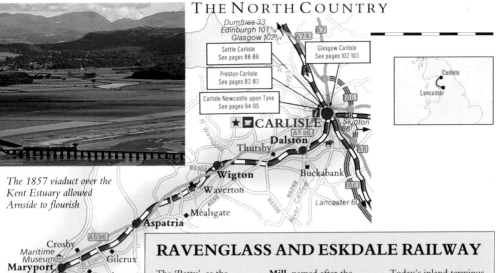

The 1857 viaduct over the Kent Estuary allowed Arnside to flourish

Dumfries 33
Edinburgh 101
Glasgow 102

Settle-Carlisle
See pages 88-89

Preston-Carlisle
See pages 82-83

Carlisle-Newcastle upon Tyne
See pages 94-95

Glasgow-Carlisle
See pages 102-103

★ CARLISLE

Thursby — Dalston

Wigton — Buckabank

Waverton

Mealsgate

Lancaster 60

Aspatria

Crosby
Maritime Museum
Maryport — Gilcrux
Dearham

Flimby

Seaton — Wordsworth House

Workington — Cockermouth
Helena Thompson

Harrington — Dean

Distington

Lowca

Parton — Arlecdon

Michael Moon's Bookshop — Whitehaven
Frizington

Corkickle — Cleator Moor

Bees Head
St Bees — Egremont

322

Beckermet
Nethertown — Nuclear Power Exhibition Centre
Braystones

Sellafield — Gosforth

Seascale — The Green
Irton Road — Beckfoot

Drigg — Miteside — ESKDALE (Dalegarth)
RAVENGLASS — Muncaster Mill
Ravensglass and Eskdale Railway — Muncaster

573 Whitfell

LAKE DISTRICT
NATIONAL PARK

Bootle — Black Combe 600

RAVENGLASS AND ESKDALE RAILWAY

The 'Ratty', as the Ravenglass & Eskdale Railway is known, started as an iron ore line in 1875 with a gauge of 3 feet. After the mines failed, it was converted by the model engineer, W J Bassett-Lowke, to a 15-inch gauge line to test his miniature steam locomotives, and services restarted in 1915. Recently the line became the first in Britain to adopt radio signalling.

The railway now runs from **Ravenglass**, where a museum is situated alongside the BR station, whose main building is now 'The Ratty Arms'. Falling gradients take the line past **Muncaster**

Mill, named after the restored building, now open to the public. The next halt, **Miteside**, uses part of an old boat to provide shelter from the rain! Views of the distant fells can be especially appreciated when open coaches are used.

The stone-built station at **Irton Road** dates from 1876 and, after crossing the river, the line reaches **The Green**, serving the Outward Bound Mountain School. At **Beckfoot** the remains of the granite quarry can be seen, and then the line passes the row of miners' cottages built when it used to serve Nab Gill mines at Boot.

Today's inland terminus lies at **Eskdale (Dalegarth)**, with a picnic area by the road leading to Ambleside.

TRAINS
Ravenglass–Eskdale (Dalegarth) 7 miles
Operates: Daily all yr
(Tel (06577) 226)
Single journey: 40mins

Walks
Walks in *Eskdale* from Dalegarth, Beckfoot, The Green and Irton Road

Places to Visit
Dalegarth By car or walk
Hardknott Roman Fort
Muncaster Mill Castle
(Etr–Sep); Muncaster
Mill (Apr–Sep)

The River Mite, one of the locomotives run by the Ravenglass & Eskdale Railway in Cumbria, known as the 'Ratty'

0   2 Mls
0   2 Kms

Green Road — Foxfield
Silecroft — Kirkby-in-Furness
Folk Museum
Millom — Ulverston — Haverthwaite — Leven Viaduct
Askam — Grange-over-Sands — Milnthorpe
Swarthmoor Hall — Holker Hall
Cumbria Crystal Glassworks — Cark & Cartmel — Kent Viaduct — Arnside
Dalton — Conishead — Kents Bank — Silverdale
Roose — Gleaston
Morecambe Bay — Steamtown — Carnforth
Bare Lane
Morecambe — Bolton le Sands
LANCASTER — A683
Heysham — Scotforth

Carlisle 60
Skipton 37½
Preston-Carlisle
See pages 82-83
Preston 21

Thurnham

with the former Windermere branch, part of which is now operated by the Lakeside and Haverthwaite steam railway (see page 83), the train crosses the Leven Viaduct. It then runs over the saltmarshes to **Cark & Cartmel**.

Carnforth
A rock cutting leads to **Kents Bank** and then the train runs along the shore to **Grange-over-Sands**, a resort developed by the Furness Railway from the 1870s. The line crosses the Kent estuary on a viaduct to **Arnside**, and then low hills take it to **Silverdale**. The line crosses marshland to Carnforth, with a good view of the Steamtown yards as it joins the main line. After a run along the coast, it turns inland again to **Lancaster** (see page 82).

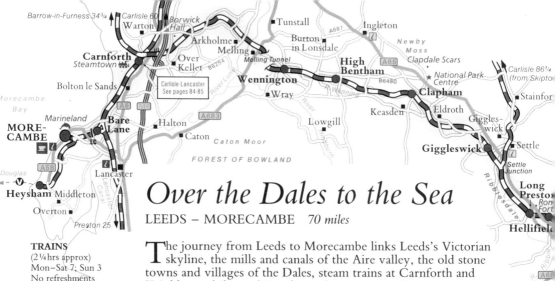

Over the Dales to the Sea

LEEDS – MORECAMBE 70 miles

The journey from Leeds to Morecambe links Leeds's Victorian skyline, the mills and canals of the Aire valley, the old stone towns and villages of the Dales, steam trains at Carnforth and Keighley and the traditional seaside at Morecambe.

Carlisle-Lancaster
See pages 84-85

TRAINS
(2¼ hrs approx)
Mon–Sat 7; Sun 3
No refreshments

Tourist Information Centres
Leeds Wellington St
(0532) 4624545
Morecambe Marine Rd
Central (0524) 414110
Skipton Victoria Sq
(0756) 2809/4357

Walks
The Dales Way from Leeds
The Lancaster Canal towpath at Carnforth
The Leeds and Liverpool Canal towpath — stations from Leeds to Gargrave
Leeds Country Way 60m walk around Leeds
The Pennine Way goes through Gargrave
Yorkshire Dales National Park information from National Park Centres, Malham and Clapham

Places to Visit
Bingley Five-rise Locks, Leeds & Liverpool Canal
Carnforth Steamtown Railway Museum (Apr–Oct, winter wkends)
Clapham Yorkshire Dales National Park Centre (Apr–Oct)
Hellifield By car or walk (5m) Yorkshire Dales National Park Centre at Malham (Apr–Oct)
Keighley Cliffe Castle Museum; East Riddlesden Hall
Leeds Art Gallery and Henry Moore Sculpture Centre; City Museum; Kirkstall Abbey; Leeds Industrial Museum; Middleton Colliery Railway; Roundhay Park
Note: For some places you may need to travel by car or bus. The Tourist Centre is near the station; bus station is about ½m.
Morecambe Marineland (Etr–Oct)
Shipley By car/bus to Bradford: Bolling Hall; Cartwright Hall; Cathedral; Industrial Museum; National Museum of Photography, Film and Television
Skipton Castle; Craven Museum

Leeds

Architecturally, Leeds is one of the richest Victorian towns in Britain. The station is at the heart of the city, but its best feature, facing on to City Square, is actually the 1937 Queens Hotel, with its Art Deco Portland stone façade. As the train leaves there are fine views over the city to the east and then the line follows the Aire valley westwards, often sandwiched between the river and the Leeds and Liverpool Canal. The ruins of Kirkstall Abbey are to the north among trees by the river. Criss-crossing the river the train then plunges into a tunnel and as it emerges there is a view of Baildon's 1848 church up on a crest, followed by Shipley's excellent Victorian townscape. From **Shipley**, a branch runs south to Bradford.

Keighley

West of Shipley the train passes close by Sir Titus Salt's 'ideal' industrial village of **Saltaire**, with its huge Italianate mills and decorative Nonconformist chapel. Salt's enlightened estate included 750 workers' houses, hospital, school and shops but no pubs, all built on the demand for alpaca wool. The next stop is **Bingley**, with good views of the famous staircases of locks that carry the canal up

towards the Pennines. After **Crossflats** the industrial landscape recedes, replaced by hills to the west and moorland to the east, and a view of 17th-century East Riddlesden Hall across the valley. **Keighley**, where there is a connection with the Keighley & Worth Valley steam railway (see opposite), is best seen after the station, as the train continues along the Aire valley. Around **Cononley** the hills close in and then the valley widens again as the train approaches Skipton.

Skipton

Skipton can be seen from the 1876 station, a good example of a typical Midland Railway building with its ironwork, decorative stonework and old water crane. The train then continues to **Gargrave**, a town set in a valley around the big Victorian church. West of the station the canal swings south, crossing the Aire on an aqueduct, and then the line swings away from the river. Moorland and hills accompany the train to **Hellifield**, once a busy junction serving the line to Blackburn. The next stop is **Long Preston**, a farming village in the Ribble valley with a Roman fort by its churchyard. The line now follows the Ribble valley to Settle Junction, where the Morecambe line branches west.

On the up and up: the Five-Rise Locks at Bingley on the Leeds and Liverpool Canal

A Keighley & Worth Valley Railway locomotive leaving Keighley, a station which the railway shares with British Rail

Change for Settle-Carlisle
See pages 88-89

Leeds-York-Scarborough
See pages 90-91

LOOK OUT FOR

The line from Leeds to Morecambe is a record of the growth of the **wool trade**. The farms in the Dales grew up to look after huge flocks of sheep, and the sturdy farmhouses still stand. Livestock markets of towns such as Giggleswick, Clapham and Skipton were the lifeblood of the region and the railways transported both sheep and fleeces. By the mid-19th century stone mills filled the Aire valley. The industry's growth is reflected by great Victorian buildings, and many mills survive as silent memorials to the textile industry.

Clapham

Leaving the Ribble valley, the train drops away to the west with **Giggleswick** in the valley in the distance. The town, with its fine church and Victorian school, is far from the station. The line now climbs with fine views of the surrounding hills and then joins the Wenning. There are panoramic views, particularly towards Newby Moss and Clapdale Scars. The National Park Centre is a good introduction to this wild and lovely landscape. West of Clapham the train begins its long descent to **High Bentham**.

Carnforth

Criss-crossing the Wenning, the train drops down past the village of Lower Bentham. Farmland and woods surround the line as it approaches **Wennington**, where a 17th-century farm stands by the station. After Melling the train crosses the Lune valley, with excellent views towards Kirkby Lonsdale. The line crosses the Lancaster Canal, with Elizabethan Borwick Hall (not regularly open to the public) to the north. With the canal alongside, the train passes under the M6 and swings sharply south to **Carnforth**, with Steamtown in view.

Morecambe

From Carnforth the train runs along the coast to Lancaster. It then reverses up the main line and swings west to Morecambe, pausing at **Bare Lane**. **Morecambe**'s pretty stone station is right on the front, and the perfect introduction to a resort created in the 19th century by the railway. A branch south leads to Heysham, a port now used for the Isle of Man service.

KEIGHLEY & WORTH VALLEY RAILWAY

Situated in a steep-sided valley off Airedale in West Yorkshire, the Keighley & Worth Valley Railway has featured in various films, the most notable being 'The Railway Children'. It also traverses the heart of the Brontë country, being very convenient for the Brontë Parsonage Museum, situated at Haworth.

The line, built largely to serve the numerous mills in the valley, was opened in 1867, and worked by the Midland Railway, whose main line passed through Keighley *en route* from Leeds to Skipton and beyond. However, so important was the valley's business for the railways that the rival Great Northern opened a line from Halifax in 1883, which used the final mile of the Worth Valley line into Keighley. The Keighley & Worth Valley branch was closed by BR in 1962, but reopened by the Preservation Society seven years later.

The line begins at **Keighley**, where the railway shares the station with BR. Curving sharply to the right, it climbs steeply for the whole of the 4¾ miles to Oxenhope. There are two short tunnels, the first coming after **Ingrow** station, while Mytholmes, the second, is a further two miles along the line. Between them are the stations of **Damems** and **Oakworth**, both excellently restored. **Haworth** station is the headquarters of the railway, while the goods yard and shed there are now used for restoring locomotives.

Oxenhope forms the terminus of the line, and there is a picnic area opposite the station. In the goods yard are two extensive modern buildings, one forming a museum, while the other is used for coach restoration and storage.

KEIGHLEY & WORTH VALLEY RAILWAY

Keighley (BR station)–Oxenhope 4¾ miles
Operates: Weekends all year, daily July to early Sep. (Tel (0535) 45214. 24hr talking timetable (0535) 43629)
Single journey: 25 mins

Tourist Information Centre
Haworth 2/4 West Ln (0535) 42329

Walks
The Brontë Way 9m between the Brontë Parsonage Museum at Haworth and Wycoller Valley near Colne

Places to Visit
Haworth Brontë Parsonage Museum (closed Feb)
Oxenhope Railway Museum (July–Aug)

Taking an Independent Line

SETTLE – CARLISLE 71½ miles

S ince its opening in 1876, the Settle and Carlisle route has always
occupied a unique position among the railways of Britain. Born
out of the ambitions of the Midland Railway to have its own direct
route from London to Scotland, the line took over ten years to carve
its way across the remote and inhospitable regions of the Pennines,
at a cost of nearly £3.5 million. It was the last main line to be built
entirely by hand by gangs of navvies armed only with picks, shovels
and brute force, living in desolate and wild shanty towns along the
route and working in conditions of wet and cold inconceivable
today. Now, its great viaducts and tunnels are a living memorial
to Victorian endeavour. British Rail, having applied for consent to
close the line, has taken the unique step of putting it up for sale
to private buyers. It is anticipated that in 1989 the future of this
always demanding, independent and unpredictable line will be
made clear.

TRAINS
Phone Carlisle Tourist
Information Centre
(0228) 25517 or any BR
Station for operating
details
Single journey: 2hrs
approx

**Tourist Information
Centres** (*summer only)
Appleby-in-Westmorland
Moot Hall, Boroughgate
(07683) 51177
Carlisle Old Town Hall,
Green Market
(0228) 25517
Horton-in-Ribblesdale Pen-
y-Ghent Café
(07296) 333
Kirkby Stephen Market Sq
(07683) 71199
Settle★ Town Hall,
Cheapside (07292) 3617

**For all information on
Carlisle see pages 82–3**

Walks
The Dales Way passes
Dent
Hadrian's Wall from
Carlisle
The Pennine Way passes
north-west of Settle and
north of Appleby-in-
Westmorland
The Yoredale Way begins
at Kirkby Stephen
*The Yorkshire Dales
National Park* stations
from Settle to Garsdale
— walks and trails
information from local
Tourist Centres and from
the Yorkshire Dales
National Park Centre at
Hawes

Places to Visit
Appleby-in-Westmorland
Appleby Castle
Conservation Centre
(Etr, May–Sep). *By car*
Burtree Crafts, Little
Asby
Dent By car Dent Crafts
Centre (mid
Mar–Christmas)
Garsdale By car Yorkshire
Dales National Park
Centre, Hawes
(Apr–Oct); Upper Dales
Folk Museum, Hawes
(Apr–Sep)
Kirkby Stephen By car
Langrigg Pottery,
Winton. At Brough:
Castle, EH; Clifford
House Craft Workshop
(Mar–Dec)
*Langwathby By car/bus to
Penrith*: see page 82
Settle Museum of North
Craven Life (June–Sep,
pm). *By car* Stainforth
packhorse bridge, NT;
Malham Tarn Estate, NT
— nature reserve and
birdwatching on Malham
Tarn

Settle

Settle has been a busy market town
since the Middle Ages, and its stone
streets look good from the station.
The line is raised high above the River
Ribble, with good views across the
valley. North of the town the train
follows the winding course of the
river, criss-crossing it through a landscape of bare fields broken by rocks
and stone walls, and climbing steadily
into the Dales between high peaks.
Horton in Ribblesdale, one of the
stations reopened for walkers under
the Dalesrail scheme, faces its little
village across the valley. Continuing
to climb through powerful Dales
scenery, the line makes its curving approach to **Ribblehead**, with the 24
limestone piers of the great viaduct
clearly visible ahead. Striding 104 feet
high across Batty Moss, the viaduct,
which took five years to build, is one
of the many excitements of the
journey. Barren Blea Moor follows,
leading to the 2,629-yard tunnel carved 500 feet below the surface and then
the train crosses Dent Head Viaduct.
Dent station, remote and isolated, is
the highest in England. More viaducts
and tunnels carry the line through the
Fells above the River Clough.

Appleby

Just north of **Garsdale** the track of the
former Hawes branch along
Wensleydale can be seen to the east
and then more viaducts and tunnels
take the line to its summit at Aisgill,
1,169 feet (356m) above sea level. The
train now joins the River Eden, and
starts the long descent to Carlisle,
with the line cut into the hillside far
above the river, and overshadowed by
the dour ridge of Mallerstang.
Descending steadily, the train passes
through Birkett tunnel and into a
softer landscape of big, bare hills. The
next stop is **Kirkby Stephen**, the
pretty barge-boarded station over a
mile west of its town, and then the
train swings west round Ash Fell and
crosses the wooded Scandal Beck and
the track of the former line from
Tebay to Barnard Castle. This route,

long closed, gave Kirkby Stephen its
second station. Just to the north is
Crosby Garrett, with its fine early
church high above the village and then
the train winds its way down to
Appleby, with two more viaducts and
one tunnel *en route*. As the Fells fall
away behind, the landscape becomes
more open. The line crosses the Eden
and the A66 outside the town, but
Appleby's castle, whose park houses
the Rare Breeds Survival Trust, and its
fine church are best seen from the
north. After Appleby the train follows
the wide Eden valley. The next stop is
Langwathby, where the red stone
station is typical of the town, and then
there are good views over the Eden to
the west.

Carlisle

The line crosses the wooded Eden on a
long viaduct and then comes to
Lazonby with its fine Victorian
church. The train now runs close to

Appleby's famous Horse Fair is held every June

LOOK OUT FOR

Built as it was by men with picks and shovels, the Settle–Carlisle line is an accurate record of the inhospitable terrain that it crosses. Throughout its 71 miles, its builders had to make use of **local materials** they found along the route, for the whole structural effort had to be virtually self-supporting. As a result, the viaducts, bridges and tunnels that are the characteristic feature of the line were built from a great variety of stone. This variation can be noted from the train, particularly the physical structure and colour of the stone, which ranges from grey to red with many tones of brown in between.

the fast-flowing Eden, with views to the east and along the river towards **Armathwaite**, its flowery station with the old signal box and goods shed is away from the town whose castle above the Eden is hidden by woods. North of the station there is another good view along the Eden valley, and then the train swings west away from the river, passes under the M6 and joins the Newcastle line for the approach to Carlisle (see page 94).

The Dalesman, a local train, calls at the remote station of Dent in Cumbria – at 1,145ft (349m) now the highest railway halt in England

Below: one of the greatest engineering achievements on the Settle–Carlisle line: the 104ft (31.7m) high Ribblehead viaduct which stretches over Batty Moss

Map labels

Glasgow 102¼
CARLISLE
Newcastle 6¾
Corby
River Eden
Cumrew
Workington 33
Cotehill
Armathwaite
Preston–Carlisle See pages 82-83
Lancaster–Carlisle See pages 84-85
Carlisle–Newcastle upon Tyne See pages 94-95
Glasgow–Carlisle See pages 102-103
Armathwaite Viaduct
Armathwaite Tunnel
Baron Wood No. 1 & 2 Tunnels
Lancaster 69
High Hesket
Kirkoswald
Lazonby
Salkeld Viaduct
Plumpton
Great Salkeld
Ousby
Langwathby
Skirwith
Penrith
Milburn
Culgaith Tunnel
Crowdundle Via.
Clifton
Kirkby Thore
Dufton
Pennine Way
Long Marton
Cliburn
Bolton
Great Strickland
Kings Meaburn
Appleby
A66
Ormside Viaduct
Wareop
Brough
Helm Tunnel
Grisburn Viaduct
Great Asby
Soulby
Winton
Crosby Garrett Tunnel
Langrigg Pottery
Burtree Crafts
Smardale Viaduct
Nateby
Kirkby Stephen
Ravenstonedale
Birkett Tunnel
Outhgill
Mallerstang
Common
Wild Boar Fell 709
Aisgill Summit 356
Shotlock Hill Tunnel
Cotterdale
Moorcock Tunnel
Dandry Mire Viaduct
Garsdale
Rise Hill Tunnel
Dent
Arten Gill Viaduct
Dales Way
Dent Head Viaduct
Pennine Way
Blea Moor Tunnel
Cam Fell
Ribblehead Viaduct
Ribblehead
YORKSHIRE DALES NATIONAL PARK
Ingleborough Hill 723
Horton Moor
693
Horton in Ribblesdale
Pen-y-Ghent
National Park Centre
Clapham
Packhorse Bridge
Stainforth
Carnforth 23
SETTLE
North Craven Life
Leeds 41¼

Line continues to Leeds For Leeds-Morecambe See pages 86-87

Scale: 0   2 Mls / 0   2 Kms

Aspects of Yorkshire

These two journeys – Leeds to York then York to Scarborough – form an exciting way to explore the many faces of Yorkshire. They link great and historic towns and cities through a dramatically varied landscape, and provide a voyage from the heart of the country to the traditional delights of the seaside.

LEEDS – YORK *38¾ miles*

After leaving **Leeds** (see page 86) the train crosses the River Aire and the Leeds and Liverpool Canal and runs to **Headingley**. The cricket ground is to the north and Kirkstall Abbey to the south. A more open landscape leads to **Horsforth** and then the train enters the great Bramhope tunnel, over two miles long and one which claimed the lives of 23 men during its building. Look back to enjoy the splendid north portal with its towers and crenellations. Embankments and viaducts now carry the line above the Wharfe valley to **Weeton.**

Harrogate

At **Pannal** there are restaurants both in the old station and in a retired Pullman carriage. The train climbs steeply before swinging out of a cutting on to the Crimple Viaduct of 1848, its 31 grey stone arches striding across the valley. Harrogate is approached through a long cutting, and the visitor gains no real feeling of this elegant former spa from the station. However, the station's central position makes it easy to explore the town. Although now rather a backwater in railway terms, Harrogate was once on a main line to Scotland, with the *Queen of Scots* Pullman calling daily.

Knaresborough

After **Starbeck** Harrogate is left behind, and then woods and cuttings lead to another fine piece of railway theatre, the castellated viaduct high over the River Nidd and, beyond it, the fine view of Knaresborough's steep old streets, church and castle. Leaving the station, the train makes its elevated way past some reservoirs with Goldsborough Hall to the south and then passes under the A1. After the remote stations at **Cattal** and **Kirk Hammerton**, the line crosses the twisting course of the Nidd and then the landscape becomes more open and flat, with long views towards Marston Moor and the site of the Civil War battle to the south and Beningbrough Hall to the north. The train then curves round past **Poppleton** and joins the main line to enter York with the Minster riding the horizon.

TRAINS
Leeds–York
(1hr 15mins approx)
Mon–Sat 16; Sun 4
No refreshments

York–Scarborough
(50mins approx)
Mon–Sat 15; Sun 11
Refreshments: some

NB Direct services Leeds–Scarborough do not go via Harrogate

Tourist Information Centres (*summer only)
Harrogate Royal Baths Assembly Rooms, Crescent Rd (0423) 525666
*Knaresborough** Market Pl (0423) 866886
Leeds Wellington St (0532) 462454/5
*Malton** Old Town Hall, Market Pl (0653) 600048
Scarborough St Nicholas Cliff (0723) 373333
York Railway Station (0904) 643700; Exhibition Sq (0904) 21756/7

For all information on Leeds see page 86

Walks
Dales Way from Leeds
Ebor Way and *Yoredale Way* from York
Wolds Way from Scarborough

Cycling
York see pages 5–7

Places to Visit
Harrogate Harlow Car Gardens; Royal Pump Room Museum
Knaresborough Castle (Etr, June–Sep); Old Mother Shipton's Cave and the Petrifying Well; Ye Oldest Chymist Shoppe (est 1720)
Malton Eden Camp Museum (mid Feb–mid Dec); Malton Museum (Apr–Oct). *By car* Castle Howard (Apr–Oct); Kirkham Priory, EH
Scarborough Castle, EH; Rotunda (Museum of Archaeology and Local History); Woodend Museum of Natural History
York Borthwick Institute of Historical Research; Castle, EH; Castle Museum; City Art Gallery; Fairfax House (Mar–Dec); Friargate Wax Museum; Guildhall; Jorvik Viking Centre; King's Manor; Merchant Adventurers' Hall; National Railway Museum; Rail Riders World (Apr–Dec); Treasurer's House (Apr–Oct); The York Story (Heritage Centre). *By car/bus* Beningbrough Hall (May–Oct)
Weeton By car Harewood House and Bird Garden

Knaresborough, set on the summit of a rocky hill and along the bank of a limestone gorge carved by the River Nidd

Designed by Vanbrugh, Castle Howard dates from the 17th and 18th centuries

Otley's memorial to the men who died building the Bramhope tunnel

YORK–SCARBOROUGH
42 miles

Malton

York-Berwick pages 96-97

Leaving **York** (see page 96) the train crosses the River Ouse with views of the Minster to the east through the trees. After Strensall the land begins to undulate then, after passing under the A64, the line swings east into the Derwent valley, to follow the river, a lovely winding wooded stretch full of pastoral pleasures. The pretty buildings of former stations, notably that built to serve Castle Howard, decorate the line as it follows the Derwent through farmland to the Georgian market town of Malton with its fine stone station, with glazed trainshed and decorative ironwork.

Seamer

The train now runs across an open landscape of wheat fields with Thorpe Bassett Wold to the south, and distant ranges of hills to north and south framing the wide Derwent valley. Seamer, with its big Norman church, is well to the west of the station, built to serve the junction with the line south to Bridlington. The line now follows the A64 into Scarborough. There is a fine view of the spires and hotels of Scarborough's skyline and in the distance the castle, high above the harbour and the bays. The station, built in 1845 and steadily extended to handle Scarborough's holiday traffic, is large and still full of interest, with a turntable, old tiled NER route maps, covered platforms and an extravagant Baroque clocktower of 1885. At its peak, Scarborough station could handle over 200 trains a day, many of which came from Middlesbrough and the north-east via the long-closed coastal line through Whitby. Developed as a spa in the 17th century, Scarborough is the Victorian seaside *par excellence*, full of grand hotels, flamboyant architecture and a traditional holiday atmosphere.

LOOK OUT FOR

The lines that link Leeds and Scarborough were built by various companies during the 1840s and subsequently became part of major routes across England. Later downgraded by closures and changes in traffic patterns, these lines are still full of **echoes of the great days of railways**. Between Leeds and York there are magnificent viaducts, a fine tunnel and other examples of ambitious Victorian engineering. By contrast, the relatively straight and flat route from York to Scarborough is marked by the stations and lineside buildings designed by the architect G T Andrews. Although most are closed, many still illustrate his elegant classicism and decorative stonework, notably those along the Derwent Valley, at Kirkham Abbey, Castle Howard, Huttons Ambo and Malton. Also stylish are the many single-storey crossing-keepers' cottages and the characteristic signal boxes. With railway history such a feature of this route, it is fitting that it is occasionally used by steam excursions from York.

Captain Cook Country

MIDDLESBROUGH – WHITBY *35 miles*

The journey from Middlesbrough to Whitby is a delightful exploration of the varied landscape of North Yorkshire. The train follows the winding course of the River Esk through wood and moorland to one of the most attractive harbours in England, a fitting end to a journey rich in Captain Cook associations.

The outline of the hill Roseberry Topping which may be seen from the line at Great Ayton

TRAINS
(1hr 20mins approx)
Mon–Sat 6; Sun 4
No refreshments

Tourist Information Centres (*summer only)
Danby* The Moors Centre, Danby Lodge, Lodge Ln (0287) 60654
Middlesbrough Albert Rd (0642) 243425
Whitby New Quay Rd (0947) 602674

Walks
The Cleveland Way passes Whitby and Kildale
North Yorkshire Moors National Park stations from Great Ayton to Whitby — walks and trails information from the National Park Centre at Danby
The Scarborough and Whitby Trailway follows a disused railway along the coast from Whitby

Places to Visit
Great Ayton Captain Cook Schoolroom Museum (Etr–Oct, pm)
Marton Captain Cook Birthplace Museum; Ormesby Hall, NT (Apr–Oct).
Middlesbrough Cleveland Crafts Centre; Cleveland Gallery; Dorman Museum; Middlesbrough Art Gallery; Transporter Bridge. By car/bus Guisborough Priory, EH; Tocketts Watermill, north-east of Guisborough (Etr–Oct)
Whitby Abbey, EH; Captain Cook's Memorial Museum (May–Oct); Dracula Experience (Etr–Sep); 199 steps and donkey road; Museum; St Mary's Church

NORTH YORKSHIRE MOORS RAILWAY

Tourist Information Centre (*summer only)
Pickering* Pickering station (0751) 73791

Walks
Dalby Forest waymarked trails, 3m from Levisham
Forestry Commission walks in Newtondale and Cropton Forest from Newtondale Halt
Historical Railway Trail from Goathland to Grosmont

Places to Visit
Goathland Mallyan Spout and Thomason Foss waterfalls
Grosmont North Yorkshire Railways engines restoration
Pickering Castle, EH; Beck Isle Museum of Rural Life (Apr–Oct)

Middlesbrough

Middlesbrough station, all heavy Gothic of 1877 with plenty of decorative details, is now rather an oasis in a desert of modern mediocrity. However, also worth seeing are the transporter bridge, a remarkable survival, the grand town hall of 1889, and the pretty terracotta façade of the old theatre. A large scale model of Captain Cook's *Endeavour* hangs in the shopping centre. Leaving the station, the train curves round the north of the town, with good views of the docks and the transporter bridge, and then turns south through suburbs to **Marton**, where the Captain Cook Birthplace Museum brings the explorer to life. Georgian Ormesby Hall is just to the north, hidden by the trees of its park. The next stations, **Gypsy Lane** and **Nunthorpe**, mark the end of the suburbs, and the line becomes a country railway, running through farmland broken by flowery hedges against the distant backdrop of the North York Moors ahead. At the former junction with the old line to Guisborough, the train turns south towards the distinctive hill known as Roseberry Topping.

Battersby

At **Great Ayton** the Captain Cook Monument, an obelisk high on a hill-top to the east, can be seen, remaining in view for some miles. The village, with its pretty houses along the River Leven and the Cook museum in the old schoolhouse, lies to the west. After passing early 19th-century Easby Hall (not open) with its pretty park and chapel, the train comes to **Battersby Junction**, with its old signal box and 1907 water crane. Here the train reverses, for the former line west to

Picton was closed long ago. With the Cleveland Hills to the south, and powerful moors all around, the train passes **Kildale**, with its church by the line, and **Commondale**. It is a dramatic landscape of bare moorland, heather and bracken, stone walls and remote farms.

Danby

At **Castleton Moor**, with the village on the hill to the south, the River Esk appears, and the line now follows its meandering course. **Danby**, the home of the North York Moors National Park Centre, is an attractive village, with its medieval bridge, fine church with 1848 chancel, ruined castle and old mill, all near the station. This, all rough stone with stepped gables, is typical of those along the line, many of which are now houses. Note the roundels where the clocks used to be. At **Lealholm** the loveliest section of the journey begins. The line follows the twisting river, criss-crossing the fast-flowing water as it tumbles over rocky ledges, with woods all around and in the distance the skyline of the moors. Lealholm has a good 1902 church by the line, a pretty Wesleyan chapel, and an 18th-century bridge. Even earlier is the humped stone Beggar's Bridge at **Glaisdale**, dated 1619 and, near by, the stone cottages built to serve the old ironworks.

Grosmont

A delightful wooded valley takes the line to **Egton**, with its big Norman-style church of 1878. The village is noted for its annual Gooseberry Show. The train crosses the river high above the cascading water and then it comes to **Grosmont**. Here is the connection with the North Yorkshire

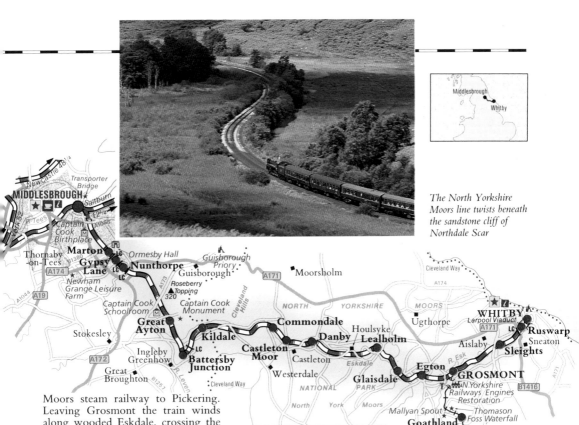

The North Yorkshire Moors line twists beneath the sandstone cliff of Northdale Scar

Moors steam railway to Pickering. Leaving Grosmont the train winds along wooded Eskdale, crossing the rocky river no less than eight times on its way to **Sleights**. Here a fine steel bridge carries the A169 over rail and river, while a footbridge from the station leads to elegant houses. Look out for leaping salmon.

Whitby

The train runs through a more open landscape to **Ruswarp**, its position marked by the tall church spire above the woods ahead. The line now curves round to pass under Larpool viaduct, built in 1885 to carry the line to Scarborough. This marks the start of the excellent approach to Whitby, with fishing boats moored in the now wide river, and the abbey high above the harbour. The journey ends in the 1847 stone station, and all around are the narrow streets of this remarkable resort famous for Captain Cook, jet and kippers.

The ruins of Whitby Abbey, founded in 657, can be seen above the seaside town

NORTH YORKSHIRE MOORS RAILWAY

The North Yorkshire Moors Railway traverses moorland, forest and valley on its way through one of our outstanding National Parks. It dates back to 1836, when George Stephenson himself engineered the line for horse-drawn coaches, which in one place had to be hauled up an incline with a rope counterbalanced by a tank of water. Closed by BR in 1965, passenger services were restarted by the preservation society in 1973.

At **Grosmont** the preserved railway's station adjoins the BR Esk Valley platform, and trains leaving for the south soon plunge into a tunnel. Alongside is the narrow Stephenson-built one, now used for the footpath to the engine sheds. Beyond is a very steep climb at 1 in 49, with fine views to the right before the train enters the steep valley of the Murk Esk. From one of the bridges there is a drop of 100 feet to the cascading water below. At the top of the steepest part of the climb is **Goathland**. Close at hand is Mallyan Spout waterfall, while there are the remains of a Roman road only 2½ miles away.

Beyond Goathland the valley opens out as the summit is reached, enabling the Early Warning station at Fylingdales to be seen near where the route of the famous Lyke Wake Walk crosses the railway. The line twists dramatically between towering sandstone cliffs before reaching the forests that can be explored by the tracks that radiate from **Newtondale Halt**. The next station is at **Levisham**, where iron was once smelted

with the aid of local charcoal. Approaching the terminus at **Pickering**, ruined limekilns remind us of another local industry, while the walls of the castle, set high on the hill above the town, are said to have guarded nearly every medieval king of England.

TRAINS

Grosmont–Pickering 18 miles
Operates: most days from Easter to end October
(Phone for details (0751) 72508)
Single journey: 1hr approx

For tourist information see left-hand panel page 92

A Borders Journey

CARLISLE – NEWCASTLE UPON TYNE 61¾ miles

TRAINS
(1½–2hrs approx)
Mon–Sat 9; Sun 8
Refreshments: some

**Tourist Information
Centres** (*summer only)
Brampton★Moot Hall
(06977) 3433
Carlisle Old Town Hall
(0228) 25517
Corbridge★ Market Place
(043471) 2815
Haltwhistle★ Sycamore St
(0498) 20351
Hexham Manor Office,
Hallgate (0434) 605225
Newcastle upon Tyne
Princess Sq
(091) 2610691

**For all information on
Carlisle see pages 82–3**

Walks
*Northumberland National
Park* Haltwhistle to
Haydon Bridge —
information from the

The Carlisle–Newcastle line, over 150 years old and Britain's first coast to coast railway, is a journey through the distinctive landscape and history of the Borders. It also threads its way through railway history. George Stephenson was born at Wylam, and *Puffing Billy* first ran near by in the 1820s.

Carlisle

When it opened in 1838 the Newcastle and Carlisle Railway connected two major cities across England at its narrowest point, but it remained isolated for some years from the rest of the growing rail network. Despite subsequent development this pioneer cross-country railway has retained much of its distinctive early character, notably

George Stephenson's cottage at Wylam

Northumberland
National Park Centre★ at
Once Brewed, Bardon
Mill

Places to Visit
Note: For Hadrian's Wall
sites near Bardon Mill or
Haydon Bridge, use the
special summer bus
service from Haltwhistle
or Hexham.
Bardon Mill Housesteads
Infantry Museum, NT &
EH; Vindolanda Museum
Brampton By car Lanercost
Priory, EH (summer
only); Naworth Castle
(May–Sep, Wed & Sun)
Corbridge Corstopitum
Museum, EH
Haltwhistle By car/bus
Carvoran Museum
Haydon Bridge By car/bus
Carrawbrough Fort and
Temple, EH
Hexham Middle March
Museum. *By car/bus*
Chesters Fort, EH
Newcastle upon Tyne
Cathedral; Hancock
Museum; John George
Joicey Museum; Laing
Art Gallery; Museum of
Antiquities; Museum of
Science and Engineering
Prudhoe Castle, EH
Stocksfield Hunday
Museum (Apr–Sep)
Wetheral Corby Castle
(grounds Apr–Sep)
Wylam George
Stephenson's Birthplace,
NT (Wed/Thurs, wkends)

its particular style of station buildings. Leaving Carlisle's handsome station, the train turns east, passing under the M6 and then by Scotby's big red stone church of 1854. The first stop is **Wetheral**, but the village with its 16th-century church and priory is best seen from the east as the train crosses the River Eden high up on Giles's five-arched viaduct of 1834. Also in view to the south is Corby Castle, a house gradually developed since the 14th century. The line climbs steadily up towards Naworth, with fine views

over the fells to the south-east interrupted by long wooded cuttings. To the north is steep rolling farmland. There are two more viaducts, the better one carrying the line at an angle over the River Gelt, before the train reaches **Brampton**. The attractive town, with its moot hall and Philip Webb church with excellent Morris & Co stained glass, is to the north and once had its own branch line.

Haltwhistle

With Lanercost Priory and Hadrian's Wall to the north the train runs through a landscape of woods and steep farmland dotted with old houses and barns and into the Irthing valley. The Wall comes nearer, with Roman forts and camps all around and then at

A view of Hadrian's Wall from Housesteads, one of Europe's finest Roman forts

Wetheral Viaduct and the River Eden

The King Edward VII railway bridge is one of six spanning the Tyne

Gilsland the line crosses it, with the old spa village to the north. Curving round, it then crosses the Wall again below the picturesque ruins of Thirlwall Castle. By Greenhead Church the train joins the A69 and follows the road close to Haltwhistle. Here the south Tyne appears, crossed by a range of good bridges, one of which carried the former branch line to Alston with its famous viaducts at Lambley and Burnstones, now to be explored on foot. Haltwhistle, with its excellent early church, spreads north from the Tudor-style station with its matching footbridge and water tower. The train now gently descends the Tyne valley between attractive hills. Look out for a fortified farm at Willimontswick, just west of **Bardon Mill**. This is the stop for Vindolanda Roman Fort and Museum, a short walk to the north.

Hexham
The train crosses the Tyne, the Allen and the Tyne again with fine woods to the south on the way to **Haydon Bridge**, where there is a Roman altar in the old church. The line continues along by the river, alternately narrow and fast-flowing and wide and meandering along the steep-sided valley, the hills broken by woodland. At Fourstones are some old limekilns with a big quarry to the north, and then the train comes to the junction of the South and North Tyne rivers. Ahead is Hexham, with the great abbey up on a hill above the town. The town looks best from the 18th-century bridge over the Tyne, near the station. Hexham was once a busy junction, with a branch south to Allendale and a line north to Scotland

via Reedsmouth, and it still has cast-iron and glazed canopies. After Hexham the big river winds its way through rolling fields. Beaufront Castle of 1841 can be seen to the north and then the train reaches **Corbridge**, with its important early church, Roman fort and 300-year-old bridge.

Wylam
Woods beside the line limit views between **Riding Mill** and **Stocksfield** but the picturesque village of Bywell with its medieval churches, castle and 18th-century hall should not be missed. East of Stocksfield the view becomes more open and soon the train is passing between Ovingham Church with its Saxon tower and 12th-century Prudhoe Castle, easily reached from **Prudhoe** station. The line approaches Wylam on an embankment, with a good view of the old steel railway bridge over the Tyne. The station is one of the oldest in Britain still in regular use. George Stephenson's birthplace can be glimpsed through the trees east of Wylam. Suburbs announce the approach of Newcastle but look out for a large power station by the line, built on the site of Blaydon racetrack. **Blaydon** is just to the east.

Newcastle upon Tyne
The train approaches Newcastle from the south, passing through the new **Metro Centre** and **Dunston** before turning north to enter the city over the King Edward VII bridge, one of the six great high and low level spans across the Tyne here. The railway's triumphal entrance into Newcastle is simply one of the most exciting in Britain, and the great stone station is the perfect introduction to the city.

Wylam Station is one of Britain's oldest

LOOK OUT FOR
As one of the first main lines to be built in Britain, the Newcastle and Carlisle had a distinctive **pioneering style**. Remarkably, this has survived the many changes of the subsequent 150 years, and much can be seen during the journey. Notable are the engineering and architectural features, particularly the great viaducts built in stone to the designs of Francis Giles during the early 1830s. The best, Wetheral, Corby and Gelt, are easily seen from the curving route of the train. Equally distinctive is the large number of original stations, designed in a general Tudor style by Benjamin Green and built in local stone. The best examples are at Haltwhistle, Wylam and Corbridge. In addition, Haltwhistle has a decorative water tower, a fitting memorial to the steam age on a railway that played its part in launching it.

To the North

YORK – BERWICK 147½ miles

The best way to enjoy this route is to change at Newcastle and take the local stopping train to Berwick, which makes it easier to enjoy the view. There is less to see from York to Newcastle, but the route as a whole is one of varied landscape, great cathedrals, splendid engineering and historic railway associations. The East Coast main line was opened throughout in 1852 and has become famous for high speed running.

York

Few cities can boast such a wealth of interest. The Minster, the city walls, the Jorvik Viking Centre, the medieval streets and the Ouse waterfront would on their own be sufficient, yet York is above all the railway city *par excellence*. The heart of a once great railway empire, it is still a major railway administrative centre, and its magnificent 1877 station is a reminder of the great days of the railway. The National Railway Museum is simply the icing on the cake. Trains for the north leave the city past the Railway Museum and then start on the long fast straight line across the Vale of York towards Darlington. There are fine views of the city and its Minster to the south until the train crosses the Ouse. The distant view of the North Yorkshire Moors to the east forms a background. The train passes Dalton with a good view of Butterfield's church of 1868, and reaches **Thirsk**. The town is away to the east, beyond the racecourse. The next station is **Northallerton**, with the powerful early church and the castle mound visible from the train.

Darlington

After Northallerton the line continues straight and level. A long curving cutting leads to the bridge over the Tees, giving a good view of Croft with its red stone church and 15th-century bridge. Darlington is now

ahead, home of the Stockton and Darlington, the first public railway to have a steam locomotive. The station, with its Dutch gables and clocktower, is a suitable memorial to the ambitions of the old North Eastern Railway. The fine 13th-century church is near by, beside the River Skerne. North of Darlington the line winds its way past moorland and mining villages.

Durham

After crossing the Wear and the Browney the line curves towards Durham and one of the visual highlights of the journey. Emerging from a cutting, the train is suddenly on the high 10-arch stone viaduct across a valley to the west, with the cathedral and all the city on display. It is a magnificent sight. The line follows the Wear to **Chester-le-Street** and then runs through Gateshead and Newcastle suburbs before crossing the Tyne for the exciting entry into **Newcastle's** grand station. (For Newcastle see pages 94–5.)

Morpeth

As the train leaves Newcastle there are good views of the city against a background of Tyneside cranes and then the surroundings are suburban until the crossing of the wooded Blyth valley, west of **Cramlington**. Morpeth's ruined castle is away from the station but there are good views west and east from the bridge over the

The glorious medieval Minster in York, standing on the foundations of a Roman fort

TRAINS
(2hrs approx)
Direct: Mon–Sat 10;
Sun 8. More frequent if
change at Newcastle
Refreshments: fast train

**Tourist Information
Centres** (★summer only)
Alnwick★ The Shambles,
Northumberland Hall
(0665) 603129
Darlington Crown St
(0325) 469858; 4773478/9
Durham Market Place
(091) 3843720
Newcastle upon Tyne
Princess Sq (091) 2610691
Thirsk★ 16 Kirkgate
(0845) 22755
York Railway Station
(0904) 643700;
Exhibition Sq
(0904) 21756/7

**For all information on
Newcastle and York
see pages 94–5 and 90–1**

Walks
Cleveland Way York, and
west of Thirsk
Ebor Way passes through
York
Foss Walk from York
Hadrian's Wall from
Newcastle
*North Yorkshire Moors
National Park* west of
Thirsk — details from
Tourist Centres
The Yoredale Way begins
at York Minster

Places to Visit
Alnmouth By car/bus
Alnwick Castle
(Apr–Sep); Warkworth
Castle and Hermitage,
EH. *By car/bus and boat*
Coquet Island
(birdwatching)
Berwick-on-Tweed
Berwick Barracks, EH;
Castle and Town Walls,
EH; Lindisfarne Wine
and Spirit Museum
Chathill By car (or by bus
from Berwick)
Bamburgh Castle
(Apr–Oct, pm); Grace
Darling Museum,
Bamburgh (May–Oct);
Seahouses Marine Life
Centre (Apr–Nov). *By
boat from Seahouses* Farne
Islands (birdwatching)
Chester-le-Street The
Ankers House. *By car/bus*
Beamish Open-air
Museum; Washington
Wildfowl Trust
Darlington Art Gallery;
Museum; Railway Centre
and Museum
Durham Castle; Cathedral
and Treasury; Light
Infantry Museum; Old
Fulling Mill Museum;
Oriental Museum
Morpeth Bagpipe
Museum; The Chantry
Silver; Clock Tower;
Northumbria Craft Centre
Northallerton By car/bus
Mount Grace Priory, EH
& NT (mid Mar–mid
Oct)

Berwick
York

Bamburgh Castle covers an area of about 4¾ acres and can be seen for miles around

Edinburgh 57½

BERWICK-UPON-TWEED

Royal Border Bridge

River Tweed

NORTH SEA

Scremerston
Haggerston
Beal
Holy Island
Lindisfarne
Lindisfarne Priory
Lindisfarne Castle
Lowick
St Cuthbert's Cave
Lighthouse
Grace Darling
Belford
Bamburgh
Marine Life Centre
Seahouses
B6348
Chathill
Chillingham Wild Cattle
Dunstanburgh
B6346
Howick Hall
Alnwick
Alnmouth
Hermitage
Amble
Acklington
A1
A1068
Widdrington
Pegswood
Morpeth
Blyth
Cramlington
Newcastle Airport
Carlisle-Newcastle See page 94-95

Newcastle-upon-Tyne
Gateshead
A1(M)
Wildfowl Trust
Washington
Beamish Open-Air Mus.
Chester-le-Street
Lumley
Plawsworth Viaduct
Durham
Thornley
A1(M)
Spennymoor
Ferryhill
Sedgefield
Bishop Auckland
A167
A177
Newton Aycliffe
Stockton-on-Tees
A66
Darlington
Croft
Great Smeaton
River Tees
North Cowton
A167
A19
Catterick Bridge
Mount Grace Priory
Kirkby Fleetham
Brompton
Northallerton
Thornton-le-Moor
Bedale
Sutton Bank
White Horse
River Swale
Thirsk
B6267
A6
Shandy Hall
Dalton
A19
Topcliffe
Newburgh Priory
A168
Dishforth
Sessay
Devil's Arrows
1322
Easingwold
Boroughbridge
Roman Town
Huby
Sollerton
A1
Beningbrough Hall
Shipton
A59
Skelton
A64
Harrogate 20½
1644
Leeds-York-Scarborough See pages 90-91
YORK
National Railway Museum
Leeds 25¾
Doncaster 32½

National Railway Museum YORK

50TH ANNIVERSARY OF THE WORLD SPEED RECORD FOR STEAM

MALLARD '88

BY TRAIN

Fifty years of the World Speed Record for Steam were marked in 1988 with specially designed Post Office stamps and postcards

---

wooded Wansbeck valley. The next stop is **Pegswood**, with the mines of Ashington forming an interesting skyline to the east before the train crosses an open landscape to **Widdrington**, with a distant view of the sea. After **Acklington**, the best of the original 1847 stations, the line sweeps over the pretty Coquet valley with Warkworth Castle on the horizon to the east.

Alnmouth

South of the station the train runs beside the sea, with good views of Alnmouth and the curving Aln estuary. Alnwick, three miles to the west, once had its own branch line. The route runs inland again to **Chathill**, another original station, where there was a branch line to the pretty fishing port of Seahouses. The landscape now improves, with long views west to Chatton Moor, while to the east is the great bulk of Bamburgh Castle against a background of the sea.

Berwick-on-Tweed

After Budle Bay the train runs by the sea and Holy Island comes into sight, low on the horizon, with the castle clearly visible as well as the lighthouse on Guile Point. As it approaches Berwick the line drops gently towards the rocky shore, seeming to pass through the dunes of this remote coastline before curving inland past Spittal towards Tweedmouth. Berwick is railway theatre at its best. The train slows round a curve and then the 28 arches of Stephenson's great Royal Border Bridge swing into view, sweeping across the Tweed high above the town. The views of the town and the valley of the Tweed to the west are excellent as the train

crosses the 2,160 feet of bridge, 126 feet in the air, to reach the station, also high up on the site of the 12th-century castle. Berwick is a very exciting town, tough, independent and yet surprisingly elegant. The complete Elizabethan town walls shelter a marvellous 17th-century church and some excellent 18th-century buildings, including the barracks of 1719.

From Berwick the main line continues to Edinburgh (see page 109).

BOMBER COMMAND
ROYAL AIR FORCE
STRIKE HARD STRIKE SURE

LOOK OUT FOR

A large number of **Second World War airfields** are near this route. They were mostly built for Bomber Command and are now largely derelict. West of York is Rufforth, but nearer the track are Linton-on-Ouse and Tholthorpe Moor, the latter clearly visible. Further to the north-west is Dishforth, but Dalton and Topcliffe are both close by. Leeming is west of Northallerton, and Croft is right by the line. Further north, Acklington can be seen by the station, while Tughall is just south of Chathill.

0   2 Mls
0   2 Kms

SCOTLAND

Scotland's landscape posed a dramatic challenge to the pioneering builders of the region's railways. On the Glasgow–Mallaig line, built in two parts by separate companies, British Rail still operate steam-hauled trains between Fort William and Mallaig: below, passing Loch Dubh, west of Lochailort

A SPIRIT OF INDEPENDENCE

RAILWAY HISTORY AND ARCHITECTURE

THE RAILWAYS OF SCOTLAND have been an integral part of the network since the formation of British Rail in 1948, but the system is very diverse. Scotland's first railway was probably a horse-drawn colliery tramway in East Lothian, opened in the 1720s. Later in the 18th century other tramways linked the Fife coalfields to the Forth but the railway age did not arrive until the late 1830s. Over the next few decades the fiercely independent Scottish railway companies spread their lines over the country. The Lowlands were well served because of the coalfields and shipyards, but lines were also opened for the north-east's fish trade. The Highlands' wild landscape and sparse population made building difficult and expensive, yet the companies carved their way to Oban, Kyle and, ultimately, Mallaig. In Scotland's remote regions the railway was often the only means of communication. But the system has been pruned throughout this century, and there were massive closures during the Beeching era. However, what remains still gives a unique view of the Scottish landscape.

Railways north of the border have retained their spirit of independence, and the landscape has always imposed its own personality. As a result, architectural features add to the excitement of the scenery.

Most striking are the viaducts and bridges; over 60 Scottish viaducts have listed building status. Some are on closed lines, with major examples at Drygrange, Glenogle, Leslie, Northwater, Connel Ferry (a viaduct which was built for the railway but now carries a road), and Ballindalloch, but many more are in use, ranging in date from the early 1840s to the early 1900s. Some reflect the styles of particular engineers; for example, Joseph Mitchell's iron lattice bridges at Tilt and Oykel.

Equally distinctive are Scottish stations. Among the earliest are the 1847 buildings between Edinburgh and Dundee, their simple classicism best seen at Cupar, Markinch and Ladybank. Among the grander stations are Ayr, Aberdeen and Perth, while croft-style stations can be seen on the Wick and Thurso line. Many are enjoyably eccentric, notably the seaside style used at Troon and the Duke of Sutherland's summer house at Dunrobin. Memorable above all are the stations built by the Highland Railway, whose styles include stone-built Tudor as at Nairn and Pitlochry, and a timber-framed design, as at Aviemore and Carrbridge. Even more attractive are those on the line from Glasgow to Mallaig with their shingled walls and two-tone green paintwork.

WALKING IN THE REGION

This section concentrates on walks that can be done in a few hours or less and are suitable for families. If you plan to follow a walk, contact the local Tourist Information Centre first.

Scotland also offers more challenging hillwalking opportunities. Most Scottish mountains can be climbed in a day. But in some mountains and regions (eg Ben Eighe and others in the north-west) a good route guide, large-scale Ordnance Survey maps and suitable clothing, equipment and experience are essential. Again, TICs will help decide whether a hill or mountain is suitable (see page 7).

Below is a list of mountains that can be reached (some by car or bus) from railway stations.

Beinn Dorain from Bridge of Orchy
Ben Cruachan from Taynuilt
Ben Eighe from Achnasheen
Ben Lui from Tyndrum
Ben More from Crianlarich
Ben Nevis from Fort William
Ben Vrackie from Pitlochry
Cairn Gorm from Aviemore
Cruach Ardrain from Crianlarich

Lairig Ghru from Aviemore
Pentland Hills from Edinburgh
Sgurr a'Mhaim from Fort William
Stob Ban from Fort William
Stobinian from Crianlarich

A selection of closed railways now designated as official footpaths is given below:

Aberdeen to Culter, Cambus O'May to Ballater on the former Deeside line from Aberdeen to Ballater

Ballindalloch-Dufftown (16 miles) on the former Speyside line from Grantown on Spey to Elgin

Dunblane to Lochearnhead (25 miles), part of the former Dunblane to Crianlarich line

Edinburgh to Dalkeith, along part of the former Waverley line

Gatehouse of Fleet to Mossdale (10 miles) on the former Dumfries to Stranraer line

Leuchars to St Andrews (4½ miles) along part of the former Leuchars to Crail line

Stirling to Kippen (10 miles) along part of the former Stirling to Balloch line

Opened in 1890, the
steel Forth Bridge
was for many years
the largest of its
type in the world;
it was designed, at
the Admiralty's
insistence, to soar
to over 360ft,
leaving room for
warships to pass
underneath

The gorge of the River Clyde slices through Lanark's Falls of Clyde nature reserve

Exploring the Lowlands

GLASGOW – CARLISLE 102¼ miles

TRAINS
(1hr 20mins approx)
Mon–Sat 18; Sun 9
Refreshments: some

Tourist Information Centres (*summer only)
Carlisle Old Town Hall, Green Market
(0228) 25517
Glasgow St Vincent Pl
(041) 227 4880
Motherwell★ Hamilton Rd
(0698) 51311

For all information on Carlisle see pages 82–83

Walks
Falls of Clyde Nature Reserve south-west of Carstairs
Glasgow parks nature trails and walks
Hadrian's Wall from Carlisle
The West Highland Way starts at Milngavie, outside Glasgow

Places to Visit
Glasgow Art Gallery and Museum; The Barras (wkend market); Burrell Collection; Cathedral; Custom House Quay; Haggs Castle; Hutchesons' Hall, NTS; Museum of Transport; People's Palace; Pollok House; Provand's Lordship; Regimental Headquarters, Royal Highland Fusiliers; Scottish Design Centre; The Stock Exchange — Scottish; The Tenement House (Apr–Oct, winter wkends pm); Third Eye Centre
For some places in Glasgow you may need to travel by car or bus. Both the bus station and the Tourist Information Centre are a short walk from Glasgow Central Station.
Motherwell Barons Haugh RSPB Reserve; Strathclyde Country Park

The first Anglo–Scottish route, opened in 1848, and now part of the high speed west coast main line, the journey from Glasgow to Carlisle explores the upper Clyde valley, the Lowther Hills and Annandale on its way to the Solway Firth and the border, linking Lowland scenery with centuries of Scottish history.

High speed trains make few stops, so for a leisurely view of the Clyde valley you have to take a local train from Glasgow to Lanark, or change at Motherwell.

Glasgow
The train leaves the splendid portals of Glasgow Central and makes the first of many crossings of the Clyde, for much of the route follows the river virtually to its source in the Lowther Hills. There are good views of the city and its spires and then the train speeds eastwards through Rutherglen, Cambuslang and Newton before it leaves Glasgow behind and enters a more rural landscape near Uddingston. There are good views of Bothwell and Hamilton from the line's elevated

A fireworks display at the Finnieston Shipyard in Glasgow

route on the eastern side of the valley, while Motherwell and the Clyde are well seen from the big stone viaduct north of **Motherwell** station. After Ravenscraig steelworks, the landscape improves, with open farmland allowing views across the Clyde valley to the hills beyond. Carluke station is well to the west of its town and then Lanark can be seen across the rolling landscape to the south, set on a hill above the river and linked by a branch line. The Lanark hills are far to the south, particularly the rounded top of Lochlyock. **Carstairs Junction**, a railway village surrounding the station, marks the connection with the line from Edinburgh and many trains to the South West and south coast of England are still joined or divided here.

Lockerbie
South of Carstairs the train crosses the Clyde and then follows the river south through an attractive and increasingly hilly landscape. The line sweeps up the Clyde valley, dominated by the conical summit of Tinto to the west and the bare rounded tops of its flanking hills. It swings round the steep sides of Scaut Hill and then follows the old Roman road up the valley. All along the route are little villages which once had stations, Symington, Lamington, Abington and Crawford and the station buildings can often be identified, attractively set against the background of flowing hills. Here and there the hillsides are defaced by particularly boring forestry plantations, looking notably out of place in this richly varied landscape. The pretty red

church at Elvanfoot stands above the line and then the train swings east into the Lowther Hills, crossing the Clyde for the last time, Glasgow's great river now little more than a stream. The line climbs steadily to Beattock summit (1,028ft/313m) and then it begins its descent along the Annan valley passing through Beattock with good views eastwards towards Moffat, which once enjoyed its own branch line. Gradually the hills recede and, as the valley widens, a more pastoral landscape of rolling farmland takes over, broken by pleasant pockets of woodland. A long cutting precedes **Lockerbie**, the only station still open of the original 18 between Carstairs and Carlisle, and so the town with its skyline of red stone spires is best seen from the south. The town hall with its Flemish-style belfry is right by the station.

Carlisle
South of Lockerbie the train crosses the wooded valley of the coffee-coloured Water of Milk and then speeds across flat farm- and woodland towards the Solway Firth, with the A74 close by. The line curves round Ecclefechan and then passes close to a Roman fort, visible to the east beside Mein Water. The former branch to Annan snakes away to the south and then Kirtlebridge Church looms above the trees, followed by Robgill Tower, an excellent fortified house set high above the Kirtle Water. Solway Firth can now be seen to the south, with the English shore clearly visible across the expanse of water. Passing Quintinshill, the scene of the worst-ever accident in British railway history, the train skirts Gretna and crosses the Sark, where a lineside notice marks the border. Just to the north is the junction with the more leisurely route from Glasgow to Carlisle via Kilmarnock and Dumfries. The line now goes straight across the low-lying estuary of the Esk, passes the extensive but little used marshalling yards at Rockcliffe, crosses the Eden and enters Carlisle with good views of the castle and the cathedral.

For Carlisle see pages 82–83

The Devil's Beef Tub in the Lowther Hills, where the line reaches over 1,000ft

Carlyle's birthplace at Ecclefechan

LOOK OUT FOR
The route from Glasgow to Carlisle reflects many of the diverse facets of **Scottish history**. Rutherglen takes its name from the legendary King Reuther, who flourished about 200BC, while Robert the Bruce met the spider in a cave near Kirkpatrick. For much of the route the line follows a Roman road and some forts survive, while medieval and later fortified towers at Beattock and Kirtlebridge underline the stormy history of the borders. Moffat is the burial place of both the famous roadmaker Macadam and the creator of the Ossian legend, Macpherson, while Thomas Carlyle was born in Ecclefechan. The reformer Robert Owen's revolutionary industrial village at New Lanark was founded in 1784, while the nearby steel mills at Ravenscraig produced the steel for the *Queen Mary* and the *Queen Elizabeth*. Finally Gretna station was for decades the introduction to Scotland for runaway lovers.

TRAINS
(2hrs 14mins approx)
Mon–Sat 2 + 2 change
at Ayr; Sun 1
Refreshments: some

**Tourist Information
Centres** (*summer only)
Ayr Sandgate
(0292) 284196
Girvan★ Bridge St
(0465) 4950
Glasgow St Vincent Pl
041–227 4880
Prestwick★ Boydfield
Gdns
(0292) 79946
Stranraer★ Port Rodie
(0776) 2595
Troon★ Municipal Bldgs,
South Beach
(0292) 317696

**For all information on
Glasgow see pages
102–3**

Walks
Culzean Country Park,
NTS walks and trails,
west of Maybole
Glasgow parks nature trails
and walks
Rozelle Nature Trails from
near the centre of Ayr
The Southern Upland Way
passes Stranraer
The West Highland Way
starts at Milngavie, on
the edge of Glasgow

Cycling
Glasgow–Irvine Cycle
Path; Stranraer circular
route (see pages 5–7)

Places to Visit
Ayr Auld Kirk
(July–Aug); Leudoun
Hall (mid July–Aug);
Tam o'Shanter Museum.
By car/bus 2m south at
Alloway: Burns Cottage
and Museum; Burns
Monument (Apr–mid
Oct); Land o'Burns
Centre
Girvan By car Bargany
Gardens (Mar–Oct)
Irvine The Heckling Shop
and Glasgow Vennel;
Scottish Maritime
Museum (mid Apr–mid
Oct). *By car/bus* Eglinton
Castle
Johnstone 1½m at
Kilbarchan: Weaver's
Cottage, NTS (Apr–Oct)
Kilwinning Dalgarven
Mill; Kilwinning Abbey,
SDD
Lochwinnoch Castle
Semple Country Park;
Community Museum;
RSPB Nature Reserve
and Visitor Centre
Maybole Collegiate
Church, SDD. *By car*
Crossraguel Abbey,
SDD; Culzean Castle and
Country Park
(Apr–Oct); Souter
Johnnie's Cottage,
Kirkoswald, NTS
(Etr–Oct)
Stranraer Museum. *By car*
Castle Kennedy Gardens
(Apr–Sep); Glenluce
Abbey, SDD

Through Burns Country
GLASGOW – STRANRAER   *101 miles*

The journey from Glasgow to Stranraer is a leisurely exploration of Scotland past and present, linking together industries old and new, ports, harbours and the seaside, golf and horseracing, the life and times of Robert Burns, distilleries and the delightfully pastoral scenery of Dumfries and Galloway.

Glasgow
Frequent fast electric trains leave Glasgow Central for Ayr but only a few diesel Super Sprinters continue to Stranraer. The train crosses the Clyde as it leaves the station and then the line runs through largely industrial surroundings to **Paisley** and **Johnstone**. West of Johnstone, suburbs and industry give way to rolling farmland as the train skirts two lochs to reach **Lochwinnoch**, set in a pleasantly rural landscape with a distant view of the moors to the west. The train now crosses a region of old mines and closed railways to **Glengarnock**, and then it runs beside the River Garnock to **Dalry** and **Kilwinning**, the latter with a good range of old stone station buildings. A branch leads to Ardrossan and Largs.

Ayr
An elevated route across the Garnoch and Irvine estuaries leads to **Irvine**. South of the station is a landscape of dunes and saltmarsh and the long curving beach that leads to **Barassie** and **Troon**, along with the first of the many golf courses that flank the line. Troon's harbour and church spires can be seen to the west, away from the jolly half-timbered station. The train continues southwards, passing the international airport north of **Prestwick**, **Newton-on-Ayr** and Ayr racecourse. Approaching **Ayr** there is a fine view west towards the

bridges and harbour as the train crosses the River Ayr. The station, large and decorative with its vast 1886 red stone French-style hotel, is a good introduction to this popular holiday resort. South of Ayr the line is immediately more rural, winding its way through a soft landscape dotted with white painted farms. After crossing the wooded River Doon the train comes to the quiet town of **Maybole**, the stop for Culzean Castle and Turnberry golf course, a few miles to the west off the A719.

Girvan
Continuing south the train passes Crossraguel Abbey to the west. The line follows the Water of Girvan with a brief view of Dailly and its castles. Approaching Girvan the valley widens, allowing sight of a skyline of spires above the twisting river. Little can be seen of the attractive harbour and beach. The best view of Girvan is from the south as the train climbs into the hills, and far out to sea is the sharp outline of Ailsa Craig, a granite rock 1,114 feet (338m) high. When clear, Arran and the Mull of Kintyre can be seen in the distance. The everwinding line swings inland, making its way up through woods to Pinmore tunnel, and then it drops steeply to the Stinchar valley, crossing the curving viaduct of 1877 with its ten stone arches. The train follows the River Stinchar through woods to Pinwherry, a

Culzean Castle, on Culzean Bay, can be reached from Maybole station

Suburban rail routes and motorway junctions in Glasgow have been omitted from this map because of limited space.

Glasgow
Stranraer

River Clyde

Gourock 26¼
Wemyss Bay 31

River Gryfe

Helensburgh 24¼

Glasgow (Abbotsinch) Airport

GLASGOW CENTRAL

Bridge of Weir

Weaver's Cottage

Kilbarchan ★

Johnstone

Paisley Gilmour Street

Glasgow–Mallaig
See pages 106-107

Glasgow–Carlisle
See pages 102-103

Edinburgh 47¼
Carlisle 102¼

Castle Semple Loch

Community Museum M

Howwood

Lochwinnoch

R Garnock

Kilbirnie Loch

Beith

Glengarnock

Dalry

Dalgarven Mill

Stewarton

Kilwinning

Abbey

Eglinton Castle

Largs 16

★ Irvine

Irvine Bay

Barassie

Troon

Ayr Bay

Prestwick Airport

Prestwick

Newton-on-Ayr

Ayr

Alloway

278 Brown Carrick Hill

281 Knoweside Hill

R. Ayr

Martnaham Loch

River Doon

B7023

Maybole

Collegiate Church

Culzean

Turnberry Golf Course ★

Crossraguel Abbey

Kirkoswald

Souter Johnnie's Cottage

Dailly

Bargany

Auchensoul Hill 314

Girvan

296 Trowier Hill

Pinmore Tunnel

Pinmore Viaduct

Lendalfoot

259

Knockdaw Hill

Pinwherry

Kildonan Convent

River Stinchar

Water of Tig

Ballantrae

Barrhill

Beneraird 437

321

Carlock Hill

A77

Mid Moile

Portencalzie

Penwhirn Reservoir

Braid Fell

234

Castle Kennedy

Loch Connell

Leswalt

STRANRAER

181

Cairn Pat

Portpatrick

Black Loch

White Loch

Former line to Dumfries

305 Benbrake Hill

Laggangairn Standing Stones

Glenwhilly

Southern Upland Way

New Luce

204 Bught Fell

Glenluce Abbey

Glenluce

Stair Haven

Luce Bay

Sandhead

0   2 Mls
0   2 Kms

Good fishing, an attractive harbour and sandy beaches can all be enjoyed at the resort of Girvan

pretty setting where the Duisk meets the Stinchar, and then it climbs again, with fine views to the east of fields broken by patches of woodland. The brown stone façade of Kildonan Convent stands in the valley, surrounded by gardens, and then the train stops at the remote **Barrhill** station, with its flowers, old clock and signal box.

Stranraer

The landscape now changes as the train winds its way up through open moorland, with long views south across Colmonell, and desolate and empty scenery as the line follows the fast-flowing Cross

The birthplace of the great poet Robert Burns in Alloway

Water of Luce. At New Luce, where the two Waters of Luce come together, the moors are left behind and the train drops down towards Glenluce and the sea through a more pastoral landscape of woods and stone-walled fields. The river valley widens steadily, and the ruins of Glenluce Abbey can clearly be seen to the east. Swinging west, the line now joins the former main line from Carlisle to Stranraer via Dumfries, its trackbed visible to the south, and suddenly the sea comes into view. The train now quickly crosses the peninsula to Loch Ryan, with Castle Kennedy hidden by woods to the north and then, after passing the junction with the former branch to Portpatrick, it runs to the east of Stranraer town and out on to the causeway that leads to the **Harbour** station, and the end of the line. There are ferries from here to Larne and the Isle of Man, but only the occasional boat trains give a hint of how busy the harbour was in its heyday.

LOOK OUT FOR

The Stranraer line has two notable features, one literary and one sporting. Linking, as it does, Glasgow with Dumfries and Galloway, the line is rich in **Burns associations**. Ayr is, above all, a Burns town. A statue of the poet stands in a park by the station, the old Tam o'Shanter Inn is now a Burns museum and the 13th-century Auld Brig of Burns's poem, *The Brigs of Ayr*, can be seen as the train crosses the River Ayr north of the station. Alloway, where Burns was born in 1759, is two miles to the south and the poet's humble birthplace is another museum. South of Ayr the landscape has distinct Burns echoes.

More tangible than Burns are the many **golf courses** close to the line. The coast from Irvine south to Girvan is one of golf's heartlands, with at least ten golf courses visible from the train, and others only a few miles away. The best known are Troon and Turnberry, both from time to time the venue for the British Open and other major tournaments.

Climbing Strathfillan en route to Tyndrum Upper

Below: Loch Shiel, on the line to Mallaig

TRAINS
(5hrs 15mins approx)
Change at Fort William
Mon–Sat 4 (additional
summer services Fort
William–Mallaig, some
steam-hauled); Sun: 2
Glasgow–Fort William
(1 on to Mallaig), plus
June–Sep (steam-hauled)
Fort William–Mallaig
Refreshments: some

**Tourist Information
Centres** (★summer only)
Fort William Tourist
Board (0397) 3781
Glasgow 35–9 St Vincent
Pl 041–227 4880
Helensburgh★ Clock
Tower (0436) 2642
Mallaig★ Information
Centre (0687) 2170
Tarbet Pier Road
(03012) 260
Tyndrum★ Car Park
(08384) 246

**For all information on
Glasgow see pages
102–3**

Walks
Caledonian Canal towpath
from Banavie
Glasgow parks nature trails
and walks
West Highland Way from
Glasgow, Crianlarich,
Tyndrum, Bridge of
Orchy, Fort William

Places to Visit
Arisaig By boat to the
islands of Rhum, Eigg
and Muck (summer only)
Banavie Neptune's
Staircase canal locks. *By
boat* pleasure cruises
along the Caledonian
Canal (summer only)
Beasdale Loch Nan Uamh
Cairn
Dumbarton Castle, SDD
Fort William Old
Inverlochy Castle, SDD;
Scottish Crafts and Ben
Nevis Exhibition
(Etr–Nov); West
Highland Museum
Glenfinnan Glenfinnan
Monument and Visitor
Centre, NTS (Apr–Oct)
Helensborough The Hill
House, NTS; *MV
Kenilworth* cruises to
Gourock, Kilcreggan and
Holy Loch (May–Sep)
Mallaig By boat summer
island cruises to Rhum,
Eigg, Muck, Skye. Skye:
Clan Donald Centre
(Apr–Oct) and Armadale
Gardens
Spean Bridge Commando
Memorial (1m)

West Highland Line

GLASGOW – MALLAIG   164¼ miles

Born out of the rivalry between the Caledonian and the North British Railways for the west coast fish trade, the West Highland line was opened in two stages, from Glasgow to Fort William in 1894, and the section to Mallaig in 1901. Now tourism is the mainstay of this spectacular route — one of the best railway journeys in Britain.

Glasgow
The train leaves the handsome glazed train shed of Glasgow's Queen Street station, and then negotiates the steep Cowlairs tunnel. It then runs west along the Clyde, passing below the Erskine Bridge, to **Dumbarton**, where there is a good view of the rock and castle just east of the fine 1896 Central station. There are views from Cardross across the Firth of Clyde to Port Glasgow and Newark Castle, with Dunoon and Holy Loch in the distance. Swinging inland to **Helensburgh Upper**, the train climbs through woods above Gare Loch to **Garelochhead**, with a good view over the Faslane naval base. The station is the first in the Arts and Crafts cum Swiss style typical of the line. Now the train crosses to Loch Long and climbs above the loch. At the head of the loch, dwarfed by the bulk of the Cobbler, is the pretty resort of Arrochar, served by **Arrochar and Tarbet** station, and then the train crosses the neck of land that separates Loch Long from the fresh water of Loch Lomond. Ahead are wonderful views of Loch Lomond, anticipating the delightful stretch high above the loch through woods and over waterfalls to **Ardlui**.

Crianlarich
The train now climbs steadily up Glen Falloch and curves over Dubh Eas on a big viaduct. From Crianlarich, the junction with the Oban branch, the train climbs up Strathfillan high above the River Fillan and the Oban line to **Tyndrum Upper**. Clinging to the hillside the line rounds the great Horseshoe Curve between Beinn Odhar and Beinn Dorain, with magnificent views from the two curving viaducts. Look back to see the Horseshoe at its best. From **Bridge of Orchy**, high above Loch Tulla, the train turns east and enters the wilderness of Rannoch Moor. This vast desert of peat bogs, heather, streams and lochs was crossed by floating the line on a bed of branches carrying thousands of tons of ash and earth. At its heart is remote **Rannoch** station. Crossing a big viaduct the train continues north to the 1,350ft (411m) summit at Corrour. **Corrour** station looks down towards Loch Ossian at the foot of Beinn na Lap.

Fort William
The line drops along Loch Treig and curves round to **Tulloch**. The train now runs west along Glen Spean into the spectacular Monessie Gorge. It

A scenic journey along the shore of Loch Eil

Crianlarich-Oban
See page 108

Glasgow-Stranraer
See pages 104-105

Glasgow-Carlisle
See pages 102-103

Suburban rail routes and motorway junctions in Glasgow have been omitted from this map because of limited space.

thunders through the vertical rock walls on a narrow ledge and then the valley opens out again to **Roy Bridge**. The next stop is **Spean Bridge**, with the old branch to Fort Augustus, and then the train runs to Fort William, passing Inverlochy Castle hotel, with Ben Nevis filling the horizon.

Fort William – Mallaig

Leaving Fort William, the Mallaig train branches west, crosses the River Lochy with the old Inverlochy Castle ruins near by, and goes on to **Banavie**. Just beyond the station is the 1901 swing bridge over the Caledonian Canal. The next stop is **Corpach**, with its huge paper mill, and then the train sets off along the shore of Loch Eil. **Loch Eil Outward Bound** and **Locheilside** overlook the loch and then the line starts to climb steeply through the rocks towards **Glenfinnan**. Set on a sharp curve is the 21-arched viaduct, with a magnificent view down to Loch Shiel and the Glenfinnan Monument. The line now winds through rock cuttings and along by Loch Eilt, and then it follows the river Ailort to **Lochailort**. It carves its exciting way past the head of the loch, coming to the Atlantic high above the rocky bays of Loch Nan Uamh. After **Beasdale** the train runs inland through rocks and woods to **Arisaig**, where there are fine views of Eigg and Rhum, far out across the wild shore. Turning north, the train now passes the sandy bays of the Morar estuary, with Loch Morar and its monster, Morag, to the east. From **Morar** station the line drops to **Mallaig**, with views out to the islands. The station overlooks the busy harbour against the background of Skye.

LOOK OUT FOR

The West Highland Railway to Fort William, although a late arrival on the national railway map, achieved a **distinctive style** and, surprisingly, this can still be enjoyed today. Notable are the stations with their blend of Arts and Crafts and Swiss styling, their walls hung with wooden shingles and their decoration in two tones of green. Good examples are at Helensburgh Upper, Arrochar and Tarbet, Garelochhead, Tyndrum Upper, Bridge of Orchy and Rannoch. Another feature of the line is the large steel viaducts on their tall masonry piers, with the most spectacular being the two on the great Horseshoe Curve north of Tyndrum. **Dramatic engineering** is also a feature of the line to Mallaig, with its numerous rock cuttings, eleven tunnels, gradients up to 1 in 48 and above all its bridges and viaducts. The best are those at Glenfinnan, Loch Nan Uamh and Morar, while the most distinctive is the castellated viaduct at Borrodale. Despite its appearance this, like all the others, was built in concrete, a pioneer use of the new material on so large a scale. Other engineering features of the line are at the Caledonian Canal just beyond Banavie station, where there is a 1901 swing bridge across the canal with its own signal box, and Telford's great flight of locks to the north.

The Glenfinnan viaduct, running through dramatic mountain scenery, is 416 yards of elegant concrete, and boasts no fewer than 21 arches

Hills and Lochs of Strathclyde

CRIANLARICH – OBAN   41¾ miles

Completed in 1880, the branch from Crianlarich to Oban was originally built as an extension of the Dunblane and Callander Railway and is now the only surviving part of that company's network. It is still a delightful journey to its terminus at Oban, an old port busy with steamer services to the islands.

TRAINS
(1hr 10mins approx)
Mon–Sat 4; Sun 2
No refreshments

All trains run through to and from Glasgow

Tourist Information
Centres (*summer only)
Oban Argyll Sq
(0631) 63122
Tyndrum* Car Park
(08384) 246

Walks
West Highland Way join at Tyndrum
Fearnoch Forest, Glen Nant Trail 2m south of Taynuilt

Places to Visit
Connel By car
Dunstaffnage Castle and Chapel, SDD
Dalmally By car Kilchurn Castle, SDD
Oban Cathedral; Highland Discovery Centre (Apr–Sep); McCaig's Tower; Oban Glass.
Taynuilt Bonawe Iron Furnace (Apr–Sep)

The train for Oban branches west off the Fort William line at **Crianlarich**, a remote station built in the 1880s to serve the meeting of the West Highland and Callander & Oban railways. The remains of the latter's main line east can be seen north of the station. The train runs along Strath Fillan, with the Fort William line visible for several miles high on the northern valley side. Entering the woods the train reaches **Tyndrum Lower** and then swings west into Argyll along Glen Lochy. The line drops through the hills, overlooked by peaks to the south, then reaches **Dalmally**, where the red stone station with its glazed canopy was in the 1870s the terminus of the line until money was raised to complete the extension to Oban. The train then swings round the head of Loch Awe, with excellent views of ruined Kilchurn Castle, a stronghold of the Campbell clan, and the loch beyond. **Loch Awe** station, recently reopened, has a small pier offering steamer trips on the loch in the summer. The line now curves along the water's edge. **Falls of**

Cruachan halt stands near the hydro-electric power station and then, as the loch narrows sharply, the train enters the narrow rock-walled Pass of Brander. With Ben Cruachan to the north and the steep screes to the south, this is a dramatic stretch. Passing white Inverawe House, the train turns west to **Taynuilt**. The line now runs beside Loch Etive, through woods and rock cuttings, with views across the water to Benderloch, and then the great steel cantilever bridge at **Connel Ferry** comes into view, striding over the Falls of Lora. Built in 1903 to carry the branch line north to Ballachulish, it is now a road bridge. The train soon winds its way into the hills and steeply down again to enter **Oban** by a circuitous route that gives ample opportunity to admire the views of the town and its harbour, its handsome Victorian stone buildings and, up above, the extraordinary colosseum known as McCaig's Tower. A traditional resort created by the railway and the steamers, Oban is a delightful place and the perfect introduction to the islands.

An autumn view of Loch Awe, towards the ruined Campbell stronghold of Kilchurn Castle

Over the Forth and the Tay

EDINBURGH – DUNDEE *59¼ miles*

The Edinburgh to Dundee line runs close to the sea for much of its route, but its main features are the original 1847 stations and the two great Victorian bridges that cross the Firths of Forth and Tay. Take a local train and sit right from Edinburgh for the best views.

The train leaves Edinburgh's **Waverley** station with the towering walls of the castle and the Scott Memorial high above the line. Leaving the suburbs, it swings north past the airport and crosses the River Almond. The great steel spans of the Forth Bridge can be seen ahead as the train climbs through **Dalmeny**. Crossing the bridge, with its 360-foot towers, is exciting, with wonderful views. Designed by Sir John Fowler and Sir Benjamin Baker and completed in 1890, the bridge used 51,000 tons of steel and cost about £3 million. The train enters Fife, passes **North Queensferry** and then curves round the Inner Bay to **Inverkeithing**, with its new station. The next station is **Aberdour**, and then the train runs along the shore past little harbours and offshore islands with, far to the south, Edinburgh and the Pentland Hills. Curving round **Burntisland** with its ancient harbour, the line hugs the rocky shore to **Kinghorn**. The domestic-style stone station of the 1840s is a happy survivor. The train reaches **Kirkcaldy** and then swings inland, a viaduct taking the line over the wooded Leven valley south of **Markinch**, the stop for Glenrothes. After **Ladybank**, the train winds through hills to **Springfield** and **Cupar**, following the River Eden down to its estuary. **Leuchars** is the stop for St Andrews, whose university, cathedral and golf courses were once served by a branch line. The train now turns inland. There are distant views of the Tay, then the train curves past Wormit as the Tay bridge comes

into view. The present bridge, completed in 1887, is the second, for the first, opened in 1878, partially collapsed during a storm in December 1879, casting a train and 75 passengers and crew into the waters below. The old piers of the original bridge can still be seen. At its northern end the bridge curves and the train makes an impressive approach to **Dundee**, along Tayside.

TRAINS
(1hr 20mins approx)
Mon–Sat 20; Sun 12
Refreshments: most

Tourist Information
Centres (*summer only)
*Cupar** Fluthers Car Park
(0334) 52874
Dundee Nethergate
Centre (0382) 27723
Edinburgh Princes St
(031) 557 1700
Kirkcaldy Esplanade
(0592) 267775

Walks
Edinburgh City Centre
Walks; Seafield Walkway
and River Almond
Walkway

Places to Visit
Aberdour Castle, SDD. *By boat* Inchcolm Abbey, SDD
Cupar Sir Douglas Bader Garden for the Disabled
Dalmeny Dalmeny House (May–Sep)
Dundee Barrack Street Museum; Claypotts Castle, SDD (Apr–Sep); RRS *Discovery* (May–Sep); Mills Observatory
Edinburgh Castle, SDD; Cathedral; Georgian House, NTS (Apr–Nov); Huntly House; John Knox's House; Museum of Childhood; National Gallery of Scotland; Outlook Tower and Camera Obscura; Palace of Holyroodhouse; Royal Botanic Garden; Royal Museum of Scotland; Scott Monument; Scottish National Portrait Gallery
Kirkcaldy Museum and Art Gallery. *By car/bus* Ravenscraig Castle, SDD
Leuchars Norman Church

The massive Forth Bridge, which celebrates its centenary in 1990

The Heart of Scotland
STIRLING – INVERNESS *151½ miles*

TRAINS
(3hrs 15mins approx)
Mon–Sat 8; Sun 3
Refreshments: some

**Tourist Information
Centres** (*summer only)
Aviemore Main Rd
(0479) 810363
*Carrbridge** Car Park
(047984) 630
*Dunblane** Stirling Rd
(0786) 824428
*Dunkeld** The Cross
(03502) 688
Inverness Church St
(0463) 234353
*Kingussie** King St
(05402) 297
Perth Marshall Pl
(0738) 38353
Pitlochry Atholl Rd
(0796) 2215/2751
Stirling Dumbarton Rd
(0786) 75019

Walks
Birnam Hill from
Dunkeld
Craigellachie Nature Trail
from Aviemore
*Craigower Hill, Dunmore
Trail* 1½m north of
Pitlochry
Glenmore Forest Park 6m
east of Aviemore
Kinnoull Hill Trail from
Perth

Cycling
Stirling, circular route
(see pages 5–7)

Places to Visit
Aviemore Aviemore
Centre; Cairngorm
Whisky Centre;
Rothiemurchus Estate
Visitor Centre
Blair Atholl Blair Castle
(Apr–mid Oct)
Carrbridge Landmark
Visitor Centre
Dunblane Cathedral, SDD
Dunkeld Bridge;
Cathedral, SDD. *By car*
The Hermitage, NTS
Inverness Cathedral;
Museum and Art Gallery
Kingussie Highland Folk
Museum; Ruthven
Barracks, SDD. *By car*
Highland Wildlife Park
(closed winter)
Perth Art Gallery and
Museum; Balhousie
Castle; Branklyn Garden,
NTS (Mar–Oct);
Caithness Glass
(Etr–Sep); Fair Maid's
House Gallery (crafts);
Round House; St John's
Kirk. *By car*
Huntingtower Castle,
SDD; Scone Palace
(Etr–Oct)
Pitlochry Power Station
and Dam. *By car*
Killiecrankie Visitors
Centre (Apr–Oct); Pass
of Killiecrankie, NTS
Stirling Argyll and
Sutherland Highlanders'
Museum; Castle, SDD;
Cathedral, SDD;
Guildhall; Mars Wark,
SDD; Smith Art Gallery
and Museum

T he route from Stirling to Inverness is probably the most exciting main line journey in Britain, a dramatic progress from gentle hills and wandering rivers to the capital of the Highlands via the bleak heights of the Cairngorms. There can be no better *entrée* to the real heart of Scotland.

Stirling
With its decorative stonework, crenellations, circular ticket office and floral displays, Stirling station is a good introduction to the town. Leaving the station the line crosses the River Forth on a pair of handsome iron bridges, built side by side by rival companies. Look back for a good view of Stirling, with the castle forming a dramatic skyline. Passing Bridge of Allan on the hillside to the east, the train comes to **Dunblane**, with the cathedral attractively set beside Allan Water. The line now follows the river's oxbow bends. **Gleneagles** is a pretty station with decorative woodwork. The train now runs through a rolling landscape, broken by woodland. Winding through the hills, the line makes a dramatic entrance to Perth.

Perth
Perth has a large and impressive station, designed by Sir William Tite in 1847, which, in its heyday, served the trains of the Highland, Caledonian and North British Railways. Queen Victoria would take her breakfast in the Royal Waiting Room here on her way to Balmoral. Leaving the station, the train passes Scone Palace and Huntingtower Castle. At Stanley Junction the line swings north, away from the former main line to Forfar and Aberdeen, and then the hills close in as the train climbs through the Pass of Birnam, high above the wooded Tay, to **Dunkeld**. The fine Tudor-style barge-boarded station of 1856 is actually in Birnam. West of the station are the decorative stone bridges and tunnel entrance built to blend with the Duke of Atholl's Hermitage pleasure garden and then the train follows the wooded Tay and Tummel valleys to **Pitlochry**. After Pitlochry's gabled station with its cast-iron fountain, the line starts its climb up towards the Pass of Killiecrankie, with the River Garry, the A9 and the remains of General Wade's military road close by. The next stop is **Blair Atholl**, with the white bulk of the castle just north of the station, and then the line continues its climb up the Garry valley and into moorland with the Badenoch mountains ahead.

Kingussie
The ascent to Druimuachdar, at 1,484 feet (452m) the highest main line summit in Britain, is a splendid journey through bare and powerful mountains. Civilisation returns at **Dalwhinnie**

with its hotel and distillery decorated with pagodas, and then the line turns north-east along Glen Truim and down into the Spey valley. The Cairngorms can now be seen in the distance as the train follows the valley of the Spey to **Newtonmore** and **Kingussie** stations, both of 1863. The line continues along the Spey, passing the Highland Wildlife Park and the sailing centre of Loch Insh with the Cairngorms filling the horizon to the east. At **Aviemore** the decorative timber and cast-iron station is well placed for the Aviemore Centre, while to the east are the locomotives and sheds of the Strathspey Steam Railway (see panel opposite). Leaving the Spey, the line makes its way through woodland to **Carrbridge**, before turning west into a more rugged landscape.

Inverness
After climbing again the train then drops down into Strathdearn to cross the River Findhorn. Continuing along the valley the train curves round towards Culloden, set into the hillside high above the River Nairn. The Moray Firth can now be seen ahead and then the great red stone viaduct comes into view, its 28 elegant arches

carrying the line high above the River Nairn. The train now passes the site of the 1746 Battle of Culloden, then drops down towards Inverness, with fine views across the Moray Firth. Inverness station marks the start of two dramatic Highland routes, the lines to Kyle of Lochalsh (pages 112–13) and Wick/Thurso (pages 116–17).

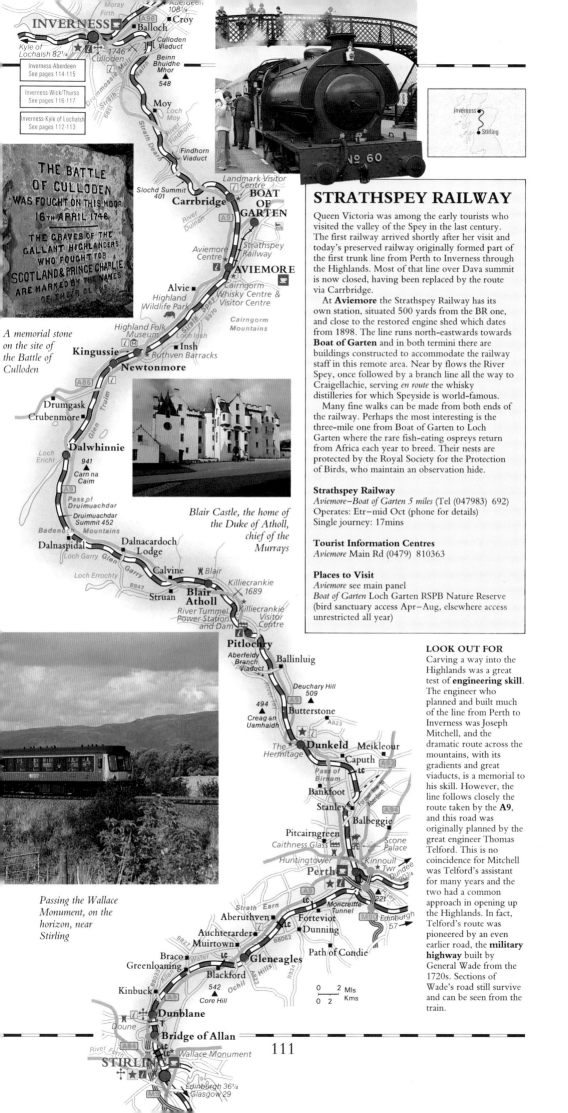

INVERNESS
Moray Firth
Kyle of Lochalsh 82¼
★ ⚓ ♿ ⌨
Aberdeen 108¼
Balloch
Croy
Culloden Viaduct
1746 ✕ Culloden
Drummossie Muir
A96
Beinn Bhuidhe Mhor
548

Inverness-Aberdeen
See pages 114-115

Inverness-Wick/Thurso
See pages 116-117

Inverness-Kyle of Lochalsh
See pages 112-113

Moy
Loch Moy
Strath Dearn
Loch Findhorn

Findhorn Viaduct

Landmark Visitor Centre
Slochd Summit 401
River Dulnan
Carrbridge
A9
BOAT OF GARTEN
RSPB
Strathspey Railway
Aviemore Centre
AVIEMORE

Alvie
Highland Wildlife Park
Cairngorm Whisky Centre & Visitor Centre
B970
Loch Insh
Cairngorm Mountains

Highland Folk Museum M
Kingussie
Ruthven Barracks
Insh
Newtonmore
A86

Drumgask
Crubenmore
Glen Truim

Dalwhinnie
941 ▲ Carn na Caim
Loch Ericht

A9
Pass of Druimuachdar
Druimuachdar Summit 452
Badenoch Mountains
Loch Garry
Dalnaspidal
Dalnacardoch Lodge
Glen Garry
Loch Errochty
B847
Calvine
✕ Blair
Struan
Blair Atholl
Killiecrankie ✕ 1689
River Tummel Power Station and Dam
Killiecrankie Visitor Centre

Pitlochry
Aberfeldy Branch Viaduct
Ballinluig
Deuchary Hill 509
A9
494 ▲ Creag an Uamhaidh
Butterstone
A923
The Hermitage
Dunkeld
Meikleour
Caputh
LC
A93
Pass of Birnam
Bankfoot
Tunnel line to Aberdeen
Stanley
A94
Balbeggie
Pitcairngreen
Caithness Glass
Scone Palace
Huntingtower
Kinnoull Twr
Perth
Dundee 20¼
A9
LC
Moncreiffe Tunnel
Strath Earn
Aberuthven
LC
Forteviot
Dunning
M90 Edinburgh 57
Auchterarder
Muirtown
B8062
Braco
LC
Path of Condie
Greenloaning
Gleneagles
B827
Water
Blackford
542 ▲ Core Hill
Ochil Hills
B933
Kinbuck
A9
Dunblane
Doune
Bridge of Allan
River Forth
A9
LC
Wallace Monument
STIRLING
✝ ★ ⚓ ℹ
M9
Edinburgh 36¼
Glasgow 29

0   2 Mls
0   2 Kms

THE BATTLE OF CULLODEN WAS FOUGHT ON THIS MOOR 16TH APRIL 1746

THE GRAVES OF THE GALLANT HIGHLANDERS WHO FOUGHT FOR SCOTLAND & PRINCE CHARLIE ARE MARKED BY THE NAMES OF THEIR CLANS

A memorial stone on the site of the Battle of Culloden

Blair Castle, the home of the Duke of Atholl, chief of the Murrays

Passing the Wallace Monument, on the horizon, near Stirling

Inverness
Stirling

STRATHSPEY RAILWAY

Queen Victoria was among the early tourists who visited the valley of the Spey in the last century. The first railway arrived shortly after her visit and today's preserved railway originally formed part of the first trunk line from Perth to Inverness through the Highlands. Most of that line over Dava summit is now closed, having been replaced by the route via Carrbridge.

At **Aviemore** the Strathspey Railway has its own station, situated 500 yards from the BR one, and close to the restored engine shed which dates from 1898. The line runs north-eastwards towards **Boat of Garten** and in both termini there are buildings constructed to accommodate the railway staff in this remote area. Near by flows the River Spey, once followed by a branch line all the way to Craigellachie, serving *en route* the whisky distilleries for which Speyside is world-famous.

Many fine walks can be made from both ends of the railway. Perhaps the most interesting is the three-mile one from Boat of Garten to Loch Garten where the rare fish-eating ospreys return from Africa each year to breed. Their nests are protected by the Royal Society for the Protection of Birds, who maintain an observation hide.

Strathspey Railway
Aviemore–Boat of Garten 5 miles (Tel (047983) 692)
Operates: Etr–mid Oct (phone for details)
Single journey: 17mins

Tourist Information Centres
Aviemore Main Rd (0479) 810363

Places to Visit
Aviemore see main panel
Boat of Garten Loch Garten RSPB Nature Reserve (bird sanctuary access Apr–Aug, elsewhere access unrestricted all year)

LOOK OUT FOR

Carving a way into the Highlands was a great test of **engineering skill**. The engineer who planned and built much of the line from Perth to Inverness was Joseph Mitchell, and the dramatic route across the mountains, with its gradients and great viaducts, is a memorial to his skill. However, the line follows closely the route taken by the **A9**, and this road was originally planned by the great engineer Thomas Telford. This is no coincidence for Mitchell was Telford's assistant for many years and the two had a common approach in opening up the Highlands. In fact, Telford's route was pioneered by an even earlier road, the **military highway** built by General Wade from the 1720s. Sections of Wade's road still survive and can be seen from the train.

111

Across the Highlands to Skye

INVERNESS – KYLE OF LOCHALSH 82¼ miles

TRAINS
(2hrs 30mins approx)
Mon–Sat 2 (+ 1 summer
only); Sun 2 (peak
summer only)
Refreshments: some
(summer only)

**Tourist Information
Centres** (*summer only)
Inverness Church St
(0463) 234353
Kyle of Lochalsh*
(0599) 4276

**For all information on
Inverness see page 110**

Walks
Achnashellach Walks from
Achnashellach station
Lochalsh Walks, Balmacara
several walks round
Lochalsh House and the
Lochalsh peninsula
(NTS)
Muir of Tarradale 1½m
east of Muir of Ord
Ord Hill 3m north of
Inverness at North
Kessock (information
from North Kessock TIC
(046 373) 505)
Rogie Walks 5m south-
east of Garve
Strathpeffer Walks around
Strathpeffer and
Dingwall
Strome Wood from
Stromeferry

Places to Visit
Dingwall Sir Hector
MacDonald's Memorial,
tel (0349) 62391 for keys
to tower. *By car/bus* at
Strathpeffer: Museum of
Dolls, Toys and
Victoriana (Etr–Oct);
Pump Room (May–Oct)
Duirinish Duirinish
Lodge wild woodland
garden (Mar–Oct)
Garve By car Rogie Falls
(see **Walks** above)
Kyle of Lochalsh By car/bus
Balmacara Estate and
Lochalsh Woodland
Garden, NTS. *By boat* at
Kyleakin: Castle Moil;
Kyle House (May–Aug)
Muir of Ord Ord
Distillery (Feb–Nov). *By
car* Beauly Priory, SDD
(Apr–Sep)

The Inverness to Kyle line was built in three stages between 1862 and 1897, at great cost and as a triumph of Victorian engineering. Although threatened with closure in the past, the line is now established as one of the greatest scenic journeys in Britain.

Inverness

With Inverness spread south along the River Ness the train swings west before slowing to a crawl across the 1909 Clachnaharry swing bridge over Telford's Caledonian Canal. The line runs along the shore of Beauly Firth, then curves round to cross the River Beauly. The first stop is **Muir of Ord**, with large grain silos for the local distilleries. The River Conon is crossed by Mitchell's fine five-arched stone viaduct of 1862, then **Dingwall** lies ahead, its spires and towers west of the pretty 1886 station with its ironwork and canopies.

Achnasheen

North of Dingwall trains for Kyle branch west off the Wick and Thurso line (see pages 116–17). As the line climbs steeply the old spa town of Strathpeffer can be seen in the valley, once served by a branch line. Dramatic woods and steep rock walls now dominate as the train enters the Highlands proper, then winds its way down to Loch Garve and along the shore of the loch, totally enclosed by woods. **Garve**, with its 1870 station house, is the first of a series of remote stops. There is a bus from here to Ullapool. Climbing again, the train

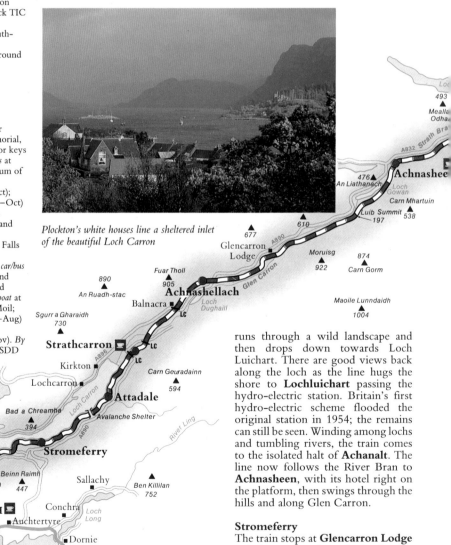

Plockton's white houses line a sheltered inlet of the beautiful Loch Carron

runs through a wild landscape and then drops down towards Loch Luichart. There are good views back along the loch as the line hugs the shore to **Lochluichart** passing the hydro-electric station. Britain's first hydro-electric scheme flooded the original station in 1954; the remains can still be seen. Winding among lochs and tumbling rivers, the train comes to the isolated halt of **Achanalt**. The line now follows the River Bran to **Achnasheen**, with its hotel right on the platform, then swings through the hills and along Glen Carron.

Stromeferry

The train stops at **Glencarron Lodge** only by request from the landowner under an original charter, and then it drops down into the Carron valley to **Achnashellach**. There is a view of Loch Dughaill from the rather primitive station, and then the line continues along the steadily widening Carron valley into a softening landscape. **Strathcarron** is set at the head of Loch Carron and there are fine views along the loch, with Skye closing the horizon in the distance. The line runs along the southern shore of the loch, with ample opportunities to enjoy the ever-changing effects of light. Passing the small halt at **Attadale** and the concrete avalanche shelter over the line the train reaches **Stromeferry**. When the Dingwall and Skye Railway reached here in 1870 the builders could afford to go no further, and so Stromeferry became the terminus of the line for the next 27 years, with steamer services to Skye and Stornoway. The final ten miles to Kyle, completed in 1897, had to be cut through virtually solid rock. There are 31 cuttings and 29 bridges, and the cost was over £20,000 per mile, then the most expensive railway ever built.

Kyle of Lochalsh

Carving its way through cuttings the train comes to **Duncraig**, with its pretty octagonal waiting room, and

The Isle of Skye, largest of the Inner Hebrides islands, seen from Kyle of Lochalsh

rock, is right on the water's edge: fishing boats, cottages, the old hotel, the ferry and the incomparable scenery must make Kyle the best placed station in Britain.

The ferry from Kyle to Skye (Kyleakin) operates frequently all day, and there are limited bus services from Kyleakin to Armadale, for the ferry to Mallaig, and the train to Fort William and Glasgow **(see pages 106–7)**

LOOK OUT FOR

Much of the Kyle line's route, being wild, bleak and inaccessible, is rich in **wildlife** and the train makes an excellent mobile hide. Buzzards are quite common, and other birds of prey include the occasional soaring eagle. Herons, oyster-catchers and other waders are common on loch shores. Herds of red deer or feral goats can be spotted, while the sharp-eyed may see otters or grey seals swimming in lochs. Another treat might be the sight of leaping salmon on the fish ladders near hydro-electric stations.

Red deer

the delightful harbour at **Plockton** comes into view. The line now makes its way inland to **Duirinish**, through vegetation that reflects the presence of the Gulf Stream, and then it returns to the shore for the last few miles to **Kyle**, with spectacular views of Skye and distant Raasay. The terminus, whose site was blasted from solid

An expansive view from the Kyle line, between Strathcarron and Kyle itself

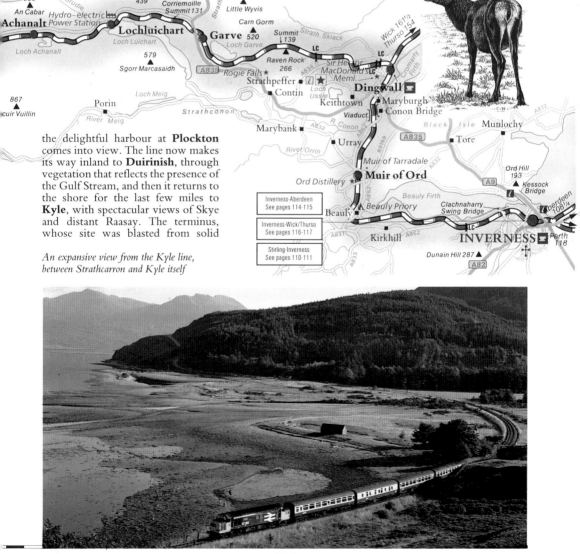

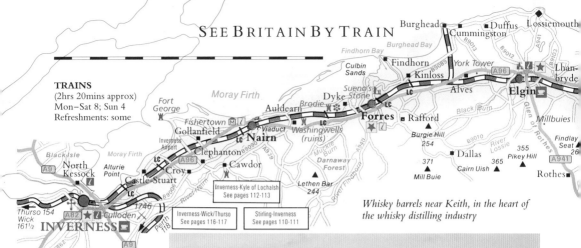

Inverness-Kyle of Lochalsh
See pages 112-113

Inverness-Wick/Thurso
See pages 116-117

Stirling-Inverness
See pages 110-111

TRAINS
(2hrs 20mins approx)
Mon–Sat 8; Sun 4
Refreshments: some

Tourist Information
Centres (*summer only)
Aberdeen Broad St
(0224) 632727
Elgin High St
(0343) 3388/2666
Forres★ Tolbooth St
(0309) 72938
Huntly★ The Square
(0466) 2255
Inverness Church St
(0463) 234353
Inverurie★ Town Hall,
Market Pl (0467) 20600
Keith★ Church Rd
(05422) 2634
Nairn★ King St
(0667) 52753

For all information on
Inverness see page 110

Walks
Elgin Town Trail in Elgin
town centre
Leith Hall Trails 7m south
of Huntly (NTS)
Millbuies 3m south of
Elgin

Places to Visit
Aberdeen Art Gallery and
Museums; Bridge of
Dee; Duthie Park Winter
Gardens; Fishmarket
(wkdays 7–8am);
Gordon Highlanders
Regimental Museum
(Sun & Wed); Marischal
College; Maritime
Museum; Provost
Skene's House. *Old
Aberdeen* Brig
o'Balgownie;
Cruickshank Botanic
Gardens; King's College;
St Andrew's Cathedral
(Jun–Sep, Sun Services);
St Machar's Cathedral
Dyce Symbol Stones,
Dyce Old Church, SDD
Elgin Cathedral, SDD;
Museum; Old Mills
Forres Falconer Museum;
Sueno's Stone, SDD. *By
car/bus* Brodie Castle and
Gardens, NTS (Apr–Sep)
Huntly Castle, SDD;
Museum. *By car/bus* Leith
Hall, NTS (house
May–Sep)
Keith G & G Kynoch
woollen mill (tours Tues
& Thurs); Mill of Towie
(May–Oct); Strathisla
Distillery (mid May–mid
Sep)
Nairn Fishertown
Museum (May–Sep). *By
car* Cawdor Castle
(May–Sep)

*Whisky barrels near Keith, in the heart of
the whisky distilling industry*

Along the Whisky Trail

INVERNESS – ABERDEEN   *108¼ miles*

The line from Inverness to Aberdeen was first planned in 1844 but
its completion ultimately involved several companies and took
over ten years. The route explores the pleasant coastal scenery of the
Moray Firth and the soft hills of Strathbogie and the Garioch, the
heart of the whisky industry.

Inverness
Leaving Inverness the train runs along
beside the Moray Firth with good
views back to the town and to the
wooded hills of the Black Isle peninsula on the northern shore. Passing
rocky Alturlie Point it swings inland
and there are glimpses of Castle Stuart
to the north. The landscape of typical
low-lying coastal farmland is briefly
interrupted by Inverness Airport,
with views beyond towards Fort
George and Rosemarkie Bay and then
the line crosses straggly woods and
marshland to **Nairn**. The pretty station, opened originally in 1855, is to
the south of the centre of this prosperous and decorative resort well
placed overlooking the River Nairn
and its estuary. The town looks good
from the east as the train crosses the
river on Joseph Mitchell's handsome
1857 stone viaduct, with the sea to the
north. Fields broken by patches of
woodland accompany the line eastwards. The ruins of Washingwells
Castle can be seen to the south but
17th-century Brodie Castle, near the
line as it crosses Muckle Burn, is
hidden by trees. Woods and the high-
sided viaduct also limit views along
the Findhorn valley. **Forres**, with its

big Victorian Gothic church, is south
of the station, which still boasts a
bypass line and the old junction with
the original Highland Railway main
line south to Aviemore.

Elgin
East of Forres the line crosses a flat
plain with views across Findhorn Bay
towards Cromarty and Caithness.
After passing the Burghead branch,
still used for grain traffic, the train
enters a more hilly landscape, with
good views to the south and York
Tower standing high above the woods
to the north. Elgin is spread to the
north, and little of the town centre,
with its ruined cathedral, can be seen.
Once the hub of a busy network,
Elgin had lines running north to
Lossiemouth, east along the Moray
coast and south along the Spey but all
that remains today is the pretty old
station with its baronial façade, north
of the present buildings. Leaving
Elgin, the train runs through rolling
farmland and then turns south
through attractive woods to the Spey
valley with a distant view of the hills
to the south. A good bridge, well seen
as the line curves to approach it, carries the train over the fast-flowing

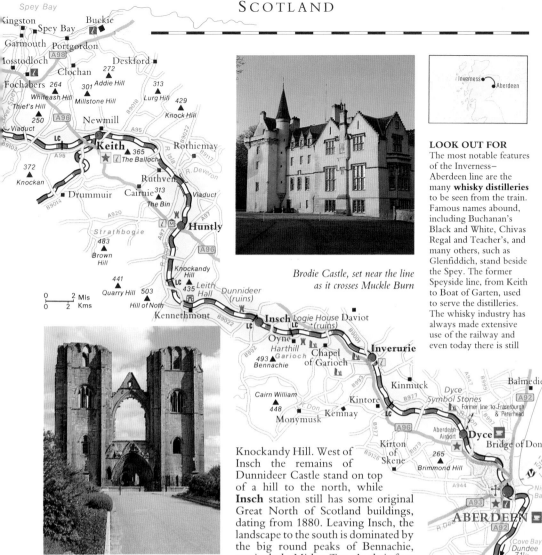

Brodie Castle, set near the line as it crosses Muckle Burn

LOOK OUT FOR

The most notable features of the Inverness–Aberdeen line are the many **whisky distilleries** to be seen from the train. Famous names abound, including Buchanan's Black and White, Chivas Regal and Teacher's, and many others, such as Glenfiddich, stand beside the Spey. The former Speyside line, from Keith to Boat of Garten, used to serve the distilleries. The whisky industry has always made extensive use of the railway and even today there is still

Elgin Cathedral is considered to have the finest design of all Scottish cathedrals

Spey and then it runs in and out of woodland to Keith, passing the first of the many distilleries that stand beside the track. **Keith** station, north of the town, was once busy with whisky trains from the Speyside line, still used occasionally to Dufftown and for fish traffic from the Moray coast ports of Buckie and Banff. Keith is also the furthest surviving outpost of the Great North of Scotland Railway, and the line from here to Aberdeen is all that remains of their once extensive network north of Aberdeen.

Huntly

East of Keith the train runs through hilly farmland along the valley of the Isla, with the distinctive flat top of Knock Hill to the north. It then joins the River Deveron, crosses it on a five-arched viaduct and follows it south to Huntly, high above the river. Huntly itself, an attractive town whose castle can be seen above the trees, is on the River Bogie, which joins the Deveron to the north. Look back for a view of the church as the train climbs southwards along the curving Bogie valley. The big hills of Strathbogie now dominate the line and then it swings east round

Knockandy Hill. West of Insch the remains of Dunnideer Castle stand on top of a hill to the north, while **Insch** station still has some original Great North of Scotland buildings, dating from 1880. Leaving Insch, the landscape to the south is dominated by the big round peaks of Bennachie, particularly Mither Tap. At their foot stands Harthill Castle, surprisingly pink, and then the train enters the Urie valley, with the ruins of Logie House to the north. The line now follows the Urie across Garioch through a region noted for its prehistoric and Pictish sites. **Inverurie** is set attractively between the Urie and the Don and the castle mound and town hall with its elaborate bell tower can be seen.

Aberdeen

South of Inverurie the train crosses the Don and then follows its meandering course through the rolling farmland of its wide valley. Passing the site of the old junction with the former branch to Peterhead and Fraserburgh, the backbone of the line's fish traffic in its heyday, the train reaches **Dyce**, with Aberdeen Airport beside the tracks. The suburbs of Aberdeen now dominate as the line swings south to enter the city through a series of granite-lined cuttings and tunnels that lead to Union Terrace Gardens, a steep-sided park deep in the heart of the city. The grand stone station, originally opened in 1867, is a handsome stone structure with a covered concourse, right in the centre of the city. The cathedral, the art gallery, the university and Aberdeen's streets of tough granite are all close by and the harbour is only a short walk to the east.

an extensive traffic in both grain and the actual spirit. Tank cars full of Chivas Regal stand in the sidings at Keith, and the huge windowless bonded stores stand by the line at every distillery. Also to be seen at Keith are fields full of old wooden barrels. Some of the lineside distilleries can be visited, while those along the remains of the Speyside line occasionally receive special trains.

Aberdeen University's granite buildings

To the Top of Britain

INVERNESS – WICK/THURSO   *161½ to Wick, 154 to Thurso*

TRAINS
(3hrs 35mins approx to Thurso; 3hrs 40mins approx to Wick)
Mon–Sat 3; Sun 2 (peak summer only)
Refreshments: some

Tourist Information Centres (★summer only)
Helmsdale★ (04312) 640
Inverness 23 Church St (0463) 234353
Lairg★ (0549) 2160
Thurso★ Car Park, Riverside (0847) 62371
Wick Whitechapel Rd off High St (0955) 2596

For all information on Inverness see page 110

Walks
Ord Hill 3m north of Inverness at North Kessock
Muir of Tarradale 1½m east of Muir of Ord
Strathpeffer Walks around Strathpeffer and Dingwall

Cycling
Thurso–Kirk–Mybster –Thurso (see pages 5–7)

Places to Visit
For *Muir of Ord* and *Dingwall* see page 112
Golspie Dunrobin Castle and Gardens (Jun–Sep)
Invershin By car/walk (3m) Falls of Shin
Tain St Duthus Church, folk museum and Clan Ross Centre
Thurso St Peter's Church (ruins); Heritage Museum (Jun–Sep). *By boat* (from Scrabster, mid May–Oct) at Stromness, Orkney: Museum; Pier Arts Centre
Wick Caithness Glass (May–Sep); Castle of Old Wick; Wick Heritage Centre (Jun–Sep)

The Inverness train passes the hills near Lairg

This journey is an adventure, a meandering exploration of the coastline, rivers, hills and moorland of the far north. Completed in 1874, the line has played its part in history, from the notorious clearances in the 19th century to the naval traffic during two World Wars and, more recently, the oil boom.
Some stops are by request only.

Inverness – Dingwall See page 112

Tain

North of Dingwall the Kyle line branches away to the west and the train runs along the shore of the Cromarty Firth. As the line rises the Firth comes into sight and the road causeway linking it to the Black Isle, to the south. The line runs inland to **Alness**, overshadowed by Cnoc Fyrish with its curious Indian-style monument, where a fine stone viaduct of 1863 carries the train over the River Alness. Look out for oil rigs in Alness Bay and in the former naval dockyard at **Invergordon**. East of the station are the huge distillery and the remains of the aluminium smelter. There are excellent views across Nigg Bay to Cromarty and the oil terminal and then the train cuts across the peninsula to **Fearn**. There is a brief view of Loch Eye and then the Dornoch Firth spreads ahead as the train approaches **Tain**, with the town on a ridge to the west. The ruins of St Duthus's Church stand by the line. The line now runs along the shore of Dornoch Firth, with views across to Dornoch.

Golspie

The next stop is **Ardgay**, with its original 1864 station and views across to Bonar Bridge and east along Dornoch Firth and then the line climbs inland along the Kyle of Sutherland after crossing the River Carron. This is the start of one of the great meanders inland that make the train's route to the north so laborious. **Culrain** is the station for Carbisdale Castle, a huge stone pile of 1914 perched wonderfully on a wooded crest, and now a youth hostel, and then the train crosses the River Oykel on a splendid iron viaduct of 1863 to **Invershin Halt**. The line now climbs through woods and rock cuttings to **Lairg**. Turning east along the River Fleet the train follows a lovely valley to **Rogart**, where an old mill and a great expanse of sheep pens stand by the cottage-like station. Dropping down through woods the line rounds the Mound Rock and runs by Loch Fleet before returning to the coast at **Golspie**, a little resort with a busy fishing harbour.

Helmsdale

As the train leaves Golspie, the fairytale towers of Dunrobin Castle come into view to the south and near the gates is the Duke of Sutherland's own station (open summer weekends for castle visitors). In the late 1860s the Duke built the line from Golspie to Helmsdale, and for years his descendants used his private train. With fine views over Dornoch Firth the train comes to **Brora**, with the little harbour tucked below the viaduct. From here to Helmsdale the train runs along the shore, remote sandy beaches broken by outcrops of rock. The cottages of Helmsdale, an early 19th-century estate village, look good as the line turns inland along the River Helmsdale.

Wick/Thurso

Following the Helmsdale north through Strath Ullie, the line crosses an empty landscape of moorland and little streams. **Kildonan** is a halt in the middle of nowhere, the scene of an unlikely gold rush in 1868, while **Kinbrace** station, looking like a croft, at least has a few houses near by. As the landscape gets wilder, herds of deer roam near the line. The next stop is **Forsinard**, with a fishermen's hotel, and the line swings into the wilds of Caithness. Stations at **Altnabreac** and **Scotscalder**, built to serve hunting lodges, now have a *Marie Celeste* quality. East of Scotscalder civilisation slowly returns. The train crosses the Thurso river with Halkirk to the north, an 18th-century model village, and then **Georgemas Junction** comes

into sight. Here the train divides, part continuing east to **Wick**, a handsome fishing village built round Telford's harbour, and part going north to **Thurso**, the most northerly town in Britain, with its ferry service to the Orkneys. Although very different in character, the two towns have similar stations, simple but elegant structures with wooden roofs, built in 1874.

Local companies operate a bus service connecting Wick and Thurso, and so it is both easy and enjoyable to visit both termini on one journey.

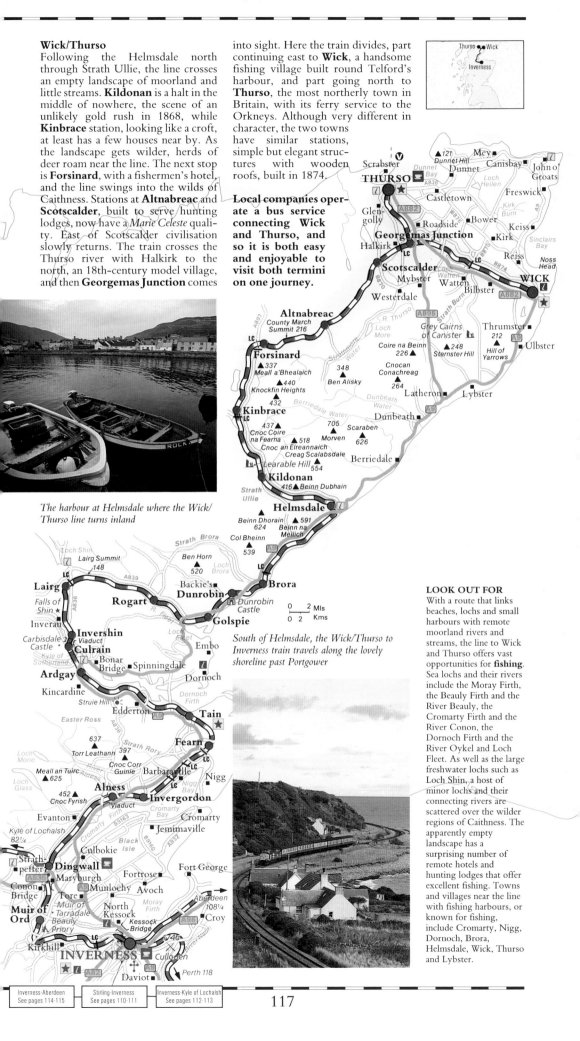

The harbour at Helmsdale where the Wick/Thurso line turns inland

South of Helmsdale, the Wick/Thurso to Inverness train travels along the lovely shoreline past Portgower

LOOK OUT FOR

With a route that links beaches, lochs and small harbours with remote moorland rivers and streams, the line to Wick and Thurso offers vast opportunities for **fishing**. Sea lochs and their rivers include the Moray Firth, the Beauly Firth and the River Beauly, the Cromarty Firth and the River Conon, the Dornoch Firth and the River Oykel and Loch Fleet. As well as the large freshwater lochs such as Loch Shin, a host of minor lochs and their connecting rivers are scattered over the wilder regions of Caithness. The apparently empty landscape has a surprising number of remote hotels and hunting lodges that offer excellent fishing. Towns and villages near the line with fishing harbours, or known for fishing, include Cromarty, Nigg, Dornoch, Brora, Helmsdale, Wick, Thurso and Lybster.

INDEX

This index includes all stations on all routes in this book, both British Rail and Preserved Railways (some on map only). Other items, of general interest, are shown in italics.

Station facilities apply to British Rail stations only

℗ No car park at station
♨ Refreshments available at station
🚖 Taxi rank at station
🚗 Immediate car hire facility at station (see also page 5)

ACKNOWLEDGEMENTS

The Automobile Association wishes to thank the following photographers, organisations and libraries for their assistance in the compilation of this book. The photographs not mentioned are from the Automobile Association's Photo Library.

J Allan Cash 85 R. Mite Loco, 86 Five Rise Locks, Bingley, 87 Keighley Stn, 93 Whitby Abbey, 94 Hadrian's Wall, 95 Newcastle bridges, 97 Bamburgh Castle; P Atterbury 32 St Pancras Stn; A Barnes 18 Eggesford; I J Belcher 55 Gt Orme Tramway; N Bentley 80 Hope Valley; C Berry 16 St Ives; R C Bishop 44/45 Friog; E A Bowness 82 M V Swan on Lake Windermere, 83 Lune Gorge, 89 Appleby Horse Fair; P H Brannlund 25 Tisbury; Britain on View 66 Malvern Stn; British Rail 28/9 Gt Bedwyn, 30 Battle Stn, Rye Stn, 31 Surbiton Stn, 60/61 Ely Cathedral & Train, 64 Malvern; W A Cousins 98/9 Loch Dubh, 106 Glenfinnan & Loch Shiel; M Esau 35 Watercress Line; D J Fowler 1 Clapham, Yorks; A Gilson 52 Knucklas Viaduct; M Grace 84 Towards Millom; D Hardley 2/3 Loch Awe, 110/1 Outside Stirling; W H Harris 23 W. Somerset Railway; Highlands & Islands Dev. Board 107 Glenfinnan Viaduct; Hulton Picture Company 10 I K Brunel, 11 Temple Mead Stn, Box Tunnel, 62 Thorpe Stn, 63 Norwich Stn; G Ibbitson 8/9 Train leaving St Ives; S D Jolly 89 Dent Stn, S King 73 Crossing the R. Yare; T Mackie 35 Lymington; Mary Evans Picture Library 10 Royal Albert Bridge, 30 Brighton Stn, 64 Thetford Stn, 76/7 High Level Bridge; C Molyneux 49 Pembroke Castle; National Railway Museum 31 Posters, 63 Poster, 64 Seat, 76 Stockton & Derby Railway Opening, 77 Shugborough Tunnel, 79 Poster; North Yorkshire Moors Railway 93 Logo; R Owen Cover & 56 Sprinter, Barmouth; Dr R L Phillips 59 Sprinter, Machynlleth; C G Prodger 36 Towards Amberley Chalk Pits; M C Pybus 74/5 Esk Valley; P W Robinson 83 Windermere Branch; RAF Museum, Hendon 97 Badge; Scotrail 100/1 Forth Bridge; Scottish Tourist Board 105 Burns' Cottage; Dr Sharma 113 Kyle Line; D Smyth 14 St Germans; Spectrum Colour Library 22 Weymouth, 39 Stringing hop poles, Rye, 48 Kidwelly Castle, 65 Stokesay Castle, 67 Worcester, 87 Badge; The Bridgeman Art Library 32 Paddington Stn; P Tickner 106 Approaching Tyndrum; M S Trigg 35 Lymington; P Underhay 12 Rounding the tunnel; V & A Museum 41 Stour Valley; A Vines Cover Kyle Line, 116 South of Lairg, 117 Portgower; R Ward 107 Loch Eilt; A J Watts 89 Ribblehead Viaduct; R Weir 109 Forth Rail Bridge, 113 Isle of Skye; Welsh Tourist Board 56 Portmerion; G C Whitwham 85 Arnside; M Wilkins 13 Dart Valley Railway, 25 Yeovil Junction